Washington
Off the Beaten Path®

Help Us Keep This Guide Up to Date

Every effort has been made by the author and editors to make this guide as accurate and useful as possible. However, many things can change after a guide is published—establishments close, phone numbers change, hiking trails are rerouted, facilities come under new management, etc.

We would love to hear from you concerning your experiences with this guide and how you feel it could be made better and be kept up to date. While we may not be able to respond to all comments and suggestions, we'll take them to heart and we'll also make certain to share them with the author. Please send your comments and suggestions to the following address:

The Globe Pequot Press
Reader Response/Editorial Department
P.O. Box 480
Guilford, CT 06437

Or you may e-mail us at:
editorial@globe-pequot.com

Thanks for your input, and happy travels!

OFF THE BEATEN PATH® SERIES

Washington

FIFTH EDITION

Myrna Oakley

The
Globe
Pequot
Press

GUILFORD, CONNECTICUT

Text design by Laura Augustine
Maps created by Equator Graphics © The Globe Pequot Press
Illustrations by Carole Drong

ISSN 1540-8442
ISBN 0-7627-2374-2

Manufactured in the United States of America
Fifth Edition/First Printing

To David, Sandra, Charlie Duane, Pene,
and friendly canine Max,
our family hosts at Hood Canal
with its great views of the water, the tides, and of morning sunrises.

To friends and family far and wide who enjoy
discovering and re-discovering the nooks and crannies
of the Pacific Northwest.

And, especially, to Suzanne Kort and Todd Litman,
who traveled the state's byways in the early 1990s
to develop the first edition of Washington: Off the Beaten Path.

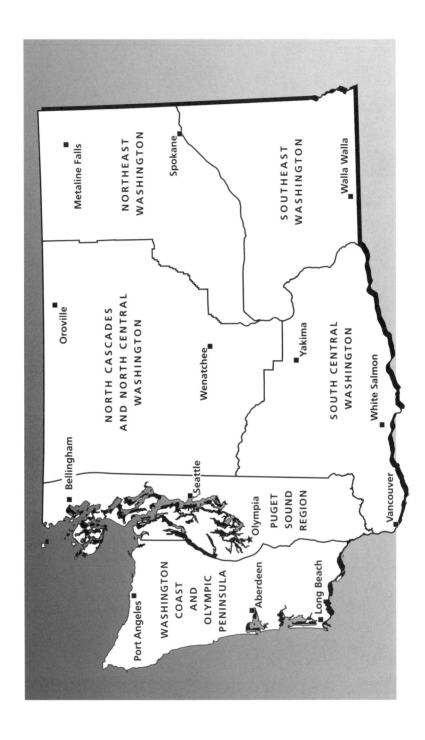

Contents

Acknowledgments

Oceans of thanks to dozens and dozens of folks who offered helpful information to update their sections of the state—restaurant, cafe, bakery, and coffee shop owners; museums and historic sites staff and volunteers; shopkeepers and innkeepers; staff and volunteers at visitor information centers throughout the state; and regional history gurus for information on train depot and lighthouse restorations, on historic hotel renovations, on ghost towns, and on rails-to-trails projects.

A special note of thanks to:

- Staff members at Fort Clatsop National Memorial (www.nps.gov/focl) in Astoria for providing information sources on the Lewis & Clark Bicentennial.

- Una Boyle, Long Beach Peninsula Visitors Bureau, for updates on the Long Beach area and about Pacific County Friends of Lewis & Clark (www.lewisandclarkwa.com).

- Julie Gangler, Tacoma-Pierce County Convention & Visitor Bureau, for help with the Tacoma area introduction.

- Loretta Martin, Langley Chamber of Commerce, for updates on south Whidbey Island.

- Sherry Baysinger, Bear Creek Homestead, for horseback rides on the Olympic Peninsula and updates on the Forks-Sappho-Clallam Bay-Neah Bay and Cape Flattery areas.

- Emily Reed, author of *Emily's Guide to the San Juans,* for help with updating eateries and lodging in the islands.

- Gig Harbor innkeeper Meri Fountain of Fountains Bed & Breakfast for planning our itinerary and ferrying us about to visit Gig Harbor–Fox Island innkeepers.

- Tacoma innkeeper Cheryl Teifke of DeVoe Mansion Bed & Breakfast for hosting and for planning my itinerary for visiting Tacoma area innkeepers.

- Leavenworth innkeepers Monty and Karen Turner, Run of the River Bed & Breakfast, and Michael and Mary Ann Zenk, Pine River Ranch, for their warm hospitality and updating their Central Cascades area.

- Lake Chelan National Recreation Area park rangers for updates on the remote Stehekin area.

ACKNOWLEDGMENTS

- Barb Drummond, Oroville Visitor Information Center, for helpful updates on the northern Okanogan region.

- Spokane innkeeper Phyllis Maguire, Marianna Stoltz House Bed & Breakfast, for updates on the Spokane-Deer Park area.

- Lori Slaybaugh and Shaun Martin, Pomeroy City Hall, for help with the Pomeroy area of far southeastern Washington.

And an extra special note of thanks to the dedicated and tenacious staff at Globe Pequot, including Paula Brisco, who has the mind-boggling task of overseeing the revisions for the entire Off the Beaten Path series.

Introduction

Washington is a generous state, offering adventures for many types of travelers. You'll find dense evergreen forests, fertile farmlands, dynamic cities, and foggy islands as well as secluded windblown beaches, waterside walks, small-town cafes and coffee shops, and tiny hamlets, particularly in the far southeast and far northeast corners. There are many well-known tourist destinations, but the real fun begins when you explore off the beaten path.

Because of my interest in cozy bed-and-breakfast inns and great public gardens along with a longtime interest in historic downtown and neighborhood renovations, historic building renovations, and live local theater, readers will find these subjects expanded in this, the fifth edition of *Washington: Off the Beaten Path.*

Using this Guide to Plan Great Trips

As you choose months and dates for your trips, plan around the Pacific Northwest's four distinct seasons: The busiest times for most destinations west of the Cascade Mountains, particularly around Puget Sound waters and the San Juan Islands, will be during July and August. Major freeways and all ferries will carry more traffic; waiting lines at ferry terminals also will be longer. If you want less traffic and fewer crowds, plan to travel mid-week or travel early spring, April through June, and early autumn, September through October. Autumn in the Northwest is sunny and warm with fall colors especially fine in October.

If you enjoy snow and winter sports, plan treks to the Cascade Mountain regions from late November through February. Be prepared with a sturdy vehicle, all-weather tires, extra-warm clothing, emergency kits, and plenty of snacks and beverages. To start your research you'll find helpful telephone numbers and Web sites in the "Mountain Passes, Valleys, and Canyons" section of North Cascades and North Central Washington, **Skiing Washington** sidebar.

The eastern half of the state offers crisp, cold winters and hot, dry summers. Travel early spring and early fall for some of the best weather east of the Cascade Mountains. Eastern Washington also offers fewer crowds, quieter byways, and many pleasant, undiscovered destinations. You'll encounter friendly locals who are glad to help travelers with directions. *Note:* Plan for long distances between services in the eastern regions—gas up often and load up on picnic foods, snacks, beverages, and ice for the cooler.

To help you plan your accommodations, within each chapter you will find lodging suggestions with telephone numbers and, usually, a Web site as well. Nearly all establishments these days are smoke-free and do not allow pets. Leashed pets are usually allowed at state campgrounds and RV parks. See Places to Stay at the end of each chapter for selected RV parks and larger motor inns. Call ahead to ask specific questions and to make lodging reservations.

A Few More Ideas & Suggestions

I suggest that, as much as possible, you maintain a flexible schedule when traveling through the Evergreen State. Allow plenty of time and leave room for interesting happenings and conversation with local folks.

Also, even with the best research you may find a place or attraction closed or discover that hours or telephone numbers have changed. If this occurs, stop at the nearest Visitor Information Center, where the staff and volunteers can offer current information and suggestions. Often these centers are open weekends during summer months. Additionally, local folks are usually willing to offer travelers information, ideas, and directions.

A Word About . . .

*P*ets: *Except for state campgrounds and RV parks, where leashed pets are usually allowed, assume that most places do not allow pets on the premises.*

Eateries: *Hours tend to range from longer in the summer to shorter in the winter, especially in the San Juan Islands and the farther off the beaten path you travel from the larger cities. If in doubt, stop at Visitor Information Centers to check on the local eateries.*

Web sites: *Generally, assume that information you obtain from travel-related Web sites is not necessarily cur-*

rent unless you see a paragraph or sentence that clearly states frequent updates. Outdated information can languish on these sites for years. If you're unsure, e-mail the Web master with specific questions.

Crossing the U.S.–Canadian border: *Expect tighter security at all customs crossings across the northern border of Washington State, and take proof of U.S. citizenship such as a voter's registration card. Carrying only a driver's license is not sufficient. No firearms are allowed into Canada. For pets have proof of recent rabies vaccination.*

If you're traveling with kids, encourage them to write notes to new friends they meet on your travels and to collect information on historic sights, attractions, geology and natural history, and whatever else tickles their fancies. In this way you can help the kids become savvy travelers who appreciate local folks and who care for preserving towns and cities as well as respecting the great outdoors.

Travel Styles & Interests

You say you and your family are rugged outdoors types? You like four-season recreation info? Go to the chapter on North Central Washington. For assistance with serious backcountry and wilderness trip planning, contact the Outdoor Recreation Information Center in the REI flagship store in Seattle (206–470–4060).

Or perhaps you and your family are water-loving types. You like salt water, surf sounds, and watching the incoming and outgoing tides. Go to the chapters on Washington Coast and Olympic Peninsula and on the Puget Sound Region.

If you have a hankerin' to pull on the Levi's, cowboy or cowgirl boots, and a wide-brimmed hat or you want to see a rodeo or ride a horse, browse Northeast Washington, Southeast Washington, and the Okanogan Valley region in the North Central Washington chapter.

What if you want to explore the routes taken by the Lewis and Clark Expedition and check on activities for the Bicentennial from 2002 through 2006? Go to Washington Coast and Olympic Peninsula, to South Central Washington, and to Southeast Washington.

A Final Word

May your travels in the Pacific Northwest be filled with great fun, much serendipity, many new vistas, and new friends from the diverse cultures that live and work in this vast region of waters, islands, mountains, rolling farmlands, deep gorges, and high deserts. Please let us know of new places you find that you'd like to recommend for the next edition of *Washington: Off the Beaten Path.*

The prices and rates listed in this guidebook were confirmed at press time. We recommend, however, that you call establishments before traveling to obtain current information.

Fast Facts about Washington

Population: 6.2 million

Area: 65,625 square miles

Capital: Olympia, located in Thurston County south of Seattle and at the southernmost tip of Puget Sound

Number of counties: 39

County names, from west to east: Wahkiakum, Pacific, Grays Harbor, Jefferson, Clallam, Mason, Thurston, Lewis, Cowlitz, Clark, Skamania, Pierce, King, Kitsap, Snohomish, Island, San Juan, Skagit, Whatcom, Okanogan, Chelan, Kittitas, Yakima, Klickitat, Benton, Grant, Douglas, Ferry, Lincoln, Adams, Franklin, Walla Walla, Columbia, Asotin, Garfield, Whitman, Spokane, Stevens, Pend Oreille

Highest point: Mount Rainier (14,411 feet), located southeast of Tacoma

Largest county: Okanogan

Least populated county: Ferry (under 8,000)

Major body of water: Puget Sound, which carves deep into the northwest section of the state from the Strait of Juan de Fuca south to Olympia

Major rivers: Columbia River/Lake Roosevelt Reservoir east of the Cascade Mountain Range; Snake River, which flows west from the Idaho border and empties into the Columbia at Pasco-Kennewick

Largest natural lake: Lake Chelan, which extends some 55 miles from Chelan to Stehekin in the North Cascades

Nickname: Evergreen State

State animal: Roosevelt elk

State bird: Goldfinch

State fish: Steelhead trout

State flower: Coastal rhododendron

State gem/rock: Petrified wood

State tree: Western hemlock

Washington Coast and Olympic Peninsula

ashington's Pacific Ocean coastline stretches from the Strait of Juan de Fuca in the north to the mouth of the Columbia River in the south. It's a region of contrasts. The Olympic Peninsula's ocean shoreline is rugged, with steep cliffs and rocky formations sculpted by wave and wind. Farther south are gentle sandy beaches lined with summer cottages and tourist communities. Grays Harbor and Willapa Bay break up the coastline and create extensive inland wetlands that are important wildlife habitats. The Olympic Peninsula rain forest has the highest annual rainfall on the continental United States, yet the Dungeness Valley on the Strait of Juan de Fuca has the lowest precipitation on the coast north of California and Oregon.

The snow-covered peaks of the Olympic Mountains provide a stunning backdrop to beaches, forests, and valleys in the region.

Most of the coastal area is thickly forested and includes some of the world's largest living trees. Many local families have been loggers, fishermen, or mill workers for three or four generations. In the coastal and inland areas of the Olympic Peninsula are several small Indian reservations including the Makah, the Jamestown, the Lower Elwah, the Quileute, the Hoh, the Quinault, the Shoalwater, and the Skokomish. Travelers can visit local historical museums, walk secluded beaches, learn about the region's unique natural environment, or enjoy busy beachside tourist areas. Outdoor activities include hiking, bicycling, fishing, birding, and beachcombing. Bring along rain gear and good walking shoes or boots so that you and the kids can take advantage of the many trails and beaches that are accessible most of the year.

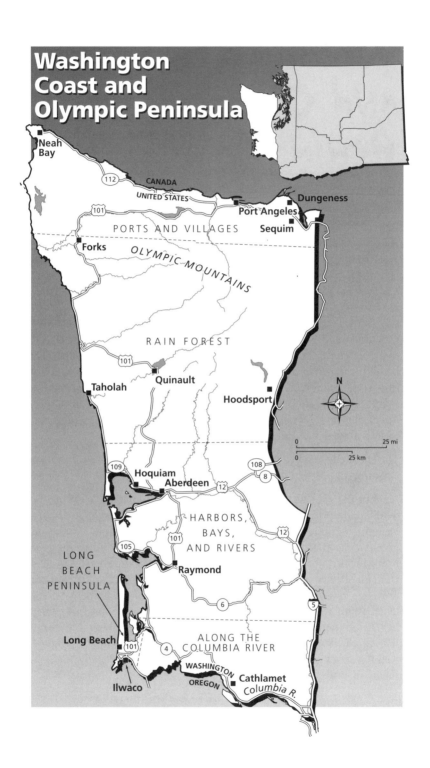

Washington Coast and Olympic Peninsula

Neah Bay

112

CANADA

UNITED STATES

101

Dungeness

Port Angeles

Sequim

PORTS AND VILLAGES

Forks

OLYMPIC MOUNTAINS

RAIN FOREST

101

Quinault

Taholah

Hoodsport

N

0   25 mi
0   25 km

109

Hoquiam

108

Aberdeen

8

12

HARBORS,
BAYS,
AND RIVERS

12

105

101

LONG
BEACH
PENINSULA

Raymond

6

5

ALONG THE
COLUMBIA RIVER

Long Beach

101

4

WASHINGTON

Cathlamet

Ilwaco

OREGON

Columbia R.

WASHINGTON COAST'S TOP HITS

Hood Canal Oysterfest & Seafood Festival, Shelton

Toad Hall Bed and Breakfast Inn, Sequim

Dungeness National Wildlife Refuge, Sequim

Arthur D. Feiro Marine Laboratory, Port Angeles

Hurricane Ridge, Port Angeles

Log Cabin Resort, Lake Crescent

Lake Ozette, Neah Bay

Makah Museum, Neah Bay

Bear Creek Homestead Bed & Breakfast, Port Angeles

Hoh River Visitor Center and Nature Trail, Forks

Aberdeen Museum of History, Aberdeen

Grays Harbor Historical Seaport, Grays Harbor

Westport Maritime Museum, Westport

Tokeland Hotel & Restaurant, Tokeland

Dennis Company, Raymond

Pacific County Historical Museum, South Bend

Ilwaco Heritage Museum, Ilwaco

Lewis and Clark Interpretive Center, Ilwaco

Shelburne Country Inn and Shoalwater Restaurant, Seaview

Klipsan Beach Cottages, Ocean Park

World Kite Museum, Long Beach

Boreas Bed and Breakfast, Long Beach

Willapa Bay Interpretive Center, Nahcotta

Leadbetter Point State Park, Oysterville

Lewis & Clark National Wildlife Refuge, Skamokawa

Puget Island, Cathlamet

Ports and Villages

The Olympic Mountains' towering peaks shelter the northernmost Dungeness Valley from the copious rainfall of the rest of the region, making it the "banana belt" of the Northwest coast.

The town of **Sequim** (pronounced *skwim*) is the commercial center of the valley and a good base from which to explore this scenic region. For an overnight stay on a secluded hilltop call the **Greywolf Inn** bed-and-breakfast (395 Keeler Road, Sequim 98382; 360–683–5889), which offers hospitality in a rural setting outside town.

For a bit of old England on the Olympic Peninsula, call friendly innkeepers Linda and Bruce Clark at **Toad Hall Bed and Breakfast,** located at 12 Jesslyn Lane, Sequim 98382; (360) 681–2534; www.northolympic. com/toadhall. You can bed down in Toad's Room, which comes with a wonderful mahogany four-poster queen bed and views of the Olympic Mountains. Or disappear into Badger's Lair, with a comfortable mahogany queen sleigh bed and its own sitting area. Ask, too, about the romantic third room that comes with a private whirlpool tub for two. On the main floor guests can relax in the comfortable common area with plush sofa and chairs and an antique bar. Coming originally from Great Britain, Linda's passion is collecting English china. She also enjoys cooking tasty breakfasts for guests—served with many cups of hot tea, of course, although you may also order freshly brewed coffee. For those who would like to be closer to the water, check out *Juan de Fuca Cottages* (182 Marine Drive, Sequim 98382; 360–683–4433), where there are six cozy cottages with kitchens and wide-angle views of the water.

Just west of the Sequim city limits at the end of Hendrickson Road is the *Dungeness River Railroad Bridge Park,* a scenic spot with nature trails to the river. On another excursion take Taylor Cut-off Road south from Highway 101 toward the mountains to reach *Lost Mountain Winery* at 3174 Lost Mountain Road, Sequim 98382. The small facility currently produces approximately 1,000 cases per year of hearty Italian-style reds, several of which have won local awards. The winery is open daily from 11:00 A.M. to 5:00 P.M. in summer and by appointment the rest of the year. Call the winery at (360) 683–5229, or visit Web sites www.lostmountain.com/home.html and www.wineryloop.com.

Also in the hills above Sequim, you'll find a delightful place to eat lunch, at *Petals Garden Cafe* located at *Cedarbrook Herb Farm* (1345 South Sequim Avenue, Sequim 98382; 360–683–4541). The twelve-acre farm planted in aromatic herbs and native plants is open year-round except for January and February. You can purchase fresh flowers, lavender plants, dried herbs, herb vinegars, dried flower bouquets and wreaths, garlic ropes, and herb sachets. Lavender lovers can stop at *Purple Haze Lavender Farm* (180 Bell Bottom Lane, Sequim 98382; 360–683–1714) to inspect a colorful display garden, collect a bouquet from the U-pick field of lavender plants, and browse a nice selection of lavender products during the summer season. Open Thursday through Sunday, 10:00 A.M. to 4:00 P.M.

To explore the historic community of *Dungeness,* head north from Highway 101 on Sequim–Dungeness Way in downtown Sequim. Dungeness is old by Washington State standards, named in 1792 by British explorer Captain George Vancouver.

Charles Seal established The Dungeness Trading Company in the 1890s and built a large country farmhouse with the proceeds. Simone Nichols has renovated Seal's home into *Groveland Cottage Bed and Breakfast Inn* (4861 Sequim–Dungeness Way, Dungeness 98382; 360–683–3565;

www.northolympic.com/groveland). Guests sleep in cozy rooms on the second floor and wake up to views of the Olympic Mountains and the inn's gardens. A delicious breakfast is served in the dining room on the main floor. Older children are allowed at the inn.

In the town of Dungeness, you'll see the historic *Dungeness Schoolhouse,* built in 1892 and used to educate local children until 1955, as well as several turn-of-the-century homes amidst fields, creeks, and wetlands. Dungeness Road ends near Cline Spit and at the ever-popular *Three Crabs Restaurant* (360–683–4264), known for its lunch and dinner seafood specialties, such as Dungeness cracked crab, smoked salmon, oysters supreme, almond red snapper, and halibut. In the downtown Sequim area, try *Oak Table Cafe* at 292 West Bell Avenue (360–683–2197) for waist-bulging breakfasts; *Cafe Cafe Coffee House* at 755 West Washington Street (360–681–3132) for homemade soups, salads, fruit smoothies, espresso, and desserts; and *Petals Garden Cafe* at 1345 South Sequim Avenue (360–683–4541) for tasty gourmet lunches in a garden setting.

Golf buffs can call ahead to plan a round of nine or eighteen holes at *Dungeness Golf & Country Club,* located at 1965 Woodcock Road, Sequim 98382; (360) 683–6344. From several fairways and greens, you can also enjoy views of the Olympic Mountains to the south.

A fun place to visit near Dungeness is the *Olympic Game Farm* located at 1423 Ward Road (360–683–4295 or 800–778–4295). Guided walking tours in summer or drive-through tours year-round will put you in the company of four-legged stars. Walt Disney Studios has employed farm residents, including grizzlies and wolves, in more than eighty wildlife productions. Many animals you'll see there, from Siberian tigers and African lions to North American timber wolves and bison, are on the endangered species list. Snacks are available for you as well as for the animals. The game farm opens daily at 9:00 A.M.

The *Dungeness National Wildlife Refuge,* located west of the game farm, offers an exhilarating immersion in an uncaged wilderness. Spring and fall are the best times to visit, when thousands of water birds make their annual migrations. From the parking lot you can take an easy quarter-mile hike to a viewpoint overlooking *Dungeness Spit,* one of the nation's largest natural sand hooks. To explore the spit, hardy and well-equipped hikers can follow the 5½-mile trail through the forest and down the beach. On the west side, you'll experience the roar of incoming waves; on the east, the quiet of a sheltered bay. Keep an eye out for playful harbor seals bobbing about as they fish and frolic offshore. The last half mile of the spit past the *New Dungeness Lighthouse* is closed to the public to ensure protection of the harbor seal adults and pups that reside there. The lighthouse, built in 1857 and automated in 1937, is the oldest one north of the Columbia River. The entrance fee to the refuge is $3.00 per family. For more information about hiking out on the Dungeness Spit, write Washington Coastal Refuges Office, 33 South Barr Road, Port Angeles 98362, or call (360) 457–8451.

The best way to go through the Dungeness Valley between Sequim and Port Angeles is on the *Old Olympic Highway.* This pleasant, less-traveled route through green farmlands offers great views of the mountains rising to the south. Those yearning for luxurious lodgings and a gourmet breakfast in the midst of all this natural beauty could arrange

Lavender Town U.S.A.

*S*equim's rich soil and low rainfall along with warm temperatures have spawned a new agricultural industry. Waves of lavender plants from pale violet to deep purple grow on farms large and small in the Dungeness Valley. To see and sniff hundreds of varieties such as Provence, Grosso, and Munstead, plan to attend the annual Lavender Festival the third weekend of July. Enjoy a host of activities that includes farm tours, a street fair, great food, art shows, and music fests. Call (800) 500–8401 or see www.lavender festival.com for details, then come and enjoy visiting lavender farms and meeting their friendly owners. Find lavender plants for your gardens and stock up on lavender soaps, bath oils, and lotions for your senses:

• Cedarbrook Herb & Lavender Farm and Petals Café (360–683–7733; www.lavenderfarms.com/cedarbrook)

• The Cutting Garden and Farmhouse Gallery (360–681–3099; www.cutting garden.com)

• Jardin du Soleil Lavender (360–582–1185, www.jardin dusoleil.com)

• Lost Mountain Lavender and The Cottage Gifts (360–681–2782; www.lostmountainlavender.com)

• Olympic Lavender Farm (360–683–4475; www.olympiclavender.com)

• Purple Haze Lavender Farm (360–683–1714; www.purple hazelavender.com)

• Sequim Valley Ranch (www.sequimvalleylavender.com)

• Willow Lavender Farm and The Weary Gardener handmade body and soap products (360–452–7342; www.theweary gardener.com) to stay at **Domaine Madeleine** (146 Wildflower Lane, Port Angeles 98362; 360–457–4174; www.domainemadeleine.com), a contemporary home situated on a bluff above the Strait of Juan de Fuca. Three of the four guest rooms have whirlpool tubs for two, and guests can wander five acres of grounds and gardens or cozy up in the living room near the huge basalt fireplace. The inn is located about 5¹/₂ miles west of Sequim, a mile off the Old Olympic Highway.

For a different perspective, turn south on Deer Park Road (3 miles east of Port Angeles) for a winding 19-mile climb over the forest-covered slopes of Blue Mountain to **Deer Park** in Olympic National Park. Here you'll find an alpine campground and ranger station (open in summer only) and the trailhead to scenic hikes overlooking the Dungeness Valley, Port Angeles, and the Strait of Juan de Fuca.

Port Angeles (www.portangeles.net), the largest city on the Olympic Peninsula, is dominated by its busy waterfront. This deepwater harbor is a port of call for international shipping, a center of ocean fishing, a major Coast Guard Station, and terminus for Black Ball's *Coho* ferry, which makes daily trips to Victoria, British Columbia, Canada. The City Pier, 1 block east of the ferry terminal, is a good starting point for your explorations. There you'll find a small park, a viewing tower, a berth for the 210-foot Coast Guard cutter *Active,* a public marine laboratory, and plenty of nearby restaurants and shops. The **Arthur D. Feiro Marine Laboratory** (360–417–6254), located on the City Pier, is the place to see and even touch the remarkable sea creatures that live on Washington's coast. You and the kids can watch the graceful movements of an octopus, stroke a stuffed sea lion, and handle a variety of living marine animals in the touch-tanks. Friendly volunteers answer questions and tell visitors about the Northwest region's marine ecology. The laboratory is open for a small admission fee from 10:00 A.M. to 8:00 P.M. daily, mid-June to Labor Day, and from noon to 4:00 P.M. on weekends the rest of the year.

To explore along the lively Port Angeles waterfront, pick up a walking-tour brochure at the Visitors Center (located next to the City Pier). The Waterfront Trail, which follows the harbor shore east along Hollywood Beach, is ideal for walking or bicycling. You can also bicycle west to **Ediz Hook,** the natural sand spit that forms the Port Angeles harbor. Bikes are available for rent at **Sound Bikes and Kayaks** (120 East Front Street; 360–457–1240; www.soundbikeskayaks.com). Not into biking today? Well, pop into **Retroville Vintage Outfitters** at 133 East First Street (360–452–1429; www.retroville.com) for a touch of nostalgia including retro clothing, kitchenware, and decorative accessories. Then, for good eats in Port Angeles, try **Bonny's Bakery** in the old firehouse at

215 South Lincoln Street (360–457–3585) for espresso, gourmet sandwiches, and French pastries; **Mermaid Cafe** at 229 West First Street (360–565–8091) for homemade soups; **Olympic Bagel Company** at 802 East First Street (360–452–9100) for freshly baked gourmet bagels; and **Landings Dockside Restaurant** at 115 East Railroad Avenue (360–457–6768) for great clam chowder and fish and chips.

If you enjoy watching the waterfront activities, you could call **Baytons' on the Bluff Bed and Breakfast** (824 West Fourth Street, Port Angeles 98363; 360–457–5569; www.northolympic.com/baytons), a large, comfortable home that offers panoramic views of the harbor, the strait, and Vancouver Island beyond. Romantics might prefer the old-world ambience of circa 1910 **Tudor Inn** bed-and-breakfast (360–452–3138; www.tudorinn.com), located a few blocks from the ferry terminal. The innkeeper is happy to help guests plan day trips and other recreation activities. Visitors can also contact innkeepers Bob and Jane Harbick at **Five SeaSuns Bed & Breakfast,** located at 1006 South Lincoln Street, Port Angeles 98362; (360) 452–8248; www.seasuns.com. The couple offers sumptuous accommodations and grounds that feature a pond, an elegant pergola for outdoor sitting, and beds and planters overflowing with colorful flowers.

Hurricane Ridge, accessible by an 18-mile paved road from Port Angeles, offers not only panoramic views of the Strait of Juan de Fuca and islands to the north but also the alpine meadows and glacier-covered

Olympic National Park

*O*lympic National Park was designated as a World Heritage Site by UNESCO on October 27, 1981, and contains the largest and best example of virgin temperate rain forest in the western hemisphere, the largest intact stand of coniferous forest in the contiguous forty-eight states, and the largest wild herd of Roosevelt elk. The park contains more than 1,200 types of plants, more than 300 species of birds, and more than 70 species of mammals. At least 8 kinds of plants and 18 kinds of animals are found only on the Olympic Peninsula and nowhere else in the world, including the Olympic marmot, chipmunk, and snow mole; the Flett's violet, Piper's bellflower, and Olympic Mountain daisy; and the Beardslee and Crescenti trout. The park's Mount Olympus is the wettest place in the continental United States, averaging an annual rainfall of 200 inches (16.7 feet). For natural history workshops and field seminars, contact Olympia Park Institute, (800) 775–3720 and www.yni.org/opi.

peaks of the Olympic Mountains to the south. During the summer park rangers lead walks and answer visitors' questions. The Hurricane Ridge Lodge, open 10:00 A.M. to 5:00 P.M. during summer and winter, includes a museum, deli, and gift shop. Rest rooms are open year-round. Camping is available in the Heart o' the Hills campground, 5 miles from the lodge on the Hurricane Ridge Road. Campfire programs are given nightly in the campground amphitheater from July 1 through Labor Day. For more information stop by the Olympic National Park Visitors Center in Port Angeles at 600 East Park Avenue (360–565–3130), open daily from 8:30 A.M. to 5:30 P.M. July 1 through September 30 and 9:00 A.M. to 4:00 P.M. the rest of the year. The helpful Web site is www.nps.gov/olym.

Nine miles west of Port Angeles, you can turn south on Olympic Hot Springs Road to explore the scenic **Elwha River Valley.** Although the lower portion of the river is now dammed, there is still much to see. Stop at the Elwha Ranger Station for information on hiking trails and the Olympic Hot Springs, or take a raft trip down the scenic Elwha River. Contact **Olympic Raft and Kayak** (123 Lake Aldwell Road, Port Angeles 98363; phone/fax 360–452–1443). Ask about rafting trips on the Elwha River and sea kayaking on Lake Aldwell. Also see www.raftandkayak.com for other seasonal trips.

Continuing west of Port Angeles, you can either follow Highway 101 inland or take Highway 112 along the coastline. If you opt for the inland route, you'll find **Lake Crescent** set in the surrounding forests. The lake is 10 miles long and more than a mile wide. Much of the area around the lake is preserved as part of the Olympic National Forest. A right turn onto East Beach Road at Lake Crescent's eastern edge takes you along a scenic, winding lakeside road to **Log Cabin Resort** (3183 East Beach Road, Port Angeles 98363; 360–928–3325). Established in 1895 on the lake's isolated north shore, the "sunny side of the lake," the resort's unpretentious cabins, RV sites, general store, and restaurant provide a secluded, friendly atmosphere. Be sure to stop by the Soda Jerk Cafe for an espresso or a thick milkshake. Guests can rent rowboats or canoes to enjoy fishing or relaxing on the lake. You can hike among giant old-growth cedars and firs or rent mountain bikes to explore forest trails. Lace up the hiking boots, grab the jackets, pack bottles of water, and head out on the 4-mile Spruce Division Railroad Trail, originally a railroad grade built during World War I to help extract spruce logs for airplane production. The trek is a great way to experience the lake's north shore.

A visitor information center is located on the lake's south shore, just off Highway 101, in a log cabin built in 1905 by Olympic Forest ranger Chris Morgenroth. From the cabin a $^3/_4$-mile trail follows a level, gravel path through the forest that ends with an uphill climb to 90-foot *Marymere Falls,* offering visitors a pleasant excursion through the rain forest. *Lake Crescent Lodge* (416 Lake Crescent Road, Port Angeles 98363; 360–928–3211), just west of the visitor center, is a classic old resort that has changed little since it was built on the lakeshore in 1916. While staying here in 1937, President Franklin Roosevelt decided to create Olympic National Park in order to preserve this area's beauty for future generations. Visitors enjoy lodge rooms or cottages, boating, fishing, and nature hikes, in addition to lounging under the shade of a lakeside tree. In the resort restaurant you can watch the sun set over the lake while savoring a fine dinner.

The *Olympic Park Institute,* located nearby at the historic *Rosemary Inn,* offers programs for children and adults on subjects ranging from creative writing to natural history and environmental ethics. The rustic resort, established on Lake Crescent in 1914, is considered an outstanding example of the Craftsman Era of American architecture. For a calendar of upcoming classes, contact the Olympic Park Institute, 111 Barnes Point Road, Port Angeles 98363; (360) 928–3720; www.yni.org/opi.

You'll find forested campgrounds, boat rentals, and groceries at Fairholm on the western edge of Lake Crescent. Farther west on Highway 101, a 12-mile drive north on Sol Duc Road takes you to *Sol Duc Hot Springs Resort* (P.O. Box 2169, Port Angeles 98362; 360–327–3583). Sol Duc means "sparkling water" in the Quileute language. Visitors have been flocking to the healthful mineral waters at Sol Duc since a magnificent spa was first built at the site in 1912 (and, sadly, burned in 1916). The resort, open mid-April through the end of September, offers three large outdoor hot mineral pools, a freshwater heated swimming pool and poolside deli, restaurant, massage therapy, a gift shop, groceries, RV hookups, and cabins. Camping, hiking trails, and naturalist programs are available at the *Sol Duc Campground* located nearby.

Take the Highway 112 turnoff at the junction west of Port Angeles if you and your travel mates hanker for more close-up views of the Olympic Peninsula's rugged northern coastline. Ten miles west of Port Angeles, turn on Camp Hayden Road to reach *Salt Creek Recreation Area,* a marine sanctuary with tide pools full of waving sea anemones, gooseneck barnacles, coal-black mussels, and colorful starfish, as well as kelp beds and rocky islands offshore. Also nearby is the Clallam County park and campground, which offers campsites, showers, and beach area. Continuing west on Highway 112, you may

Lake Crescent Lodge Sun Room

see a gray whale spouting offshore or, perhaps, a pod of orca or a California sea lion swimming by. Watch for crowds of harbor seals relaxing on the small offshore islands.

Continue west to **Neah Bay** or take the turnoff on Hoko-Ozette Road, just past the fishing village of Sekiu on Clallam Bay, to **Lake Ozette.** The lake, which is the largest natural body of freshwater in Washington State, is a great place to enjoy a canoe or rowboat. By boat you can explore miles of wild shoreline and secluded campsites not accessible by land. The 10-mile loop trail around the lake to the ocean beach makes a long day hike, or you can pack in food, water, and gear and stay overnight at secluded coastal campsites. The ranger station at Ozette can provide tide tables and other important information you need before heading out on these potentially dangerous beach trails. The park offers interpretive programs in the summer as well as a pleasant twenty-two-site campground at the lake's north end.

Or contact **Lost Resort Campground** (20860 Hoko-Ozette Road, Clallam Bay 98326; 360–963–2899); it's about ¼ mile from the Ranger Station. For even more civilized accommodations, contact **Winters Summer Bed & Breakfast** overlooking the Strait of Juan de Fuca at 16651 Highway 12, Clallam Bay 98326; (360) 963–2264; www.northolympic.com/winters.

For an easy day hike from Ozette, walk along the 3-mile boardwalk over coastal wetlands to Cape Alava, the site of an ancient Makah Indian fishing village that was buried by a mud slide 500 years ago and recently excavated. The well-preserved contents of the village, exposed by tidal action in the 1970s, are housed at the **Makah Museum** (360–645–2711), which is part of the Makah Cultural and Research Center in Neah Bay, on the Makah Indian Reservation located about 60 miles from Port Angeles. Owned and operated by the Makah Tribe, museum exhibits tell the story of people who lived a rigorous life hunting whales, seals, and fish. The museum craft shop and other shops in town display the work of Neah Bay's resident Makah artists. The museum, which charges a small entrance fee, is located on Bayview Avenue and is open from 10:00 A.M. to 5:00 P.M. daily in summer and Wednesday through Sunday during the rest of the year.

Neah Bay is also the site of the annual Makah Days celebration, held the last weekend in August, which features traditional salmon bakes along with dancing and singing and canoe races.

There are several motels and small RV parks in Neah Bay—try **Silver Salmon Motel & RV Park** (360–645–2284), **Cape Motel & RV Park** (360–645–2250), and **Tyee Motel** (360–645–2223).

Follow signs to the Makah Air Force Station west of Neah Bay and take the right-hand fork to reach the renovated ¾-mile trail to **Cape Flattery,** the northwesternmost point in the contiguous United States. Along the trail are several observation decks, and you'll find two picnic tables at trail's end. This rocky point has great views of Tatoosh Island, a half-mile-long volcanic outcropping that was once a favorite Makah retreat and is now home to a century-old lighthouse and nesting seabirds. This is a good place to get a close-up view of gray whales, which are often sighted feeding in the area during their annual migrations up the coast from May through June. Blustery Cape Flattery is well known for its average of 215 days of precipitation a year—be sure to bring rain gear and sturdy boots.

To reach the more primitive and scenic ocean beaches, take the south fork at the Air Force Station. **Hobuck** and **Sooes Beaches** are located on the outer coast a few miles south of Neah Bay. From Makah Bay south the beaches are primitive and untouched by tourism. *Note:* Pack hearty snacks and beverages before leaving Port Angeles. The **Makah National Fish Hatchery,** located on a dirt road just south of Sooes Beach, is open daily year-round and welcomes visitors to its salmon-spawning facilities. When you're ready to continue your peninsula journey, return east on Highway 112 and take the turnoff south on Burnt Mountain Road, located 6 miles south of Clallam Bay, back to Highway 101.

Rain Forest

Burnt Mountain Road connects to Highway 101 at Sappho. A mile farther west you can take Pavel Road 2 miles to the **Solduc Salmon Hatchery.** The hatchery has a small interpretive center with colorful dioramas illustrating the life cycle of Soleduck salmon and the challenges facing the fisheries industries. Just north of the community of Forks, La Push Road connects Highway 101 with **Rialto Beach, Mora Campground** (part of Olympic National Park), and the Quileute native community of **La Push.** A short distance from the beach is **Manitou Lodge** (813 Kilmer Road, P.O. Box 600, Forks 98331; 360–374–6295; www.manitoulodge.com). Visitors to this rain-forest hideaway can take advantage of its proximity to forests, rivers, and unspoiled beaches to enjoy a variety of outdoor activities. Or just hole up with a good novel and relax by the huge lodge fireplace. Breakfast is served in the lodge's pleasant dining room. To get to Manitou Lodge, follow La Push Road 8 miles west of Highway 101, turn right onto Mora Road, and then right again onto Kilmer Road after crossing the single lane bridge over the Sol Duc River. To bed down closer to the ocean, try **La Push Ocean Park Resort** (700 Main Street, P.O. Box 67, La Push 98350; 360–374–5267 or 800–487–1267), a Quileute tribal enterprise. Guests enjoy ocean views and access to miles of sandy and rocky beaches ideal for beachcombing. Whale watching is a popular activity during the spring months.

Located on Highway 101, **Forks** is primarily a logging town. The **Forks Timber Museum** located south of town offers a comprehensive introduction to the history, economy, and culture of logging. Historical photographs, old logging equipment, and dioramas give a glimpse of what life was like in old logging camps and pioneer homes and how simple tools and hard work were employed to fell, transport, and cut timber into commercial lumber. The old-fashioned Fourth of July celebration in Forks highlights traditional logging skill competitions. For more information contact the Forks Chamber of Commerce, Route 101 North, Forks 98331; (360) 374–2531; www.forkswa.com.

For a pleasant place to stay in Forks, call Susan and Bill Brager at **Miller Tree Inn Bed-and-Breakfast** (P.O. Box 953, Forks 98331; 360–374–6806), a 1917 homestead on three parklike acres located at 654 East Division Street, 6 blocks east of the only stoplight in town. You could also call the Baysingers and their gaggle of horses and pets at **Bear Creek Homestead Bed & Breakfast,** located north of Forks at 2094 Bear Creek Road (800–485–1721; www.bearcreekhomestead.com). Ask about the comfy guest rooms in the main house and about the cozy canvas tent-cabins near the meadow. At *Misty Valley Inn Bed & Breakfast,* located at 194894 Highway 101 North (360–374–9389 or 887–374–9389; www.mistyvalleyinn.com), guests enjoy pastoral views and gourmet breakfasts. If you'd like a cozy self-contained cottage right in Forks, contact Deannie Hoien at *Shady Nook Cottages* (81 Ash Avenue, P.O. Box 483, Forks 98331; 360–374–5497; www.shadynookcottage.com). *Note:* Unless you are camping or driving a self-contained RV and to avoid being disappointed during July, August, and September, be sure to arrange your overnight accommodations well ahead of visiting the Forks–Neah Bay area. If all facilities are full, call the Forks Visitors Center (360–374–2531 or 800–443–6757) for assistance.

Accessed 10 miles south of Forks, Upper Hoh Road follows the Hoh River Valley 18 miles east into the thickest part of the rain forest. At the end of the road is the Olympic National Park *Hoh River Visitor Center and Nature Trail.* This area receives more than 120 inches of rain annually, creating a lush multilayered environment highlighted with every shade of green imaginable. Even a short excursion through the Hall of Mosses Trail or along the Spruce Nature Trail offers an opportunity to experience the grandeur of the old-growth hemlock forest that once covered much of western Washington. To reach more secluded parts of the forest, you can walk a few miles toward the Blue Glacier or—well prepared with food, water, and gear—hardy folks can take

Storm Watching 101

*T*he best times to head to coastal areas for watching Pacific storms are mid-November to mid-February. When big winter storms are forecast, they can unleash walloping wave action, towers of foamy spray, and hours of howling winds. Joining the gaggle of intrepid stormwatchers is easy—just dress in warm sweaters, windbreakers, boots, hats, and gloves, grab the cameras, and head to safe places along the coastline to have a gander. Check these travel sources for current information on the safest perches from which to watch Washington coast storms:

• *Long Beach Peninsula Visitors Bureau (360–642–2351 or 800–646–2351; www.funbeach.com)*

• *Fort Canby State Park at Ilwaco (360–642–3078)*

• *Westport/Grayland Visitors Information Center, Westport (360–268–9422)*

• *Westport Maritime Museum and Lighthouse, Westport (360–268–0078)*

• *Forks Visitors Information Center, Forks (360–374–2531 or 800–443–3677; www.forkswa.com)*

longer hikes to backcountry campsites such as Olympus (9 miles from the visitor center) or Glacier Meadows (an additional 8 miles). Contact the Hoh River Visitor Center at (360) 374–6925.

Located 7 miles south of Upper Hoh Road near Milepost 172 is the *Hoh Humm Ranch* (171763 Highway 101, Forks 98331; 360–374–5337), a working farm owned by the Huelsdonk family and situated on the banks of the Hoh River along with llamas, deer, goats, and cattle, plus the resident ranch cats. Two ranch-house rooms share a bath, and a hearty farm breakfast is included. You and the kids can fish from the riverbank or just relax and enjoy the scenery.

The *Rain Forest Hostel* (169312 Highway 101, Forks 98331; 360–374–2270), located 23 miles south of Forks on Highway 101, offers basic accommodations at a minimal price; reservations are required. It's a popular base for young travelers exploring the Olympic Peninsula, so part of the fun is meeting visitors from around the world. Host Jim Conomos helps his guests explore the region, including arranging tours, rain-forest hikes, fishing on the Hoh River, and visits to lumber mills and Indian reservations. A half mile south of the hostel is the turnoff west to the *Hoh Reservation Tribal Center and Gallery,* at 2464 Lower Hoh Road (360–374–6582). Stop by the center to see examples of traditional baskets and beadwork and find out about the work of tribal artists.

Highway 101 curves west to follow the cliffs above *Ruby* and *Kalaloch* (pronounced *Clay-lock*) *Beaches,* offering magnificent views of the Pacific Ocean. It's a rugged coastline littered with sea stacks and rock pillars where waves leap, foam, and crash against rocks, driftwood, and offshore islands. At night you'll see flashes from the lighthouse, which has provided a warning to coastal mariners since it was built in 1891, on distant Destruction Island.

At Queets the highway turns inland to Lake Quinault. This is the densest part of the rain forest. To experience this lush and green place with its giant trees, you can stay at *Lochaerie Resort Cabins* (638 North Shore Road, Amanda Park 98526; 360–288–2215; www.lochaerie.com), located 4 miles east of Highway 101 on the lake's north shore. The six rustic cabins have changed little since they were built on the cliffs above the lake in the 1920s and 1930s. Each cabin has a fireplace, kitchen, and views of the lake—everything needed for a romantic sojourn. Guests can explore the driftwood-covered beach, canoe, or hike nearby on rain-forest trails. Additional information about day hikes can be obtained from the Quinault Ranger Station (360–288–2525) and from the Quinault River Ranger Station (360–288–2444).

Good eateries nearby suggested by locals include **Salmon House Restaurant** at Rain Forest Resort Village (360–288–2535); **Camp Seven Restaurant** (360–288–2662); and **J. J.'s Cafe** (360–288–2275). Rain Forest Resort Village also offers lake-view cabins.

On the south side of the lake, 2 miles east of the highway, sits **Lake Quinault Lodge** (South Shore Road, P.O. Box 7, Quinault 98575; 800–562–6672 or 360–288–2900), a ninety-two–room waterfront resort built in 1926. Guests can rent boats and canoes for exploring the lake, enjoy a game of badminton on the grass, soak in the swimming pool, and enjoy gourmet dining in the semiformal restaurant. For more rustic accommodations ask about the **Boathouse Annex** built in 1923. Pets are allowed in the Annex, which offers eight guest rooms. None of the resort's rooms has a TV or a telephone.

Harbors, Bays, and Rivers

The twin port cities of Hoquiam and Aberdeen on Grays Harbor are hardworking communities where logging, fishing, and shipping are nearly everybody's business. On a hillside above residential Hoquiam sits the splendid **Hoquiam Castle Bed and Breakfast** (515 Chenault, Hoquiam 98550; 360–533–2005; www.hoquiamcastle. com), built in 1897 by lumber baron Robert Lytle and now listed on the State and National Registers of Historic Places. The restored mansion is filled with opulent antiques, lovely cut-glass windows, a restored turn-of-the-century saloon, and five spacious guest rooms outfitted with antique furnishings and finery from the late 1800s.

For other comfortable overnight accommodations in the area, try the historic **Cooney Mansion Bed & Breakfast** (1705 Fifth Street, Cosmopolis 98537; 360–533–0602); **Aberdeen Mansion Bed & Breakfast** (807 North M Street, Aberdeen 98520; 360–533–7079); and **The Abel House Bed & Breakfast** (117 Fleet Street South, Montesano 98563; 360–249–6002).

Downtown Hoquiam has a waterfront park where you can watch work and pleasure boats on the river. Or you and the kids can climb the viewing tower at the end of Twenty-eighth Street on Grays Harbor to see the ocean-going container ships. Continue west past Hoquiam to follow the coast north on scenic Highway 109, past a series of small resort towns, including Ocean City, Copalis Beach, Pacific Beach, Moclips, and the native community of Taholah. Along the way you'll find windswept beaches, art galleries, antiques and gift shops, and resorts. For more information on places to stay, contact the Washington Coast Visitor

Information Center, P.O. Box 562, Copalis Beach 98535; (800) 286–4552 or (360) 289–4552.

A few miles east of Hoquiam, the **Aberdeen Museum of History,** located at 111 East Third Street, Aberdeen 98520 (360–533–1976), includes an eclectic variety of curiosities and displays from Grays Harbor's past. You'll see yesteryear's logging and farming equipment, period clothing, and toys. Exhibits include a blacksmith's shop, a general store, and a one-room schoolhouse. The museum is managed by an enthusiastic corps of volunteers, and it is open Wednesday through Sunday from 11:00 A.M. to 4:00 P.M. during the summer and weekends from noon to 4:00 P.M. during the winter.

Grays Harbor was a major shipbuilding center during the days of sail, when locally milled lumber was in great demand for hulls, masts, and spars. Three- and four-masted schooners, wooden steamships, and tugboats were constructed along the bay, and they crowded the harbor's docks. At the **Grays Harbor Historical Seaport** (712 Hagara Street, Aberdeen 98520; 360–532–8611), you can absorb this sea history and tour a full-scale reproduction of the *Lady Washington,* one of the ships used by explorer Robert Gray to sail into the harbor in 1792. The replica was built in 1989 as part of the state's centennial celebration and now sails regularly along the coast. Log onto www.ladywashington. linsect.com for information about dockside tours, educational programs,

Hoquiam Castle

adventure sail training, and the current sailing schedule for ports in Washington State and also in the neighboring state of Oregon. For additional information about the Hoquiam, Aberdeen, and Cosmopolis areas, contact the Grays Harbor Visitor Information Center, (800) 621-9625; www.graysharbor.com and www.graysharbor.org.

Twenty miles west of Aberdeen just off Highway 105, you'll find the town of **Westport,** where maritime life abounds. At the bustling marina the fishing and charter boats prepare for offshore tours or return loaded with fish and crabs. During the summer, catch the passengers-only ferry from Westport across the mouth of Grays Harbor to the tourist community of Ocean Shores. The Westport boardwalk is an ideal place to stroll and watch the waterfront activity, and there's a tower to climb for a bird's-eye view. The Colonial Revival structure located at 2201 Westhaven Drive was built in 1939 to house the Coast Guard's Lifeboat Station at Grays Harbor. The building now houses the **Westport Maritime Museum** (360–268–0078) and is open from 10:00 A.M. to 4:00 P.M. Memorial Day weekend to Labor Day. Tours of the **Grays Harbor Lighthouse,** located nearby at Point Chehalis, have been suspended due to heightened security, but you can still see it from a roadside viewing platform. The 107-foot-tall structure is more than a hundred years old, and its automated light, at 123 feet above the water, ranks as the highest light on the Washington coast.

March through May is the time to catch sight of migrating gray whale families as they swim north past Westport from their breeding lagoons in Baja California to the krill-rich waters of the Bering Sea near Alaska. The gray whale population once again numbers in the thousands due to international protection. To find out about whale-watching cruises, call the Westport-Grayland Chamber of Commerce (800–345–6223 or 360–268–9422; www.westportgray land-chamber.org).

Following the coast south on Highway 101 you'll have wide views of the Pacific Ocean before turning east at Willapa Bay. This long, shallow bay is rich with wildlife and shellfish. You can sample this bounty by following the turnoff at the Shoalwater Indian Reservation to the *Tokeland Hotel & Restaurant* located at 100 Hotel Road in Tokeland; (360) 267–7006. The hotel's dining room offers a panoramic view of Willapa Bay as well as hearty food. Established in 1889 as the Kindred Inn, this is the oldest operating hotel in Washington State, offering simple but satisfying accommodations.

Johns River

Elk River

Satsop River

Wynoochee River

Wishkah River

Hoquiam River

Humptulips River

Copalis River

Raymond, located just south of the junction of Highways 101 and 105, is a pleasant town on the Willapa River serving loggers, fishermen, and tourists. The old *Dennis Company* building at Blake and Fifth Streets offers a glimpse of the region's history in an 85-foot-long mural depicting shipping and logging activity in 1905. It's a friendly, small-town general store with walls lined with tools and turn-of-the-twentieth-century photographs. A collection of antique farm machinery and wagons across the street makes this a colorful corner to explore.

Continuing west on Highway 101, you'll pass through the picturesque riverside village of *South Bend.* The town's shoreline is worth a leisurely stroll to view the rough wooden fishing docks, piles of discarded oyster shells, and busy crab-processing plants. The *Pacific County Historical Museum,* located on the highway at 1008 West Robert Bush Drive in South Bend (360–875–5224; www.pacificcohistory.org), offers glimpses of the area's colorful past. The museum is open daily 11:00 A.M to 4:00 P.M.

Surf's Up Near Westport

*T*he seals, sea lions, and gray whales that make the waters of Westport home have recently been joined by another species of sea creature: surfers. This isn't the California-style surfing celebrated in Beach Boys songs—far from it. The waters here rarely top the high fifties in temperature, making wetsuits mandatory year-round, but the quality of the waves on this wild-and-woolly coast is what keeps thousands of the hardiest surfers coming back each year, both winter and summer. You can see some 200 of the best surfers around competing at Westhaven Park during the annual Longboard Surfing contest the first weekend in August. And if you have a hankering to hang ten yourself, lessons are available from The Surf Shop (207 North Montesano 98563; 360–268–0992).

Walk up the hill behind downtown, past some of the town's stately old houses, for great views of the Willapa River and the forested hills that lie beyond. On the corner of Memorial and Cowlitz Streets, you can visit one of Washington's finest county courthouses. Open during business hours, the elegant 1910 building sports an impressive art-glass dome and historical scenes painted in the 1940s.

The highway follows Willapa Bay's southeastern shore past South Bend. You'll pass rich wetland scenery including beds of eelgrass, feasting grounds for migrating black brant geese. The estuary environment supports a mind-boggling array of life-forms, from mud-dwelling clams, shrimps, and oysters to the millions of marine birds that consume them. After crossing the Naselle River, you'll pass pristine Long Island, part of **Willapa National Wildlife Refuge** (360–484–3482) and accessible only by private boat. The island supports a coastal rain forest that includes a stand of old-growth cedars as well as deer, bear, elk, grouse, beaver, and a diverse songbird population. Stop by the refuge headquarters east of the highway across from the island's south end for more information.

Long Beach Peninsula

The Long Beach Peninsula is an inviting place to explore for day or weekend rambles. The roar of the surf is never far off, the air is washed clean by ocean winds, and there are activities galore. The larger beachside communities are popular tourist destinations, but you don't have to go far to find lesser-known treasures and quiet walking trails.

You can enjoy a public art treasure hunt by searching for the numerous historical murals that grace the exterior wall surfaces of department stores, cafes, and public buildings in Ilwaco, Seaview, Long Beach, and Ocean Park. A free Muralogue guide is available from the Long Beach Peninsula Visitors Center (P.O. Box 562, Long Beach 98631; 800–451–2542 or 360–642–2400; www.funbeach.com).

Ilwaco is a fishing community at the peninsula's south end. The town's harbor is a great place to browse. You'll see charter boats with folks aboard heading out to fish for salmon, sturgeon, bottom fish, or tuna. In the harbor area are canneries for fish and crab processing, fresh-fish markets, gift shops, and eateries. Stop by **Festivals Coffee Net** at 151 Howerton Avenue (360–642–2288) for freshly baked cinnamon rolls, scones, and cookies and specialty coffee drinks with views of the bustling marina. For gourmet eats served up with Northwest wines and microbrews, the locals suggest *Rebecca's Canoe Room Cafe,* also near the Ilwaco marina at 161 Howerton Avenue (360–642–4899); open daily for lunch and open on Thursday, Friday, and Saturday for dinner.

Between 1889 and 1930 the Ilwaco Railroad and Navigation Company transported goods and people up and down the peninsula, first by coach along the beach, then by narrow-gauge railway from Ilwaco to Nahcotta. On your rambles around Ilwaco, stop by the *Ilwaco Heritage Museum,* housed in the old telephone utilities building at 115 Southeast Lake Street (360–642–3446). You and the kids can see a scale model of the 1890s narrow-gauge railway that ran along the beach from Ilwaco about 12 miles north to the small town of Nahcotta. Often referred to as the Clamshell Railway, its schedule ran according to the incoming and outgoing tides. The old railway depot is on display in the museum's courtyard. The museum is open year-round from 9:00 A.M. to 5:00 P.M. Monday through Saturday and noon to 4:00 P.M. Sunday. You can spot the first outdoor mural produced on the peninsula, a 1920s railway scene, on the north side of the Doupe Brothers Hardware Store at Ilwaco's only traffic light.

The *Inn at Ilwaco Bed & Breakfast* (120 Willams Street NE, Ilwaco 98624; 360–642–8686) is located within walking distance of the port and marina. Housed in a refurbished 1928 New England–style church, the nautically decorated guest rooms, each with private bath, were once Sunday-school rooms. Two and a half miles southwest of Ilwaco, off Highway 101, *Fort Canby State Park* offers beaches, forest trails, campsites, and two historic lighthouses. Although you can camp at Fort Canby without reserving your spot, the sites by the ocean and each of the sixty hookups must be reserved. Reservations are recommended in summer. Call Washington State Parks Campground reservations toll-free at (800) 452–5687. If you need more information, call the Fort Canby Park rangers at (360) 642–3078 or log onto www.parks.wa.gov.

Waikiki Beach, a sheltered cove well supplied with driftwood and smooth sand near the Fort Canby Park entrance, is a great place to watch the Columbia River's busy shipping activities. For even more dramatic views, hike along the established trail to the North Head Lighthouse. The *Lewis and Clark Interpretive Center* offers views of the Columbia River between the north and south jetties. A stroll through the center takes you on Lewis and Clark's heroic journey from Camp Du Bois in Wood River, Illinois, to the Pacific Ocean. The party's mainly river routes took them through sections of the states of Illinois, Missouri, Kansas, Nebraska, Iowa, South Dakota, North Dakota, Montana, Idaho, Washington, and

Oregon. In his journal Clark calculated the main group of thirty-three members had traveled 4,132 miles in 554 days. Twelve other members, boatmen, had taken the main group via the Missouri River as far as Fort Mandan, North Dakota, then returned to Camp Du Bois with plants and items collected from that first leg of the journey.

North on Highway 101 the small town of Seaview offers several more outdoor murals. If you are in the mood for a leisurely stroll, Seaview's

Lewis & Clark Corps of Discovery 200th Anniversary

*O*n November 7, 1805, William Clark wrote in his journal: "Great joy in camp we are in view of the Ocian...." For the record, the party was still some 20 miles from the Pacific Ocean, but they finally arrived at the mouth of the Columbia River on November 15 and set up Station Camp. Although Clark scouted up the Long Beach Peninsula some 9 miles for a possible winter headquarters site, the party backtracked upriver and, on the advice of Clatsop Indians about food sources, they started crossing to the Oregon side of the river on November 26. By December 7 the whole party was hunkered down at the Fort Clatsop site, and they began building their winter quarters. The Fort Clatsop National Memorial is near Astoria, which was established as a trading site in 1811 at the confluence of the Columbia River and the Pacific Ocean. Planning your Corps of Discovery travel itineraries is easy. Check these sites for Bicentennial events and activities, which range from 2002 through 2006:

Fort Clatsop National Memorial— Living-history programs mid-June through Labor Day (92343 Fort Clatsop Road, Astoria, OR 97103; 503–861–2471; www.nps.gov/focl)

Pacific County Friends of Lewis & Clark— A living-history event about the expedition over Veteran's Day weekend, November 9–10, 2002, at the Ilwaco Heritage Museum; a large Destination 2005 event planned by both Clatsop (OR) and Pacific Counties (www.lewisandclarkwa.com)

Lewis & Clark Trail Heritage Foundation (www.lewisandclark.org)

National Coast Trails Association— Lectures, hikes, and kayak trips in Pacific and Clatsop Counties (888–920–2777; www.coasttrails.org)

Discovering Lewis & Clark— A multimedia site incorporating the entire route from east to west (www.lewis-clark.org)

Lewis & Clark Bicentennial— This official national Web site lists Signature Events, activities, and other happenings from 2002 to 2006 for the eleven states encompassing the journey, plus other states involved in preparation for the journey (www.lewisandclark 200.org)

First Signature Bicentennial Event— Scheduled for January 18, 2003, at Monticello, Thomas Jefferson's home in Virginia (www.monticello.org)

meandering back roads offer pleasant views of quaint cottages, many established during the late nineteenth century as summer retreats. The **Shelburne Country Inn and Shoalwater Restaurant** (4415 Pacific Highway, P.O. Box 250, Seaview 98644; inn: 360–642–2442; restaurant: 360–642–4142) was built in 1896 and restored in the 1970s. Along with antiques, homemade quilts, and a bountiful herb garden, the inn features hearty country breakfasts and gourmet meals.

Long Beach, the largest town on your way up the peninsula, has a wooden boardwalk stretching several blocks along the beach from South Tenth Street. The boardwalk provides easy access to the roaring surf, rustling dune grass, and the wide, sandy beach. Subtle lighting along the way makes the boardwalk ideal for a romantic evening walk. From here you can also spot the array of multicolored kites that folks of all ages fly on the beach in late August during the **Washington State International Kite Festival.**

Stop by the **World Kite Museum and Hall of Fame** at 112 Third Street (360–642–4020; www.worldkitemuseum.com) in Long Beach, which features displays from delicate butterfly and dragon kites to huge fighting kites and videos showing kites flying high on local beaches. The museum's impressive collection numbers more than 1,300 kites representing cultures around the world. You can visit daily from 11:00 A.M. to 5:00 P.M. in summer and on weekends in winter. Look in a small alley between Second Street and Third Street South and between Pacific Highway 3 and Boulevard Street to see if the kids can find **Fish Alley Theater.** Tell them it's close to **Boo-Boo's Putt-Putt Golf.** Great fun for the whole family, this outdoor theater space offers local storytellers, clowns, jugglers, face painters, and musicians during the summer months.

There's the Beef!

If you're up for an eating challenge, the Corral Drive-In in Long Beach has one for you—in sheer volume, if not culinary inventiveness. Owner Don McGuire's Tsunami Burger is 22 inches across and weighs four pounds before cooking. Add a bun custommade by the local bakery and all the condiments, and a finished Tsunami Burger can weigh in at close to eight pounds! This monstrous, $27 burger is a hit with local Long Beachers, who order it like a big sandwich for parties and cut it into eight pieces to share. The Corral is open for lunch and dinner, 11:00 A.M. to 8:00 P.M. daily, takeout only. It's at North Pacific Highway and Ninety-fifth Street, Long Beach 98631; (360) 642–2774; www.corraldrivein.org.

Fun places to grab a bite to eat on the Long Beach Peninsula include *42nd Street Cafe* (4201 Pacific Way in Seaview; 360–642–2323); *The Berry Patch* (1513 Bay Avenue in Ocean Park; 360–665–5551); *Sand Dollar Deli & Pizza* (401 South Pacific in Long Beach; 360–642–3432); *The Crab Pot* (1917 Pacific Highway; 360–642–8870); and *Dooger's Seafood & Grill* (900 Pacific Highway South; 360–642–4224).

Continuing north, travelers can find access to the beach at both Loomis Lake and Pacific Pines State Parks, where you walk on sandy paths lined with wild strawberry plants. The beaches are great spots for seaside picnics. In this quieter section of the peninsula, *Blackwood Beach Cottages* at 20711 Pacific Way in Ocean Park (888–376–6356; www.blackwood beachcottages.com) offers five cottages with ocean and sunset views and three woodland cottages, all with kitchens and such pleasant amenities as Seattle's Best Coffee, Fran's chocolates, Tazo teas, and fresh flowers. If you like being closer to the action, check out *Boardwalk Cottages* at 800 Ocean Beach Boulevard South in Long Beach (800–569–3804; www. boardwalkcottages.com); *Gabrielle's Beach Units* (360–642–3433 or 360–642–8466) also near the boardwalk in Long Beach; or *The Seaview Motel & Cottages* at 3728 Pacific Way in Seaview (360–642– 2450). To bed down in the former digs of the lighthouse keepers, located just inland from North Head Lighthouse and Fort Canby State Park, inquire at (800) 452–5687. For other cottages, motels, and beachside RV parks, contact the Long Beach Peninsula Visitor Information Center, (360) 642–2400; www.funbeach.com.

Romantics can contact innkeepers Susie Goldsmith and Bill Verner at *Boreas Bed and Breakfast,* also close to the ocean at 607 North Boulevard, Long Beach 98631; (360) 642–8069; www.boreasinn.com. Guests are invited to take turns using the whirlpool spa located a few steps from the inn and housed in an enclosed cedar-and-glass gazebo. Breakfast is a lively event, with guests gathering on the main level for such tasty treats as roasted Washington pears stuffed with pecans, dried cranberries, cinnamon, and brown sugar; peach kuchen baked in custard; a three-mushroom frittata sautéed with sherry; and fresh-roasted organic coffee. Other pleasant bed-and-breakfast inns on the Long Beach Peninsula include *Whalebone House,* restored circa 1889, located at 2101 Bay Avenue in Ocean Park 98640 (888–298–3330; www.whalebonehouse.com); the circa 1911 Craftsman-style bungalow *Lion's Paw Inn,* located at 3310 Pacific Highway South in Seaview 98644 (800–972–1046; www.thelionspawinn.com); and the circa 1929

Moby Dick Hotel & Oyster Farm located at 24814 Sandridge Road in Nahcotta 98637 (360–665–4543 or 800–673–6145).

Head east (right) from Ocean Park on Bay Avenue and then north (left) on Sandridge Road to the tiny town of *Nahcotta,* the center of the peninsula's oyster industry. Native oysters, a tribal staple for centuries, were wiped out by the 1920s through overharvesting, disease, and freezing weather. The introduction of Japanese oysters and new cultivation techniques have made this Willapa Bay area one of the foremost oyster-growing places in the world.

Nahcotta's *Ark Restaurant and Bakery* (3310–273rd, Nahcotta 98637; 360–665–4133) is famous for regional culinary delights. In the modest blue building on the Nahcotta dock, travelers enjoy meals featuring Willapa Bay oysters, Washington wild blackberries, Columbia River salmon, and sturgeon. The restaurant is open daily for dinner at 5:00 P.M. and for Sunday brunch from 11:00 A.M. to 3:00 P.M. The place fills up fast when it opens so it's best to call for reservations.

Just beyond the Ark Restaurant, stop to visit the *Willapa Bay Interpretive Center* at 273rd Place. The center, open from 10:00 A.M. to 3:00 P.M. on weekends Memorial Day through Labor Day, replicates an oyster station house and inside shows the chronology of 150 years of oyster growing on the bay. You'll also see the walls covered with old photographs, memorabilia, oyster-harvesting tools, maps, and a 20-foot mural of Willapa Bay. From here continue north on Sandridge Road to visit *Oysterville,* which was established in 1854 to house those early workers and families. You can see the local church, a one-room schoolhouse, the general store, and early 1900s houses as you stroll through this quiet bayside village.

Three miles north of Oysterville on Stackpole Road find *Leadbetter Point State Park,* part of the Willapa National Wildlife Refuge and located at the far point of the 28-mile long peninsula. A favorite place for bird-watchers, Leadbetter Point's tidal flats overflow with migrating shorebirds and geese in April and May.

Along the Columbia River

The little town of *Chinook* was one of the most prosperous communities in Washington during the 1880s when fish traps lined the river, catching tons of fish to be processed in waterfront canneries. The traps were banned in 1935, but the port of Chinook is one of the

On the Coastal Trail with Lewis & Clark

*C*aptain William Clark's journal entry, November 26, 1805, describes the area that now comprises the **Lewis & Clark National Wildlife Refuge** near Skamokawa and Cathlamet: "Great numbers of Swan Geese Brant Ducks & Gulls in this great bend which is Crouded with low Islands covered with weeds grass etc. and overflowed every flood tide." This wild and scenic area today remains very much like it was in 1805 when Clark penned these words in his journal.

major fishing centers on the Long Beach Peninsula. You can still see many old homes built in the late 1800s. The old Methodist church on the corner of Highway 101 and Hazel Street in Chinook has been converted into the **Sanctuary Restaurant** (360–777–8380), offering excellent food that highlights Scandinavian cuisine. You can try *fiskekaker* (fish cakes), *Svenska kottbullar* (meatballs), or the nightly seafood, meat, and produce specials. The Sanctuary is open for dinner daily except Monday. It draws diners from all over the area, so call well ahead for reservations.

Scenic Highway 4 winds eastward through forestlands along the Columbia River, past the communities of Naselle, Grays River, Skamokawa, and Cathlamet. Plan to stop at the **Columbia White-tailed Deer National Wildlife Refuge,** with its 4,757 acres of diked floodplain and islands covered with thick grass and woodland habitat for birds and land animals. There are trails for walking or bicycling around the refuge.

Travelers can also find comfy lodgings at **Skamokawa Inn Bed and Breakfast,** 1391 West Highway 4, Skamokawa 98647 (360–795–8300 or 888–920–2777; www.skamokawainn.com). The nine light and airy guest rooms are situated in the historic Skamokawa General Store building, constructed on a wide deck that extends about 40 feet over the Columbia River, on its north bank. The river views are splendid from your lofty perch on the second floor. You're looking out onto one of the main sections of the **Lewis & Clark Columbia River Water Trail** (see www.coasttrails.org) and to the adjacent 40,000-plus acres of **Lewis & Clark National Wildlife Refuge** (360–795–3915). Ask the innkeepers or the refuge rangers about kayak rentals, instruction, and guide services for paddles on the scenic water trails.

The town of **Cathlamet** sits above the Columbia River, well situated for watching the parade of river traffic and enjoying views of the rural farmland of **Puget Island.** The 4-mile-long island is perfect for an easy bicycle ride, and from the south end you can board the last of the Columbia River ferries to the Oregon side of the river. Puget Island innkeeper Winnie Lowsma welcomes birders and butterfly watchers to **Redfern Farm Bed & Breakfast** (277 Cross Dike Road, Cathlamet 98612; 360–849–4108). You'll find two second-floor guest rooms (each with private bath), an outdoor spa, and a back deck overlooking the family garden and orchard. The **Wahkiakum County Historical Museum** at 65 River Street in Cathlamet offers artifacts of work and daily life from when the town was young. From Cathlamet you can take the Puget Island ferry across to the Oregon side of the Columbia River and head east on Highway 30 into the Portland environs. Or you can continue east on Highway 14 to Longview and reconnect with Interstate 5 for trips north to Olympia, Tacoma, and Seattle or south to Vancouver and Portland.

PLACES TO STAY ON THE WASHINGTON COAST

CATHLAMET
Redfern Farm Bed &
Breakfast
277 Cross Dike Road
98612
(360) 849–4108

Skamokawa Inn Bed &
Breakfast
1391 West State
Route 4 98647
(888) 920–2777
or (360) 795–8300

DUNGENESS
Groveland Cottage Bed
and Breakfast
4861 Sequim-
Dungeness Way 98382
(800) 879–8859
or (360) 683–3565

FORKS
Bear Creek Homestead Bed
& Breakfast
2094 Bear Creek Road
Port Angeles 98362
(Sappho)
(800) 485–1721

Manitou Lodge
Kilmer Road
Forks 98331
(360) 374–6295

Shady Nook Cottages
81 Ash Avenue
Forks 98331
(360) 374–5497

ILWACO
Inn at Ilwaco Bed &
Breakfast
120 Williams Street NE
Ilwaco 98624
(360) 642–8686

KALALOCH
Kalaloch Lodge
157151 Highway 101
Forks 98331
(360) 962–2271

LA PUSH
La Push Ocean Park Resort
700 Main Street
La Push 98350
(800) 487–1267
or (360) 374–5267

LAKE CRESCENT
Lake Crescent Lodge
416 Lake Crescent Road
Port Angeles 98362
(360) 928–3211

Log Cabin Resort
3183 East Beach Road
Port Angeles 98362
(360) 928–3325

Sol Duc Hot Springs Resort
P.O. Box 2169
Port Angeles 98362
(360) 327–3583

LAKE QUINAULT
Lake Quinault Lodge
Boathouse Annex
South Shore Road
Lake Quinault 98575
(800) 562–6672

Lochaerie Resort Cabins
638 North Shore Road
Amanda Park 98526
(360) 288–2215

LONG BEACH PENINSULA
Boardwalk Cottages
800 Ocean Beach
Boulevard South
Long Beach 98631
(800) 569–3804

Boreas Bed and Breakfast
607 North Boulevard
Long Beach 98631
(360) 642–8069

Oceanaire RV Park
25918 R Street
Ocean Park 98640
(360) 665–4027

Seaview Motel & Cottages
3728 Pacific Way
Seaview 98644
(360) 642–2450

Whalebone House Bed &
Breakfast
2101 Bay Avenue
Ocean Park 98640
(888) 298–3330 or
(360) 665–5371

NEAH BAY
Silver Salmon Motel &
RV Park
Bayview Avenue
Neah Bay 98357
(360) 645–2284

PORT ANGELES
Baytons' on the Bluff Bed
and Breakfast
824 West Fourth Street
Port Angeles 98362
(360) 457–5569

Red Caboose Getaway
24 Old Coyote Way
Sequim 98382
(360) 683–7350

SEQUIM
Juan de Fuca Cottages
182 Marine Drive
Sequim 98382
(360) 683–4433

Toad Hall Bed and
Breakfast
12 Jesslyn Lane
Sequim 98382
(360) 681–2534

TOKELAND
Tokeland Hotel
& Restaurant
100 Hotel Road
Tokeland 98590
(360) 267–7006

WESTPORT
Chateau Hotel Westport
710 Hancock
Westport 98595
(360) 268–9101

The Islander Motel &
RV Park
421 Neddie Rose Drive
Westport 98595
(800) 322–1740

**PLACES TO EAT ON
THE WASHINGTON COAST**

ABERDEEN
Billy's Bar and Grill
322 East Heron Street
Aberdeen 98520
(360) 533–7144

Bridges Restaurant
112 North G Street
Aberdeen 98520
(360) 532–6563

Helpful Web Sites on the Washington Coast

The Olympic Peninsula
www.northolympic.com/

Olympic National Forest
www.fs.fed.us/r6/olympia

Olympic National Park
www.nps.gov/olym/

Grays Harbor County
www.graysharbor.com/

Cranberry Coast
www.cranberrycoast.com

Long Beach Peninsula
www.funbeach.com

Lewis & Clark Bicentennial
www.lewisandclarkwa.com

CHINOOK
The Sanctuary Restaurant
Highway 101 and
Hazel Street
Chinook 98614
(360) 777-8380

DUNGENESS
Three Crabs Restaurant
11 Three Crabs Road
Dungeness 98382
(360) 683-4264

FORKS
Forks Coffee Shop Cafe
Highway 101
Forks 98331
(360) 374-6769

Kalaloch Lodge Restaurant
157151 Highway 101
Forks 98331
(360) 962-2271

Smoke House Restaurant
193161 Highway 101
Forks 98331
(360) 374-6258

HOQUIAM
The Levee Street
709 Levee Street
Hoquiam 98550
(360) 532-1959

ILWACO
Festivals Coffee Net
151 Howerton Avenue
Ilwaco 98624
(360) 642-2288

Harbor Lights Restaurant
Port of Ilwaco
Ilwaco 98624
(360) 624-3196

LAKE CRESCENT
Lake Crescent Lodge
416 Lake Crescent Road
Port Angeles 98362
(360) 928-3211

Selected Chambers of Commerce

Port Angeles Chamber of Commerce
121 Railroad Avenue, Port Angeles 98362
(360) 452-2363; www.portangeles.net

Westport/Grayland Chamber of Commerce
2985 South Montesano, Westport 98595
(800) 345-6223 or (360) 268-9422

Long Beach Peninsula Visitors Bureau
P.O. Box 562, Long Beach 98631
(800) 451-2542 or (360) 642-2400

Log Cabin Resort
3183 East Beach Road
Port Angeles 98362

LONG BEACH
Cottage Bakery & Deli
118 Pacific Highway
Long Beach 98631
(360) 642-4441

42nd Street Cafe
Pacific Highway and
Forty-second Street
Long Beach 98631
(360) 642-2323

NAHCOTTA
The Ark Restaurant
and Bakery
273rd Street and
Sandridge Road
Nahcotta 98637
(360) 665-4133

OCEAN PARK
Back Porch Garden Cafe
1517 Bay Avenue
Ocean Park 98640
(360) 665-5732

PORT ANGELES
Bella Italia
117-B East First Street
Port Angeles 98362
(360) 457-5442

Bonny's Bakery Cafe
215 South Lincoln Street
Port Angeles 98362
(360) 457-3585

C'est Si Bon
23 Cedar Park Road
Port Angeles 98362
(360) 452-8888

SEAVIEW
Julie's Loose Caboose Diner
Pacific Highway and Forty-
Sixth Street
Seaview 98644
(360) 642-2894

Shoalwater Restaurant
4415 Pacific Highway
Seaview 98644
(360) 642-4142

SEQUIM
El Cazador Restaurant
531 West Washington Street
Sequim 98382
(360) 683-4788

Oak Table Cafe
292 West Bell Avenue
Sequim 98382
(360) 683-2197

Petals Garden Cafe
1345 S Sequim Avenue
Sequim 98382
(360) 683–4541

WESTPORT
Islander Restaurant
421 Neddie Rose Drive
Westport 98595
(360) 268–9166

Sourdough Lil's
301 Dock Street
Westport 98595
(320) 268–9700

ALSO WORTH SEEING

The Cranberry Museum &
Farm, Long Beach

Moclips, Highway 109,
South Coast

Lewis & Clark
Discovery Dunes Trail,
Long Beach

Fort Clatsop, Lewis &
Clark's Winter
Headquarters, Astoria

Purple Haze Lavender
Farm, Sequim

Puget Sound Region

You could spend a lifetime exploring the Puget Sound region and still have more to discover. Puget Sound's inland waterways, cut by huge glaciers, offer travelers hundreds of miles of shoreline and friendly waterfront communities as well as numerous islands. The region's moist maritime climate supports lush forests and farms. A dynamic economy based on natural resources, agriculture, and industry has attracted a diverse culture. Many families live on the sound's larger islands, such as Anderson, Vashon, Bainbridge, Whidbey, Fidalgo, Guemes, Lummi, Shaw, Lopez, Orcas, and San Juan. It's a way of life that's slower, less frantic. Checking ferry schedules, waiting in ferry lines, and riding the small county ferries or the enormous green and white Washington State ferries consume a good bit of time. But it's an activity that visitors also can enjoy because ferry rides come with fresh salt water smells, dipping seagulls, busy shorebirds, and other happy travelers along with wide-angle views of distant mountains, the swirling waters, and the smaller islands. And, if we're very lucky, we get to see a pod of whales, particularly the striking black and white Orcas.

You can still find old-timers who'll tell stories of life in the mid- to late-1800s decades ago, when logging, fishing, and homesteading were the region's primary occupations; when the "mosquito fleet" of small steamships provided transportation between communities scattered along the extensive shoreline; when the rhythm of the tides was a dominant force in every resident's life, including the lives of native peoples, many of whom live in tribal communities on small reservations scattered around Puget Sound and the Olympic Peninsula.

The cities of Olympia, Tacoma, Seattle, Bellevue, Edmonds, and Everett form an urban corridor along the east side of Puget Sound.

South Puget Sound

Mount Rainier is a dominant feature of the lower sound. There are many interesting places to visit in the area around Mount

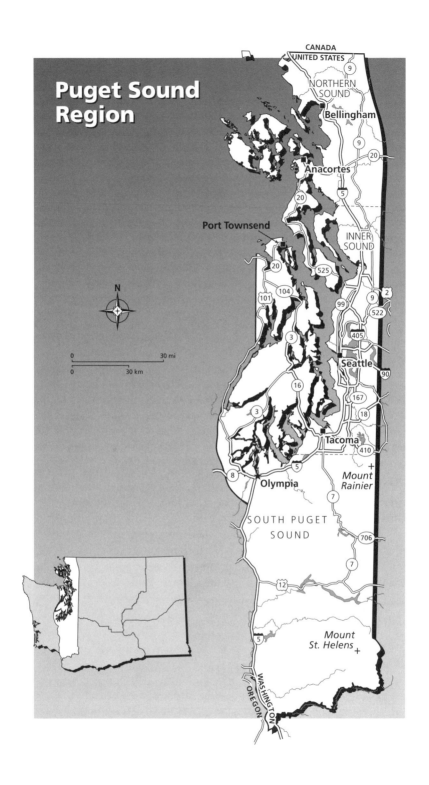

Puget Sound Region

CANADA
UNITED STATES
9
NORTHERN SOUND
Bellingham
9
20
Anacortes
20
5
Port Townsend
INNER SOUND
525
20
104
101
99
2
9
522
3
405
Seattle
90
16
167
3
18
Tacoma
410
5
+ Mount Rainier
8 **Olympia**
7
SOUTH PUGET SOUND
706
7
12
5
Mount St. Helens +
WASHINGTON
OREGON

N

0 ____ 30 mi
0 ____ 30 km

Puget Sound's Top Hits

Mount Rainier Scenic Railroad, Elbe

Pioneer Farm Museum, Eatonville

Hands-on Children's Museum, Olympia

Wolf Haven Wildlife Sanctuary, Tenino

Alice's Restaurant, Tenino

Mason County Historical Society
   Museum, Shelton

Bair Restaurant, Steilacoom

The Johnson Farm, Anderson Island

Museum of Glass, Tacoma

Center for Wooden Boats, Seattle

Elanden Gardens and Gallery,
   Bremerton

Sidney Art Gallery, Port Orchard

Suquamish Museum, Suquamish

Rothschild House, Port Townsend

Port Townsend Marine
   Science Center, Port Townsend

Meerkerk Rhododendron Gardens,
   Whidbey Island

Island County Historical Museum,
   Coupeville

The Anacortes Murals, Anacortes

La Conner Quilt Museum, La Conner

The American Museum of Radio,
   Bellingham

Hovander Homestead Park, Ferndale

Lynden Pioneer Museum, Lynden

Mount Constitution, Orcas Island

Point Roberts

Rainier National Park. The steam-powered **Mount Rainier Scenic Railroad** excursion train takes riders on a slow jaunt from Elbe to Mineral Lake at the mountain's base. On this one-and-a-half-hour roundtrip, you'll pass through thick evergreen forests, cross the bubbling Nisqually River, and enjoy spectacular views of the sleeping volcano's summit. Passengers can either sit in an open carriage or, if the weather is cool, relax in a closed, heated car.

Trains leave at 11:00 A.M, 1:15 P.M., and 3:30 P.M. weekends from Memorial Day through the end of September, and daily from June 15 through Labor Day. For further information call (360) 569–2588, or write to P.O. Box 921, Elbe 98330. You can also check the Web site, www.mrsr.com, which has good links for railroad buffs.

Back in the Elbe railroad yard, you'll find the two classic dining cars of the **Mount Rainier Dining Company** permanently parked on the tracks—a 1922 Southern Pacific and a 1910 Great Northern, offering a railroad dining car experience for any meal. You can watch the steam engine switching in the yard while feasting on specialties such as salmon or baby-back ribs cooked over a fragrant wood-pit barbecue. Cooking takes place in a renovated 1910 baggage car. There is also a lounge named the Side Track Room located in a late 1930s Chicago, Burlington, and Quincy coach. The dining car is open Wednesday through Sunday for breakfast, lunch, and dinner. Call (360) 569–2500 for reservations.

Six miles farther east on Highway 706 is Ashford, a small community of artists, outdoor enthusiasts, and old-timers who appreciate living at the entrance to Mount Rainier National Park. The *Mountain Meadows Inn* (28912 Highway 706 East, P. O. Box 291, Ashford 98304; 360–569–2788; www.mt-rainier.net) is a friendly yet elegant bed-and-breakfast. Located in a house built in 1910, it was the home of the superintendent of National Mill, once the biggest lumber mill west of the Mississippi River. Guests wake to a hearty, gourmet country breakfast of, perhaps, smoked king salmon and herbed cream cheese omelets. Wildlife is often visible from the generous front porch or while strolling on trails through the forest.

Another favorite lodging in these parts is *Alexander's Old Country Inn & Restaurant* (37515 State Route 706 East; 800–654–7615 or 360–569–2300), just 3 miles east of Ashford. Luminaries such as Theodore Roosevelt and William Howard Taft have bunked down at this twelve-room homestead, the oldest historic structure in the area.

Alexander's restaurant (360–569–2300) is touted as one of the best in these parts. The pan-fried trout comes from its own glacier-fed pond, and the baked salmon or beef tenderloin in a green pepper and mango chutney are highly recommended as well. Diners also enjoy freshly baked breads and desserts.

Stormking Bed and Breakfast & Spa (37311 State Route 706 East, P.O. Box 126, Ashford 98304; 360–569–2339; www.stormkingspa.com) is located on Goat Creek in a rustic 1890 homestead that once provided lodging for turn-of-the-century mountain visitors. The newly renovated inn offers four rooms and is just 1 mile from the Nisqually entrance to Mount Rainier National Park. There are plenty of art galleries in Ashford, and they all open their doors for Arttrek on the first Saturday of the month from 11:00 A.M. to 6:00 P.M. year-round, offering visitors an opportunity to discover the works of artists inspired by the grandeur of their mountain home. Highlights along the way include *Pottery by Jana,* whose charming studio on a quiet country road (30803 Mount Tahoma Canyon Road; 360–569–2933) offers functional stoneware enlivened with irises.

If all this exploring has tied your muscles in knots, consider being pampered at *Wellspring Spa and Log Cabins* (54922 Kernahan Road, Ashford 98304; 360–569–2514; www.wellspringspa.com), where licensed massage therapist Sunny Thompson has created a mountain paradise of saunas, waterfalls, hot tubs, and comfortable rooms and cozy log cabins (and even a treehouse nest). The outdoor hot tubs overlook

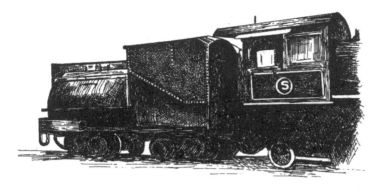

Mount Rainier Scenic Railroad

landscaped gardens with terraced waterfalls and cooing doves. The wood-heat saunas or professional massage can do wonders to revitalize even the weariest traveler.

Jasmer's Guest House (30005 SR 706 East, Ashford 98304; 360–569–2682) offers cozy cabins along Big Creek. Other accommodations close to Ashford include *Nisqually Lodge* (360–569–8804) for comfy lodge-style rooms and *Mounthaven Resort* (360–569–2594 or 800–456–9380) for cabins and RV spaces. On the far north side of Mount Rainier, *Alta Crystal Resort* (68317 SR 410 East, Greenwater 98022; 800–277–6475) offers cabins and chalets near Crystal Mountain Ski Area and also near hiking and mountain biking trails through an old-growth forest within the Mount Baker–Snoqualmie National Forest.

Mount Rainier National Park celebrated its centennial anniversary in 1999; its capstone, Mount Rainier, rises to a whopping elevation of 14,411 feet. This mountain is not one to take lightly. It commands respect; it makes its own weather. Because it is also an active volcano covered with ice and snow (like Mount St. Helens), geological and weather-related changes can happen here almost without warning. But during summer months, from late June to early September, you can enjoy two scenic drives that lead safely to panoramic locations on the mountain. The first, *Paradise,* is accessed from the Ashford area; the second, *Sunrise,* is accessed from the east side near the Chinook Pass highway. Sunrise is the more arduous and winding drive, but the rewards are many, including wonderful wildflower meadows with environmentally sensitive paths and trails among the native plantings. Both Paradise and Sunrise are above 5,000 feet in elevation, so travelers should take warm sweaters and jackets on this trek. There are six developed campgrounds in Mount Rainier National Park; check the Web sites www.nps.gov/mora/ and www. mount.rainier.national-park. com for helpful information about camping, hiking, horse camping, and backpacking in the park. Additional information can be obtained from park headquarters in Ashford (360–539–2211). During winter avid cross-country skiers can contact the *Mount Tahoma Trails Association* about skiing hut-to-hut on some 100 miles of logging road trails; call (360) 569–2451, Mount Tahoma Ski Trail office, for a recorded message and current information.

Good places to grab a bite to eat include *Rainier Overland Restaurant and Lodge,* open summers in Ashford (360–569–0851); *National Park Inn Restaurant* in nearby Longmire (360–569–2275); and *Scaleburgers* at 54109 Mountain Highway in Elbe (360–569–2247). Located in a weigh-station building renovated circa 1939, Scaleburgers has been serving juicy hamburgers since 1987.

In the lowlands near Eatonville you can enter a time warp at the *Pioneer Farm Museum* (7716 Ohop Valley Road, P.O. Box 1520, Eatonville 98328; 360–832–6300). The museum offers hands-on experience in pioneer living. Visitors forge horseshoes, grind wheat, or milk a cow. The museum's one-room schoolhouse is a reminder of the intimacy of education in rural communities. One-and-a-half-hour tours are run from 11:15 A.M. to 4:00 P.M. daily in summer and on weekends during spring and fall. The museum gift shop, housed in an 1888 trading post cabin, brims with old-fashioned treats.

North of Eatonville off Highway 161 is *Northwest Trek* (11610 Trek Drive East; 360–832–6117; www.nwtrek.org), an unusual park where you can see a wide variety of wildlife living in a woodland setting. Endangered sandhill cranes and caribou roam free amid moose, bison, and bighorn sheep, while elusive cougar, lynx, and bobcat prowl in Cat Country. You may catch sight of playful raccoons, river otters, or beavers as you explore the park's nature trails adorned with ferns, native berries, and trees. The park opens at 9:30 A.M. daily from March through October, with tram tours every hour beginning at 10:00 A.M.

Your perspective of the natural world may change after visiting *Mount St. Helens,* located just south of Mount Rainier. At 8:32 A.M. on Sunday, May 18, 1980, St. Helens exploded in a massive outpouring of lava and dust. The eruption measured 5.1 on the Richter scale. Since then, a total of 110,000 acres has been preserved for research, education, and recreation.

The best way to get oriented to the *Mount St. Helens National Volcanic*

FAVORITE ATTRACTIONS

*Mount Rainier
National Park,*
Ashford; (360) 569–2211

*Mount St. Helens National
Volcanic Monument,*
Castle Rock;
(360) 274–2131

Fort Worden,
Port Townsend;
(360) 385–4730

*Ebey's Landing National
Historical Reserve,*
Whidbey Island

Museum of Glass, Tacoma;
(253) 396–1768

Monument is to turn east from Interstate 5, exit 49 at Castle Rock, onto Highway 504 and drive 43 miles east to the Coldwater Ridge Visitor Center (3029 Spirit Lake Highway, Castle Rock 98611; 360–274–2131; open daily 10:00 A.M.– 6:00 P.M. with shorter hours during winter months; nominal fee). Here you see displays on the area's geology, the May 18 eruption with eyewitness accounts, lava dome growth, and current monitoring of the mountain. Folks also have close-up views of the volcano, crater, and landslide area. From here drive 9 miles farther to *Johnston Ridge Observatory* (open May 1 to November 1, nominal fee) for even closer, more dramatic views. Hardy folks with four-wheel-drive vehicles can access other dramatic sights, including 11 miles of blown-down timber, on the eastern flank of the mountain. You can also find some of these back roads from Randle via Highway 12, accessed about 15 miles north of Castle Rock. Check with the Cowlitz Valley Ranger District (360–497–1100) in Randle for directions and current road conditions on these narrow and winding routes. The monument's Web site offers current information: www.fs.fed.us/gpnf/mshnvm. For a guided trek into the volcano's blowdown area and a hardy over-night adventure to boot, call the Smith family at *Mount St. Helen's Tent & Breakfast Adventure* (14000 Spirit Lake Highway, P.O. Box 149, Toutle 98649; 360–274–6542). The family's ninety-acre Eco-Park facility at the 4,200-foot elevation level near Toutle opens May through September and offers cozy tent cabins with wood floors, tent sites, RV spaces (no hookups and no generators permitted in the wilderness area), and a backwoods cafe.

For bedding down easy distances from both Mount Rainier and Mount St. Helens, contact *Cowlitz River Lodge,* 13069 Highway 12, Packwood 98361 (888–305–2185); *Mountain View Lodge,* 13163 Highway 12, Packwood 98361 (360–494–5555); and *Timberline Village Motel & RV Park,* 13807 Highway 12, Packwood 98361 (360–494–9224). Good eats in the Packwood area can be gotten at *The Gourmet Cup & Bistro* at 105 Main Street East (360–494–6310); *Blue Spruce Saloon & Diner* on Highway 12 at Willame Street (360–494–5605); and *Peters Inn* on Highway 12 near Skate Creek Road (360–494–4000). Also check the Web site www.destinationpackwood.com for helpful mountain recreation information.

The Venerable Capitol

Olympia's opulent Legislative House, completed in 1927, was one of the last domed capitols built in the United States. Forty-two steps lead to the entrance, symbolizing the fact that Washington was the forty-second state to join the Union. The granite for the steps and foundation were quarried in the town of Index, and the sandstone of its face is also from the Cascade foothills. The dome weighs thirty million pounds and sits 287 feet above the ground. A Visitor Information Center at Fourteenth and Capitol Way offers more information about the Capitol grounds; call (360) 586–3460.

Continuing east on Highway 12 takes you from Randle to Packwood, then over the high mountain wilderness areas of White Pass, past the fishing resorts along Rimrock Lake, and down the Tieton River Canyon toward Yakima.

Because **Olympia** is the state capital and the home of Miller beer (orginally the Olympia Brewery), many visitors simply tour the capitol building, then move on. But there are many lesser-known sights worth experiencing. Start with a sidewalk tour of downtown as described in "Olympia's Historic Downtown: A Walking Tour," which highlights outstanding buildings, homes, and parks. This brochure is available from the Olympia Thurston County Visitor Information Center located at 1600 East Fourth Avenue, Olympia 98507; (360) 357–3362; www.olympiachamber.com.

Families with young children will want to stop at Olympia's **Hands-on Children's Museum** (106 Eleventh Street, Olympia 98507; 360–956–0818). This creative place offers a diverse collection of interactive exhibits for kids ten years old and younger. The kids may get to "swim through Puget Sound" in a miniature maze—complete with goggles to wear, sea creatures to identify, and trash to clean up—or learn how to make everything from submarines to ice cream. The museum is open June 1 through September 30 on Wednesday and Thursday from 10:00 A.M. to 5:00 P.M., Friday until 6:00 P.M., Saturday until 4:00 P.M., and Sunday from noon to 4:00 P.M. From October through May, hours are Tuesday through Saturday from 10:00 A.M. to 5:00 P.M. Admission is $3.50. To get there, continue north from exit 105 on Plum, turn left (west) on State Street, then left on Franklin Street for half a block. Exhibits and workshops change regularly.

After your visit to the museum, grab a bite to eat at the **Urban Onion** (116 Legion Way SE; 360–943–9242), which reportedly has the best kids' menu in town. You'll find it downtown at Washington and Legion Streets in the old Olympian Hotel. If you're there for breakfast, don't pass up the famous U.O. Smoothie, a concoction of orange juice, bananas, and yogurt, or the veggie stir-fry served over hash browns. Lunch and dinner entrees range from traditional burgers to vegetarian burritos.

Stroll along **Percival Landing** boardwalk on Olympia's waterfront to see the arrival and departure of boats and ships and occasionally view the playful antics of a seal. A three-story tower at the landing's north end offers great views of the port, the city, and, on a clear day, the Olympic Mountains. You'll find several places to eat, including the **Olympia Farmers' Market,** located at the north end of Capitol Way, where you can enjoy just-harvested produce, fresh seafood, and locally cooked specialty foods. The spacious, covered market is open from 10:00 A.M. to 3:00 P.M. weekends in April, Thursday through Sunday from May through September, and Friday through Sunday in October.

To absorb the atmosphere of Olympia's past, enjoy a meal at the historic **Spar Cafe, Bar and Tobacco Merchant** (114 East Fourth Avenue; 360–357–6444). The Spar retains many details from its early days; chairs have a clip on the back to hold the patron's hat, sports scores are announced on a chalkboard, and the walls are decorated with old logging photos.

You can enjoy a number of other eateries and coffee shops in the Olympia area, including **Tugboat Annie's Restaurant** located at 2100 West Bay Drive (360–943–1850); **Budd Bay Cafe** at 525 Columbia Street NW (360–357–6963); **Oyster House, Inc.** at 320 Fourth Avenue West (360–753–7000); **Twisters Cafe and Espresso** at 703 Legion Way SE (360–753–1050); **Crazee Espresso** at 124 Fourth Avenue East (360–754–8187); and **Wagner's European Bakery & Cafe** at 1013 Capitol Way (360–357–7268).

For fine lodgings near the downtown area, call the innkeepers at **Swantown Inn Bed & Breakfast,** a circa-1893 Queen Anne/Eastlake Victorian mansion located at 1431 Eleventh Avenue SE, Olympia 98501; (360) 753–9123. View the elegant guest rooms at www.olywa.net/swantown/. A sumptuous gourmet breakfast is served in the grand dining room, or you can have a continental repast delivered to your door.

From the **Puget View Guesthouse** (7924 Sixty-first Avenue NE, Olympia 98506; 360–413–9474), located a few miles northeast of Olympia on Puget Sound, guests enjoy wide water views of Nisqually Reach, Anderson Island, and Longbranch Peninsula. They can also walk the nearby beaches and trails of **Tolmie State Park** and watch for marine wildlife. The Nisqually River, which flows from glaciers on Mount Rainier, empties into Puget Sound at the nearby **Nisqually National Wildlife Refuge.** Visitors can enjoy walking on public trails, including the 1-mile Twin Barn Loop to the Education Center (open weekdays from 10:00 A.M. to 2:00 P.M.). For more information contact the refuge office at 100 Brown Farm Road NE, Lacey 98506 (360–753–9467) from 7:30 A.M. to 4:00 P.M. weekdays.

More splendid nature trails are found a few miles south of Olympia at **Mima Mounds Natural Area Preserve,** an unanswered "whodunit" carved into the landscape. There is an interpretive center built into one of these 6-foot-high geological bumps. You'll find an observation deck, a barrier-free interpretive path, and hiking trails among the riot of colorful wildflowers and native grasses that bloom in the spring. For a scenic route to the preserve, take Mud Bay Highway west from Olympia and turn south just past the Evergreen Parkway onto picturesque Delphi Valley Road. In about 5 miles veer right on Waddell Creek Road and follow signs south through the Capital Forest. After about 2 miles you'll see the turnoff to Mima Mounds on your right.

A few miles east of Mima Mounds is the **Wolf Haven Wildlife Sanctuary** at 3111 Offut Lake Road, Tenino 98589 (360–264–4695; www.wolfhaven.org), open from 10:00 A.M. to 5:00 P.M. daily, May through September, and until 4:00 P.M. Wednesday through Sunday, October through April. Wolf Haven is a privately owned refuge for abandoned wolves and other feral animals that can't be returned to the wild. For a small fee you can take a tour. Volunteers describe wolf biology and lore as well as the personalities of individual wolves living at the sanctuary. You can experience a campfire sing fest and howl-in on Friday and Saturday nights in summer (except in cases of heavy rain) from 7:00 to 10:00 P.M.

Nearby, visit **Lattin's Cider Mill** and purchase freshly made cider, homemade pies, jams, and syrups as well as fresh seasonal fruits and

---

Resident Wolves of Wolf Haven

*F*olks can "adopt" a resident Wolf Haven wolf either singly, as pairs, or as packs. This is a personal way to connect with and make a difference in the lives of these extraordinary animals, which are no longer able to live in the wild. Lone wolves are paired whenever possible for companionship. See www.wolfhaven.org for current information or call (360) 264–4695.

Selected list of resident wolves:

Pairs
Onyx and Tahoma
Solo and Denali
Marius and Morning Star
California Girls: Grey and Brita

Packs
California Boys: Stormy, Cherokee, and Sequoia
Idaho Pack: Kooskia, Siri, Mahina, Miwok, and Zuni

Lone wolves
Ramses
Moose

vegetables. Stop by before 10:00 A.M. on weekends to sample home-made doughnuts. If you would like to stay overnight in the area, call **Blueberry Hill Farm Guest House Bed & Breakfast,** (360) 458–4726; www.blueberryhillfarmguesthouse.com. The innkeeper makes Grandma's Gourmet Berry Jam and also serves guests delicious farm breakfasts (at a nominal charge of $5.00 per person) that are health-ful as well as waist-bulging. Travelers in RVs can check with **Offut Lake Resort,** also near Tenino (360–264–2438; www.offutlakeresort.com), for scenic RV sites close to the lake as well as fishing, boating, and canoeing.

South of Wolf Haven on Highway 99 is the town of **Tenino,** a friendly community famous around the turn of the century for its sandstone quarries. The scenic **Tenino City Park** was built around one of the retired quarries. Water cascades down moss- and vine-covered sand-stone walls into a pond, now used each summer as the community's public swimming pool (open from 12:30 to 6:30 P.M., Tuesday through Sunday, from mid-June through August).

Tenino was a railroad town named, some say, after the Number 10-9-0 engine that pulled local trains. Located on the main north-south line, all Olympia rail traffic used to change trains in Tenino. The **Tenino Depot Museum** (360–264–4321), adjacent to the city park, is one of many local sandstone buildings. Museum exhibits illustrate techniques used in the old quarries to transform raw stone into everything from bricks to flower pots, as well as railroad lore and local history. The museum is open Thursday through Sunday, from noon to 4:00 P.M., from mid-March to mid-October.

For outstanding dining call **Alice's Restaurant** (19248 Johnson Creek Road SE, Tenino 98589; 360–264–2887; www.alicesdinners.com). To get there, go south from Tenino on Highway 507, turn left at 184th Avenue (which becomes Skookumchuck Road), and in about 5 miles turn left onto Johnson Creek Road. The menu at Alice's highlights country game—including braised rabbit, catfish, roast pheasant, and venison—in addition to more conventional fare. While waiting to be seated, you can stroll around the trim gardens, complete with gazebo and ponds.

Fifteen miles west and north of Olympia on Highway 101 is the lumber town of **Shelton,** dominated by a lumber mill that sprawls along the waterfront. You can view the whole complex from the hilltop viewpoint adjacent to the huge sawmill wheel that stands as a monument to the lumber industry and a welcome to visitors who approach town from the east. A good place to start your exploration of Shelton is at the Visitors

TOP ANNUAL EVENTS IN THE PUGET SOUND REGION

Mystery Weekend,
Langley, mid-February;
(360) 221-5676

Skagit Valley Tulip Festival,
Mount Vernon, all of April;
(360) 428-5959

Rhododendron Show,
Shelton, early May;
(800) 576-2021

Scottish Highland Games,
Ferndale, early June;
(360) 384-3444

Capitol Area
Lakefair-Bed Race,
Olympia, mid-July;
(800) 753-8474

Bumbershoot,
Seattle, Labor Day
weekend; (206) 684-7200

Information Center located in an old caboose on Railroad Avenue in the center of town. Across the parking lot from the caboose, you can order a juicy hamburger or fresh seafood at **Shooters Bar & Grill** (328 West Railroad Avenue; 360–426–2186).

Across the street, the **Mason County Historical Society Museum** offers exhibits of the region's logging and frontier past. Located in a library building constructed in 1914, the museum features family photographs, pioneer tools and artifacts, and a nineteenth-century schoolroom. The museum is open from noon to 5:00 P.M., Thursday through Sunday from June through September, and Thursday through Saturday from October through May. Stroll down Railroad Avenue and Cota Street to get a feel for the town and its eclectic antiques and secondhand shops.

From Shelton you can continue north on Highway 101 along Hood Canal, passing through waterside communities such as Hoodsport, Lilliwaup, and Quilcene on your way to Port Townsend, Sequim, and Port Angeles in the northernmost section of the Olympic Peninsula.

Steilacoom, located just north of Olympia via Interstate 5, is a small town perched on a bluff overlooking the southernmost part of Puget Sound and nearby Anderson Island. Established in 1854 by Maine sea captain Lafayette Balch, Steilacoom was the first incorporated town in the Washington Territories, and during the late nineteenth century, it was an important seaport, county seat, and commercial center. Stroll through the downtown National Historic District, with more than thirty buildings on the Historic Register. For all-out elegant dining, enjoy a sumptuous dinner at **E.R. Rogers Restaurant,** which commands a fine view of the water at 1702 Commercial Street; (253) 582–0280. You can sample shrimp-stuffed artichoke, feast on charbroiled Northwest salmon, or try a combination platter of prime rib and Australian lobster tail. Dinners are served Monday through Sunday. The Sunday brunch offers a buffet that includes hot dishes, shellfish, seasonal fruits, and fresh breads and pastries. The restaurant occupies the restored mansion built by Steilacoom pioneer businessman Edwin R. Rogers in 1891 for his bride, Catherine.

The **Bair Restaurant** at 1617 Lafayette Street (253–588–9668; www.

thebairrestaurant.com), offers great breakfasts, delicious lunch fare, and Northwest-style gourmet dinners. The former hardware store and pharmacy, built in 1895 by W. L. Bair, was a popular gathering spot for those early commuters who caught the Tacoma trolley that stopped across the street. The store's lights would dim just before the trolley arrived, giving patrons a few minutes' warning to pay their bills. The restaurant is open daily, but call for seasonal hours.

The indigenous people of south Puget Sound, the Coast Salish, had a main village where the town of Steilacoom is now situated. Despite being officially ignored in the Medicine Creek Treaty of 1854, the Steilacoom tribe has preserved its identity and traditions. You can learn more by visiting the *Steilacoom Tribal Cultural Center,* in a lovely old church in downtown Steilacoom (1515 Lafayette Street; 253–584–6308). The center is open daily except Monday from 10:00 A.M. to 4:00 P.M. The gift shop sells Indian crafts and artwork. There is a small admission charge for some of the gallery exhibits.

Steilacoom's history is rich with stories of fast ships, quick business deals, and slow trains. To learn more about the town, visit the *Steilacoom Historical Museum,* in the basement of the Town Hall at 112 Main Street; (253) 584–4133. The museum, open from 1:00 to 4:00 P.M. Tuesday through Sunday, offers a glimpse of the town's 140-year history, including displays of a turn-of-the-twentieth-century kitchen, a blacksmith's shop, and a barber shop.

From Steilacoom you can take a twenty-minute ferry ride across the waters of Puget Sound to *Anderson Island.* The island is only 4 miles from end to end, but there are plenty of little nooks to explore. At the center of the island you'll find *The Johnson Farm* (253–884–4905), which was operated by the Johnson family from 1912 to 1975 and is now maintained by the Anderson Island Historical Society to display the labors and comforts of traditional rural life. A community garden on the property brims with homegrown vegetables and fruit in summer and fall. Tools and artifacts are on display, including the wheelhouse of the ferry *Tahoma,* which plied the Anderson Island route for decades. The farm is always open and tours of the farmhouse are available on summer weekends. Browse in the cozy gift shop nestled in one of the renovated chicken coops.

Anderson Marine Park, on the island's southwest shore, is a delightful and secluded place to explore. The park offers a nature trail through the woods and down to Carlson's Cove. Well-marked signs point out the diverse plant life and bird activity in the evergreen forest. Along the way you'll step on short stretches of the trail marked "skid road," "corduroy," and "puncheon." These terms, which describe the shape of the logs under your feet in the muddier parts of the walk, demonstrate historic road surfacing techniques to show how logging roads were once built. The last stretch includes a steep descent down to a small dock floating in the secluded cove rich with intertidal life. Beware of the poison oak beyond the marked path along the shore, and be sure to wear good walking shoes.

Ken and Annie Burg offer families the fun and comfort of their large log home, *Inn at Burg's Landing Bed & Breakfast* (8808 Villa Beach Road; 253–884–9185), located near the island ferry dock. From the inn's large decks, you can watch the boat traffic passing on the waters of Puget Sound, with a backdrop of Mount Rainier and the Cascades on blue-sky days. The inn's private beach is ideal for strolling and seashell collecting. Ken Burg, who grew up on Anderson Island and attended its one-room school, can tell stories of island life "back in the good old days." Annie guarantees that no guest goes hungry for breakfast.

Inner Sound

Historically the home of the Puyallup and Nisqually Indian tribes, the Tacoma area's first white settlers arrived in 1833 when the British Hudson's Bay Company established a fur trading post, Fort Nisqually. In the early 1850s the first permanent settlers arrived, mainly lumbermen. These workers built sawmills along the Commencement Bay waterfront, which soon bustled with cargo ships and workers of many nationalities, including American, English, Scottish, Irish, Hawaiian, Native American, and Chinese. Back then the old Whiskey Row area sported saloons, brothels, and gambling houses. By the early 1870s the fledgling town successfully courted the Northern Pacific Railroad to designate Tacoma its western terminus. The railroad was completed in 1883, thus linking Tacoma to the rest of the country, and the city's population soared from some 5,000 in 1884 to 50,000 by 1892.

And what about today? A twenty-first-century renaissance is under way in Tacoma, the welcome mat is out, and travelers will find many new shops, cafes, restaurants, and hotels downtown and in several historic neighborhoods. A new museum district is in the making along the Thea Foss Waterway, where visitors can find one of its stunning centerpieces, the newly opened *Museum of Glass* at 1801 Dock Street (253–396–1768; www.museumofglass.com). Its impressive tilted 90-foot tall cone wrapped in shimmering stainless steel offers a reminder of the sawmill wood burners of the mid-1800s and symbolizes the city's transformation from an industrial to a cultural enclave. Reflecting pools, walkways, and outdoor spaces invite visitors to linger along the waterway. Indoors you can see glassblowing demonstrations in the Hot Shop Amphitheater and enjoy rotating exhibits in the gallery spaces, as well as browse in the museum store and linger in the cafe that overlooks the waterway.

The *Washington State History Museum* at 1911 Pacific Avenue (888–238–4373; www.wshs.org) is connected to the Museum of Glass by the spectacular Chihuly Bridge of Glass, a 500-foot pedestrian walkway over I–705 that showcases the work of renowned glass artist and Tacoma native, Dale Chihuly. Next door is historic Union Station, also displaying Chihuly glass in its rotunda, and soon home to the *Tacoma Art Museum* (253–272–4258; www.tacomaartmuseum.org). Other nearby museums include the *Working Waterfront Museum* at 705 Dock Street (253–272–2750); *Karpeles Manuscript Library Museum* at 407 South G Street (253–383–2575); and the *African American Museum* located at 925 C Court (253–274–1278). You can also explore downtown Tacoma's historic *Broadway Theater District* and adjacent Antiques Row on Broadway between Seventh and Ninth Streets. In this area you'll see two restored circa 1918 theaters and a contemporary theater, along with several architectural treasures such as the 1886 Old City Hall clock tower and the 1888 Northern Pacific Railroad headquarters.

From here head north to the Stadium District, named for the imposing 1906 chateau-like fortress that began as an elegant hotel but now houses Stadium High School. Continue to Old Town to see the *Job Carr Cabin Museum* at 2305 North Thirtieth Street (253–627–5405), a replica of the 1864 home of Tacoma's first mayor, public notary, and postmaster. Next you can visit the *Proctor Historic District,* with its intriguing shops, cafes, and restaurants. At the far northern tip of the city *Point Defiance Park* at 5400 North Pearl Street offers a zoo, aquarium, and colorful perennial gardens along with *Camp 6 Logging Exhibit & Museum* (253–752–0047) and *Fort Nisqually Living History Museum* (253–591–5339). You could also check on the projected opening dates of the *Harold LeMay Classic Car Museum* (www. lemaymuseum.org) and the *Pioneer Museum of Motorcycles* (www.museumofmotorcycles.com).

For good eats and libations in the Tacoma area, there are several options: *Antique Sandwich Company* at 5102 Pearl Street (253–752–4069) serves good specialty sandwiches and is a popular hangout; and *Spar Tavern* at 2121 North Thirtieth Street (253–627–8215) offers tasty pub fare and local microbrews and ales. *The Swiss,* a blues pub

Estates, Mansions, Villas, & Castles

A number of Pacific Northwest timber, ship, and industrial barons of the late 1800s and early 1900s exhibited a tendency to the immense, ornate, and showy when it came to building their houses. Many of these palatial homes eventually fell into disrepair, some were razed, but a number of these fine structures have recently been renovated. Here are six among the top-drawer variety, five of them open as bed-and-breakfast inns and one as a splendid estate garden, also open to the public. Each offers a fascinating history.

Branch Colonial House Bed & Breakfast Inn,
6,000 square feet
Circa 1904 home restored by
Robin Soto
2420 North Twenty-first Street
Tacoma 98406
(253) 752–3563 or (877) 752–3565
www.colonialhousebnb.com

Chinaberry Hill Victorian Inn,
6,000 square feet
Circa 1889 home restored by
Cecil and Yarrow Wayman
302 Tacoma Avenue North
Tacoma 98403
(253) 272–1282
www.chinaberryhill.com

DeVoe Mansion Bed & Breakfast Inn, 6,000 square feet
Circa 1911 home restored by
Dave and Cheryl Teifke
208 East 133rd Street
Tacoma 98445
(253) 539–3991 or (888) 539–3991
www.devoemansion.com

Thornewood Castle Inn Bed & Breakfast, 27,000 square feet
Circa 1911, renovation ongoing by
Wayne and Deanna Robinson
8601 North Thorne Lane SW
Lakewood 98498
(253) 584–4393
www.thornewoodcastle.com

Villa Bed & Breakfast,
10,000 square feet
Circa 1925 home renovated by Greg
and Becky Anglemyer
705 North Fifth Street
Tacoma 98403
(253) 572–1157 or (888) 572–1157
www.villabb.com

Circa 1907 Lakewold Gardens Estate
Ten-acre estate gardens developed
beginning in 1938 by owners Corydon and Eulalie Wagner. Gardens
and Georgian-style manor house
now conserved by Friends of Lakewold; splendid gardens and gift
shop open to the public.
12317 Gravelly Lake Drive SW
Tacoma 98499
(253) 584–3360 or
(888) 858–4106
www.lakewold.org

and coffeehouse offering polka breakfasts with live accordion music, is located at 1904 Jefferson Avenue (253–572–2821). **From the Bayou Restaurant,** located at 506A Garfield Street (253–539–4269) and open for lunch and dinner, offers Cajun cuisine such as crab-stuffed halibut with Cajun roux. For the seriously romantic, **The Lobster Shop at Dash Point,** at 6912 Soundview Drive NE (253–927–1513), is open daily for lunch and dinner and features steak and seafood along with tasty appetizers with a Pacific Rim touch.

Pearl Street ends to the north at Point Defiance, where the ferry leaves every hour until late evening for **Vashon Island,** one of the largest of Puget Sound's islands. When you ferry over to visit this relaxing island of artists and outdoor lovers, stop at the **Blue Heron Art Center** (19704 Vashon Highway; 206–463–5131; www.vashonalliedarts.com) to get a feel for the thriving arts community and its myriad events. Next, call the **Brian Brenno Blown Glass Studio & Gallery** (17630 Vashon Highway; 206–463–4525) to ask if they're blowing glass. Among other creations at the gallery, you'll see life-size glass hats in fabulous colors. If you're ready for a snack, pop in to **Stray Dog Cafe** (17530 Vashon Highway; 206–463–7833) or **Fred's Homegrown Restaurant & Deli** (17614 Vashon Highway; 206–463–6302). Then don't miss visiting **The Country Store and Farm** (20211 Vashon Highway; 888–245–6136; www.tcsag.com) to enjoy the Ceiling Museum of antique kitchen implements and kitchenware as well as all kinds of natural foods, preserves, and

Other Friendly B&Bs, Tacoma–Gig Harbor–Vashon Island Area

Green Cape Cod Bed & Breakfast
(circa 1929)
2711 North Warner Street
Tacoma 98407
(253) 752–1977
www.greencapecod.com

Plum Duff Bed & Breakfast
(circa 1901)
619 North K Street
Tacoma 98466
(253) 627–6916
www.plumduff.com

The Fountains Bed & Breakfast
926–120th Street NW
Gig Harbor 98332
(253) 851–6262
www.fountainsbb.com

Aloha Beachside Bed & Breakfast
8318 Highway 302
Gig Harbor 98329

(888) 256–4222
www.alohabeachsidebb.com

Rosegate Victorian Bed & Breakfast
9409 Eighty-sixth Avenue NW
Gig Harbor 98335
(253) 851–3179
www.rosegatebb.com

The Betty MacDonald Farm
Bed & Breakfast
12000 Ninety-ninth Avenue SW
Vashon Island 98070
(206) 567–4227 or
(888) 328–6753
www.bettymacdonaldfarm.com

Angels of the Sea Bed & Breakfast
(circa 1917)
26431 Ninety-ninth Avenue SW
Vashon Island 98070
(800) 798–9249
www.angelsofthesea.com

garden goodies. Head down to **Point Robinson** at the southeast tip of the island, called Maury Island, to see the working lighthouse situated there. Call the president of the Keepers of Point Robinson (206–463–6672) well ahead if you'd like to arrange a tour.

Linger overnight on Vashon Island by arranging for cozy rooms at **Teahouse Guest Cottage** (5313 Point Robinson Road; 206–463–3398) or at **Artist's Studio Loft** (16529 Ninety-first Avenue SW; 206–463–3881; www.asl-bnb.com). For additional information browse the Visitors Information Center site, www.vashonchamber.com.

Gig Harbor is a delightful fishing village nestled in a protected bay on the northwest side of the Tacoma Narrows. The harbor is crowded with both pleasure and fishing boats. Harborview Drive, which hugs the shore, is lined with shops, sidewalk cafes, and galleries, making it a great place to stroll.

Gig Harbor's **Rent-A-Boat and Charters** (8827 North Harborview Drive; 253–858–7341) offers several fun ways to explore Puget Sound, from pedal boats and seagoing kayaks to large sailboats and powerboats. Located below Neville's Restaurant, the operation is open daily (weather permitting) in spring and summer from 9:00 A.M. to 7:00 P.M. and by reservation in winter. Galleries featuring local artisans are scattered throughout town. The **Ebb Tide Co-operative Gallery** (3106 North Harborview Drive; 253–851–5293), open daily from 10:00 A.M. until 5:00 P.M., displays colorful woven clothing, jewelry, watercolors, wood carvings, and pottery. You'll find great gifts at the **White Whale** (888–858–3286), **The Beach Basket** (253–858–3008), **Seasons on the Bay** (253–858–8892), or **Strictly Scandinavian** (253–851–5959)—all located in the heart of Gig Harbor. For comfortable lodgings, most with views of Henderson Bay, Carr Inlet, or Colvos Passage, check with these friendly Gig Harbor innkeepers: Suzanne Savlov at **Peacock Hill Guest House** (9520 Peacock Hill Avenue, 800–863–2318); Tom and Laura Yarborough at **Rosedale Bed & Breakfast** (7714 Ray Nash Drive NW; 888–337–1504); and Jenny Santori at **Bear's Lair Bed & Breakfast** (13706 Ninety-second Avenue Court NW; 877–855–9768; www.bearslairbb.com).

Recommended eating spots in the Gig Harbor area include **Green Turtle Restaurant** at 2905 Harborview Drive (253–851–3176); **Anthony's Seafood Restaurant** at 8827 North Harborview Drive (253–853–6353); **Tides Tavern** at 2925 Harborview Drive (253–858–3982); and **Kimball Espresso Gallery** at 6950 Kimball Drive (253–858–2625). For those interested in live local theater, check out the local plays and outdoor summer musicals offered by *Encore! Theatre Company* (253–858– 2282) and *Paradise Cabaret Theatre* (253–851–7529).

From Gig Harbor you can backtrack a few miles to Tacoma via the Tacoma Narrows Bridge and rejoin Interstate 5 heading north to Seattle environs. *Seattle's International District,* south of downtown and east of the Kingdome, includes a large and well-established Asian community. Visitors enjoy touring the many small shops and sampling the excellent food. *Uwajimaya,* at 519 Sixth Avenue South, is a unique department store where you'll find an amazing assortment of Asian foods, artwork, furniture, books, and household goods. To learn about Seattle's Chinese community, contact *Chinatown Discovery Tours* (425–885–3085), which offers both day and night guided tours of the Chinese/Asian Museum, specialty shops, and the district's best restaurants.

At the south end of Lake Union, the *Center for Wooden Boats* (1010 Valley Street; 206–382–2628; www.cwb.org) has a fleet of classic wooden boats, which are available for rent by the hour or the day. You can explore waterway attractions and join the colorful flotilla of small boats on the lake. The center also sponsors workshops where enthusiasts share ancient skills and historical knowledge, from boatbuilding and knot work to traditional music and lore of the seven seas. The center's pavilion is an ideal place to enjoy a picnic and view lakeside activities.

Also located along the shores of Lake Union, northwest of the Center for Wooden Boats, is the free-spirited *Fremont Neighborhood.* On Fremont Avenue you'll discover a number of funky, Bohemian, and fun gift shops, boutiques, cafes, and coffeehouses.

For bedding down in the Seattle area, try *Chambered Nautilus Bed & Breakfast Inn,* a Georgian Colonial inn located in the University District at 5005 Twenty-second Avenue NE, Seattle 98105 (206–522–2536); *The Bacon Mansion,* a grand Edwardian-style inn located at 959 Broadway East, Seattle 98102 (206–329–1864); or homey but elegant *Salisbury House Bed & Breakfast* in the Capitol Hill area located at 750 Sixteenth Avenue East, Seattle 98112 (206–328–8682).

The *University of Washington* and its environs offer numerous day and evening activities. Explore paths and nature areas on the campus and wander among colorful perennials in the *Medicinal Herb Garden* (take the Fifteenth Street and Fortieth Avenue entry gate into the campus near Meany Hall, then bear right onto Stevens Way to the garden). Spend hours walking pathways and waterside boardwalks at the renowned *Washington Arboretum,* visit several fine museums on campus, and attend performances at the university's several concert halls. Sporting events range from crewing races on nearby Lake Washington to Husky football and basketball games. The U.W. Visitors Information Center (206–543–9198) can provide maps and current information about cultural and sporting events. Nearby University Village Center offers interesting shops, delis, cafes, galleries, bookstores, and an excellent weekend farmers' market.

The Capitol Hill area is also great for walking with all sorts of parks, shops, cafes, and coffee shops. *Volunteer Park,* located nearby and designed by the East Coast Olmstead brothers, offers paths for walking, places to picnic, and a superb orchid collection at the park's handsome glass conservatory. At the western edge of the extensive grounds, you can enjoy marvelous views of the city and Puget Sound and also take in gorgeous sunsets. Also plan an hour or more to enjoy the splendid *Bellevue Botanical Gardens,* located at 12001 Main Street, Bellevue 98005 (425–452–2750; www.bellevuebotanical.org). Here, folks stroll

For Wine & Microbrew Aficionados

*T*he grand dutchess of wineries in the Seattle area is the elegant Chateau Ste. Michelle located at 14111 Northeast 145th in Woodinville (425–415–3300 for events and directions; www.ste-michelle.com). Tall Douglas fir, colorful rhododendrons, and lush beds of annuals and perennials greet visitors entering the chateau gates. There are shady picnic areas, and folks also can browse in the gift shop, attend seasonal events, and take a tour of the wine-making process. Wine and microbrew aficionados can also check out other fine establishments:

Columbia Winery,
14030 Northeast 145th,
Woodinville 98072
(800–488–2347;
www.columbiawinery.com)

Hedges Cellars,
195 Northeast Gilman Boulevard,

Issaquah 98027
(800–859–9463;
www.hedgescellars.com)

Redhook Ale Brewery,
14300 Northeast 145th Street,
Woodinville 98072
(425–483–3232)

Northwest Brewhouse and Grill,
7950–164th Avenue NE,
Redmond 98052
(425–498–2337)

Rock Bottom Brewery and Restaurant,
550–106th Avenue NE,
Bellevue 98004
(425–462–9300;
www.rockbottom.com)

For additional information check the informative Web site www.eastkingcounty.org.

along a lush perennial border garden, a summer dahlia display, a traditional knot garden, a meditative Japanese garden, an alpine rock garden, and a loop trail through the reserve. For other helpful information about the Bellevue-Redmond-Kirkland area, browse the informational Web site www.eastkingcounty.org. For a pleasant day trip, head down to the Seattle waterfront and board the ferry for a thirty-minute ride to nearby *Bainbridge Island.* Browse the shops and boutiques in Winslow, the island's main town, and enjoy eats or beverages at one of these friendly spots located in downtown Winslow along Winslow Way: *Bainbridge Coffee Company* (206–842–2557); *Sweet & Savory Cafe* (206–842–5532); *Blackbird Bakery* (206–780–1322); *Island Ice Cream & Coffee* (206–842–2557); and *Winslow Way Cafe* (206–842–0517). To stay overnight on the island, check with *Monarch Manor Cottages* (ask about the Carriage House, Stable Suite, and Beach Cabana), located at 7656 Madrona Drive NE (206–780–0112); *Agate Beach Guest House* (ask about the Beachfront Studio), located in nearby Suquamish at 17230 Angeline Avenue South just 8 miles from the ferry landing (360–598–2047 or 877–864–7630;

Brimming with rich scenery and history and just a thirty-minute ferry ride from Seattle, Bainbridge Island is the perfect day-trip destination. It's also the gateway for the get-away-from-it-all activities on the Kitsap and Olympic Peninsulas. One of the most lovely and historic places on the island is the Bloedel Reserve (7571 Northeast Dolphin Drive; 206–842–7631). Once a private estate, the 150-acre reserve offers a feast for the senses with its beautifully maintained grounds, including a bird marsh, English landscape garden, moss garden, reflection pool, Japanese garden, and woodlands. The reserve is open to the public Wednesday through Sunday; reservations are required.

www.guesthouse-agatebeach.com); or, contact the friendly folks at *Buchanan Inn Bed & Breakfast,* 8494 Northeast Odd Fellows Road, Bainbridge Island 98110 (800–598–3926; www.buchananinn.com). From the island you can access other Kitsap Peninsula destinations such as Poulsbo, Port Orchard, and Gig Harbor.

The picturesque *Snoqualmie Valley,* a few miles east of Seattle, is surrounded by the foothills of the Cascade Mountain range. The Snoqualmie River, flowing down the valley, creates the spectacular 270-foot Snoqualmie Falls. Above the falls is a public overlook and the trendy and posh *Salish Lodge* (6501 Railroad Avenue, P.O. Box 1109, Snoqualmie 98065; 800–826–6124) hotel and restaurant. The *Honey Farm Inn* (9050–384th Avenue SE, Snoqualmie 98065; 425–888–9399; www.myenchantedmoments.com/honeyfarm.html) offers comfortable bed-and-breakfast accommodations. Travelers find nine guest rooms with private baths on the second floor, a fireplace in the Master Suite, and an outside deck with views of Mount Si to the east. At the inn's Wildflower Restaurant, you can enjoy a sumptuous gourmet dinner.

The *Snoqualmie Valley Railroad & Northwest Railway Museum,* located at 38625 Southeast King Street in downtown Snoqualmie, offers train rides from the restored Victorian train station through scenic evergreen forests, to the nearby community of North Bend and past Snoqualmie Falls. There are runs each weekend from April through October (Sunday only before Memorial Day and after Labor Day). Call (425) 888–3030 for the current schedule and fare information; www.trainmuseum.org and www.snovalley.org.

For toothsome treats after visiting the railway museum, be sure to stop by *Snoqualmie Falls Candy Factory* (8102 Railroad Avenue SE; 425–888–0439) for not only delicious fudge and taffy but also hamburgers, sandwiches, espresso, and a great selection of ice cream. You could also plan a stop at *Gilman Village* in nearby Issaquah to sample chocolate confections at *Boehm's Candies* (255 Northeast Gilman Boulevard, Issaquah 98027; 425–392–6652; www.chocoholic.com). Gilman Village offers a gaggle of shops, boutiques, and eateries. For a cozy place to spend the night, call the friendly folks at *Roaring River Bed & Breakfast,* 46715 Southeast 129th Street, North Bend 98045; (425) 888–4834 or (877) 627–4647; www.theroaringriver.com. All four rooms have private entrances, sitting areas, and decks overlooking the bubbling Middle Fork of the Snoqualmie River. For evening dining in the North Bend area, try *Gordy's Steakhouse* at the Cascade Golf Course (425–831–2433) and *Robertello's Italian Cafe* (425–888–1803), both recommended by the locals.

Near *Carnation,* 6 miles north of Fall City on Highway 203, *Remlinger Farms* is a diverse 270-acre fruit, vegetable, and berry farm that welcomes families. There's a farm-animal petting zoo for children, picnic tables, a farm-fresh produce store, restaurant, and bakery. Remlinger Farms offers a Ripe 'n Ready Report of in-season produce by calling (425) 451–8740 or browsing the farm's Web site, www.remlingerfarms.com. The farm is located half a mile off Highway 203 on Northeast Thirty-second Street, just south of Carnation.

From Seattle take a ferry to Bremerton, and from here explore the *Kitsap Peninsula* and the western sections of Puget Sound. It has 236 miles of shoreline, more than any other county in the state. Most of its towns have splendid water views. When you reach Gorst, a tiny town on the edge of Sinclair Inlet, you'll find an ex-landfill and log dump transformed into the remarkable *Elandan Gardens and Gallery* at 3050 West State Highway 16, Bremerton 98312 (360–373–8260). The garden's extensive bonsai collection and gallery, which offers elegant antiques and art treasures, are open from 10:00 A.M. to 5:00 P.M. Tuesday through Sunday.

Port Orchard, located southeast of Gorst on Highway 16, has a hospitable downtown ideal for window shopping. Bay Street, the main commercial street, has old-fashioned sidewalks with a wooden canopy for comfortable strolling, rain or shine. Murals on downtown walls illustrate life during the late nineteenth century when Port Orchard was a major stop for the mosquito fleet, the small steamboats that were once a common form of transportation on the sound. At the north end of Sidney Avenue, you can catch the modern version of the fleet, which carries pedestrians and bicycles across the bay to Bremerton every half hour. A waterfront observation deck offers views of marine activities in the bay and across the water to Bremerton's naval shipyards.

To get a taste of Port Orchard's early days as well as the richness of local artistic talent, stroll a few blocks south on Sidney Avenue to the *Sidney Art Gallery* at 202 Sidney Avenue (360–876–3693), open Tuesday through Saturday from 11:00 A.M. to 4:00 P.M. and on Sunday from 1:00 to 5:00 P.M. The first floor of this former Masonic Temple, built in 1903, features monthly exhibits highlighting the works of Northwest artists. Learn more about Port Orchard history at the *Log Cabin Museum,* located just up the hill at 416 Sidney Street, and at the *Sidney Museum* (360–876–3693), featuring exhibits of turn-of-the-century stores and coastal scenes. The latter is located in the art gallery building on Sidney Street, on the second floor.

Bicyclists can enjoy a splendid ride on the *Manchester Bike Route.* This quiet, winding, beachfront road goes 15 miles to Manchester. Along the way you'll find beaches to explore, a restaurant where you can refuel, and a pleasant state park for play. For an all-day adventure, you can bicycle approximately 8 miles farther to the Southworth Ferry Dock and ride a ferry to Vashon Island or to downtown Seattle.

Reflections Bed and Breakfast (3878 Reflection Lane East, Port Orchard 98366; 360–871–5582; www.portorchard.com/reflections), a spacious home filled with New England antiques, offers wide views of Bainbridge Island and Port Orchard Passage from each guest room, the deck, or the hot tub. Guests can choose from the Chesapeake Room, the Sudbury Room, the Fairfax Room, and the honeymoon suite complete with a private sitting room and deck.

Poulsbo is a friendly community on the shores of Liberty Bay. Settled in the 1880s by Norwegians, the Poulsbo business community has revived this heritage to create a Scandinavian theme town. Scandinavian delights await at every turn in the town's historic district, from *potato lefse* (pancakes) to the painted folk art designs *(rosemailing)* adorning shutters and doorways. Be sure to visit **Sluy's Poulsbo Bakery** (360–779–2798) on Front Street, Poulsbo's main street and also close to the water and the marina, for delicious Poulsbo bread and Scandinavian pastries galore.

The **Marine Science Center** at 18743 Front Street (360–779–5549), celebrates Poulsbo's proximity to the sea. Established in 1966, the center offers a hands-on introduction to coastal marine life. The kids will be fascinated by the touch-tanks filled with living sea creatures such as kelp crabs, sea cucumbers, and anemones. You'll find a number of eateries and coffeehouses in Poulsbo to tempt the palate and quench the thirst for a freshly brewed cup of coffee or a steaming latte, among them **New Day Seafood Eatery** at 325 Northeast Hostmark Street (360–697–3183) for seafood and hamburgers; **Benson's Restaurant** at 18820 Front Street near the city docks (360–697–3449; www.bensonsrestaurant.com) for fine dining; **Checkers Espresso and Gallery** at 18881 Front Street, Suite E (360–697–2559); **Sir Bean Coffee & Tea Co.** at 18851 Highway 305 (360–779–4838); and the funky and fun **Poulsbohemian Coffeehouse** in the Egan Rank Building at 19003 Front Street (360–779–9199; www.silverlink.net/pbch/).

After browsing in the shops or learning about marine biology, head for **Anderson Parkway** with its large wooden gazebo (Kvelstad Pavilion), where you can relax and see the marina, the boats, Liberty Bay, and the green hills beyond. A 612-foot boardwalk leads from the Viking statue, along the shore, and up the forest-covered bluff to the serene **Arboretum Conservatory.** As you stroll you may see loons or cormorants dive for fish offshore.

After all this waterside exploration, you may want to take to the waves yourself. The **Olympic Outdoor Center** (18971 Front Street; 360–697–6095), across from Poulsbo's Marina and Waterfront Park, can outfit and prepare you for an adventure on Liberty Bay. The shop rents kayaks and canoes of all sizes for $10 to $20 per hour with instruction. Experienced naturalists are also available for scheduled or self-designed day (or full-moon) trips.

The **Cascade Marine Trail** links more than fifty kayak-accessible sites, from comfy bed-and-breakfasts to campgrounds, throughout Puget Sound. Kayaking visionaries foresee the day when this network of trails and campsites will take paddlers from Olympia north as far as

Skagway, Alaska. Trail updates are available at the Olympic Outdoor Center, or you can contact the Washington Water Trails Association at 4649 Sunnyside Avenue North, Room 305, Seattle 98103-6900; (206) 545–9161; www.wwta.org.

To find out more about the early people who first used these waters for food and travel, take a right (south) turn off Highway 305, south of Poulsbo, to the **Suquamish Museum** at 15838 Sandy Hook Road, Suquamish 98392 (360–394–5275; www.suquamish.nsn.us/museum). The museum's premier museum exhibit, *The Eyes of Chief Seattle,* will introduce you to the history and traditional lifestyle of the Suquamish Nation. Visitors can watch *Come Forth Laughing, Voices of the Suquamish People,* an award-winning media production that lets tribal elders tell their own stories. The museum is open daily from 10:00 A.M. to 5:00 P.M., May 1 to September 30; and during the rest of the year on Friday through Sunday, 11:00 A.M. to 4:00 P.M.

Three miles northeast of the museum off Highway 305 is **Old Man House State Park,** where Chief Sealth (who gave his name to the city of Seattle) lived and died. The Old Man House was a huge plank building that once stretched along the beach. A display explains how local tribes built and used the gigantic house. The small park is ideal for picnics and quiet reflection alongside Agate Passage.

For a relaxing rural interlude, contact the **Manor Farm Inn** (26069 Big Valley Road NE, Poulsbo 98370; 360–779–4628), a comfortable country-style bed-and-breakfast. The inn offers seven spacious guest rooms. See the rooms and pastoral grounds on the inn's Web site, www.manorfarm inn.com. For other comfortable overnight stays in the Poulsbo area, contact **Murphy House Bed & Breakfast** near the bustling waterfront at 425 Northeast Hostmark Street (360–779–1600 or 800–799–1606; www. bbonline.com/wa/murphy/) and **Foxbridge Bed & Breakfast,** an elegant Georgian manor close to town at 30680 Highway 3 NE (360–598–5599, www.sfox.com/foxbridge).

Shine Road becomes Paradise Bay Road north of Highway 104, which winds through the forests above Hood Canal, offering occasional glimpses of the water along the way. Past Port Ludlow and Oak Bay, you can turn off to Indian Island and Fort Flagler, or you can continue straight toward Port Townsend. The bridge to **Indian Island** offers great views of the narrow strait separating this island from the mainland. The road beyond the bridge follows the southern shore, with several places to pull off and admire the scenery. Turn right at the JEFFERSON COUNTY DAY USE sign, and follow the gravel road down to the beach to

Family Excursions on the Kitsap Peninsula

Anna Smith Children's Park
Creative demonstration garden
7601 Tracyton Boulevard NW
Bremerton 98312
(360) 337–4595

Kitsap Harbor Tours
Navy ships and sea life
Bremerton, Keyport, and Poulsbo
(360) 377–8924 or (360) 297–8200

Point Defiance Zoo & Aquarium
Picnic and play areas, gardens
5400 North Pearl Street

Tacoma 98407
(253) 591–5337; www.pdza.org

More information:

Kitsap County Parks & Recreation
(360) 337–4595

Kitsap Peninsula Visitors Information
(360) 297–8200; www.visitkitsap.com

Washington State Ferries
(206) 464–6400;
www.wsdot.wa.gov/ferries

explore the pebbly tidelands, scattered with driftwood and salt marsh plants. Myriad water birds are especially abundant during their fall migration. Just above the shore you'll find the trailhead to the South Indian Island Trail, an ideal hike if you want to explore more of the island's beauty.

The causeway from Indian Island to **Marrowstone Island** crosses lush wetlands and a lagoon between the two islands. Nearby sits **The Ecologic Place Beach Cottages** at 10 Beach Drive, Nordland 98358 (360–385–3077; www.ecologicplace.com), a rustic retreat surrounded by tall grass and wild beaches, ideal for wildlife lovers. Eight cedar guest cabins encircling the meadow come with kitchens and windows that offer views of Oak Bay. The caretakers recommend that guests bring boots, warm clothing, blankets, and, if possible, a canoe or kayak. Linens, towels, basic kitchen utensils, and firewood for the woodstoves are provided.

Fort Flagler covers the entire north end of Marrowstone Island with forests, former gun batteries, and rugged coastline. The fort was used off and on for military training until it became a park in 1954. Although the campground is busy during the summer (call 360–385–1259 for campsite reservations), the park is big and diverse enough to offer seclusion for those who seek it. Numerous hiking trails go through the forest to cliffs overlooking Admiralty Inlet, where you might spy colorful harlequin ducks feeding offshore or perhaps watch a peregrine falcon soaring overhead. The **Roots of a Forest** interpretive trail, a short distance past the campground entrance, provides an inside look into forest ecology. There's an indoor interpretive display, open weekends from 1:00 to 4:00 P.M., across from the park office and a wild, expansive beach to explore at **Marrowstone Point,** down the road at the northeast corner of the park.

The **Ajax Cafe** in Port Hadlock (271 Water Street; 360–385–3450; www.ajaxcafe.com) is an unexpected delight. With its funky decor the much-loved cafe offers superb dinners, including shark, scallops, salmon, duck, or beef. The public wharves, ships, and boatyards across the street add to the ambience. A sign at the dock tells of the history of this now-quiet oceanside spot as a booming industrial site from 1878 to 1916. The cafe is open daily for dinner from 5:00 to 9:00 P.M. and for lunch Friday to Sunday from 11:30 A.M. to 3:30 P.M.

In **Port Townsend** there's plenty of northwest history to discover, and also a plethora of arts events, open houses, and festivals. Contact the Port Townsend Visitors Center at 2437 East Sims Way, Port Townsend 98368 (360–385–2722; www. ptguide.com) for seasonal information. Residents enjoy meeting one another and visitors for coffee and delicious sweets at the **Bread and Roses Bakery** (230 Quincy Street; 360–385–1044) or for a fresh, healthful breakfast at the **Salal Cafe** (634 Water Street). Both establishments open onto **Franklin Court,** a courtyard with flowers, wooden walkways, and fruit trees.

Because Port Townsend's scenic location has spawned a lively community of artists, visitors find many fine galleries located downtown in the waterfront area as well as uptown, on the bluff overlooking the Puget Sound. Try **Ancestral Spirits Gallery** at 701 Water Street (360–385–0078) for Inuit and Native American art; **The Bird's Nest Gallery** at 715 Water Street (360–385–9297) for a comfortable jumble of garden art, unique jewelry, and handcrafted home accessories; **Fountain Cafe** at 920 Washington Street (360–385–1364) for monthly exhibits of local northwest artists' works along with tasty food; and the **Open Studio Gallery** located near the Visitors Center at 2409 Jefferson Street (360–379–8110) for showings from some thirty local artists and artisans.

Berries

Western Washington's climate is conducive to growing a wide array of fresh berries, beginning in early summer with strawberries and raspberries and ending in the fall with wild blackberries and huckleberries. You'll find U-pick farms and stands throughout your journeys in the Puget Sound area. Berries are especially abundant in the Pierce, Skagit, Snohomish, Snoqualmie, and Whatcom County areas. When you're at a restaurant and the server says there's fresh berry pie, don't pass it up. You could also try the loganberry, a cross between a blackberry and a raspberry.

The *Jefferson County Historical Museum* is located at 540 Water Street (360–385–1003; www.jchsmuseum.org) in the circa 1891 city hall building. The four-story brick structure houses exhibits that describe the area's nautical, native, and Victorian history. The museum is open Monday through Saturday from 11:00 A.M. to 4:00 P.M. and Sunday from 1:00 to 4:00 P.M. Admission is by donation.

Be sure to explore the historic neighborhoods on the hill above downtown Port Townsend. Just follow the stairs up Taylor Street or take either Quincy or Monroe Streets up the hill to see the many Victorian homes that once housed the cultural and financial elite of territorial Washington. Stop to see the Old Bell Tower on Tyler Street on the bluff, which once summoned the volunteer fire department. At the corner of Jefferson and Taylor Streets, you'll find the 1868 *Rothschild House,* which

Live Local Theater in the Puget Sound Region

*F*rom producing Laughter on the Twenty-Third Floor *(Neil Simon) and* Ten Little Indians *(Agatha Christie) to* Crazy for You *(George Gershwin) and* South Pacific *(Rogers & Hammerstein), live local theater groups are alive and well in the greater Puget Sound region. These avid thespians also offer warm welcomes to visitors traveling to their towns and cities. Call for seasonal play dates.*

Driftwood Players, Aberdeen (360–538–1213)

The Playhouse Theatre, Bainbridge Island (206–842–8578)

Bellingham Theatre Guild, Bellingham (360–733–1811; www.bellinghamtheatreguild.com)

Everett Community Theater, Everett (425–257–6766)

San Juan Island Community Theatre, Friday Harbor (630–378–3211; www.sanjuanarts.org)

Paradise Cabaret Dinner Theatre and Summer Theatre, Gig Harbor (253–851–7529; www.paradisetheatre.org)

Key City Players, Port Townsend (360–385–7396)

American Cabaret Theatre, Seattle (206–325–6500; www.americancabarettheatre.com)

Fifth Avenue Musical Theatre Company, Seattle (206–292–2787; www.5thavenuetheatre.org)

Seattle Children's Theatre, Seattle (206–441–3322; www.sct.org)

Snoqualmie Falls Forest Theater, Snoqualmie (425–222–7944)

Tacoma Little Theatre, Tacoma (253–272–2281; www.tacomalittletheatre.com)

Whidbey Playhouse, Oak Harbor, Whidbey Island (360–679–2237; www.whidbeyplayhouse.com)

has been preserved as it was a century ago, when it was home to the Rothschild family. You can tour the house from 11:00 A.M. to 4:00 P.M. daily during spring and summer to see the large kitchen, the formal dining room and parlor, and bedrooms filled with the family's original furniture and clothing. Be sure to stroll through the rose garden with its fragrant, many-petaled varieties, some dating back to the early 1800s. Call the Visitors Information Center (360–385–2722) for the current dates of Port Townsend's favorite annual events including the *Annual Victorian Festival* in mid-March, the *Gallery Walk* in early May, the *Great Main Street Garage Sale* in late May, the *Secret Garden Tour* in late June, the *Historic Homes Tour* in mid-September, and the *Cabin Fever Quilt Show* in late September.

If you can't spend a night at the opulent *Ann Starrett Mansion Victorian Bed and Breakfast Inn* (744 Clay Street, Port Townsend 98368; 360–385–3205; www.starrettmansion.com), you may call to see if tours are currently scheduled. It is a splendid example of Victorian architecture, complete with octagonal tower, sweeping circular staircase, and formal sitting rooms. Ask about the comfortable carriage house guest rooms on the garden level.

Within walking distance, on Jackson Street, find lovely *Chetzemoka Park* and its rose garden, including a splendid rose arbor walkway, large swings, and views of Admiralty Inlet and the Cascade Mountains to the east. Picnics are a favorite pastime here. Other comfortable places to stay overnight in Port Townsend include *The James House,* a home built by a prominent businessman circa 1889 and now renovated, located on the bluff at 1238 Washington Street (360–385–1238), and *Ravenscroft Inn Bed & Breakfast,* also located on the bluff and overlooking the water at 533 Quincy Street (360–385–2784). From the bluff you can walk down a series of concrete stairs to the downtown waterfront area and its eclectic assortment of shops, galleries, boutiques, and eateries.

Consider the much-loved *Fountain Cafe* at 920 Washington Street (360–385–1364) for seafood and pasta specialties; *Port Townsend Fudge & Espresso* at 1046 Water Street (360–385–9955) for lattes, teas, and goodies; *Nifty Fifties* at 817 Water Street (360–385–1931) for juicy hamburgers and old-fashioned sundaes, shakes, malts, and sodas; and *Elevated Ice Cream & Candy Shop,* also on Water Street (360–385–1156), to enjoy homemade ice cream, Italian ices, espresso, and pastries and to see local art on display.

While you are in Port Townsend, be sure to inquire about events at *Fort Worden State Park* (360–344–4400). Like Fort Flagler to the east, Fort Worden was once part of the fortifications that protected Puget Sound from sea invasion. Located just 2 miles north of downtown, the fort is the site of *Port Townsend Marine Science Center* (360–385–5582) and of Centrum Foundation (P.O. Box 1158, Port Townsend 98368; 360–385–3102; www.centrum.org). Events offered by Centrum include writing, music, and dance conferences, which usually offer activities open to the public. There is also a rhododendron garden, an artillery museum, nature walks, and a public beach to explore. You can stay in the old barracks or in comfortable officers' quarters, in the youth hostel, or at the campground. For information about vacation housing or camping, call (360) 385–4730.

Whidbey Island, the largest of the Puget Sound islands, has been populated for 10,000 years by Native people and was one of the first areas on the sound to be settled by Europeans. Its extensive coastline, lush forests, and location midway between the snow-capped Olympic and Cascade mountain ranges create outstanding views everywhere you look. Whidbey Island has long been a favorite retreat for city dwellers,

The Nautical Life: Wooden Boats, Tall Ships, Schooners, Wooden Boatbuilding, & Wooden Boat Festivals

*T*he *Wooden Boat Foundation*—A center for maritime education located in the Cupola House at Point Hudson at 380 Jefferson Street, Port Townsend 98368 (360-385-3628, www.woodenboat.org).

Wooden Boat Festival—Held the first weekend of September in Port Townsend (www.woodenboat.org); includes the Symposium on Wooden Boatbuilding.

Tall ship **The Lady Washington**— Ninety-ton trading vessel that was built on the Essex River, Massachusetts, in 1750 and was first named Washington; find the current schedule for ports of call up and down the west coast on the ship's Web site, www.ladywashington.linsect.com.

Northwest Maritime Education Alliance—Offers collaborative programs: lecture series, summer workshops, restora-

tion projects, and historic vessel tours (www.nwmaritime.org).

The Northwest School of Wooden Boatbuilding—Offers classes and workshops at 251 Otto Street, Port Townsend 98368 (360-385-4948; www.nwboatschool.org).

Sound Experience—Offers environmental sailing programs in the waters of Puget Sound aboard the historic schooner Adventuress (2310 Washington Street, Port Townsend 98368; 360-379-0438; www.soundexp.org).

Center for Wooden Boats—Located on Lake Union, offering exhibits, programs, and classic wooden boats to rent for informal paddling excursions on the lake (1010 Valley Street, Seattle 98105; 206-382-2628, www.cwb.org).

offering visitors plenty to do and see. Small working farms, artist studios, and innovative home businesses are scattered among meadows, shoreline, and evergreen forests. There are several historic communities and small-scale resorts. Whidbey Island is accessible from both the Seattle and Port Townsend areas by short ferry rides and also from the north across the Deception Pass bridge. To get to Whidbey Island from the Seattle area, take exit 189 (Mukilteo ferry) from I–5 and follow signs through Mukilteo to the ferry terminal. Join the lineup in the right-hand lane. Ferries leave about every half hour and take twenty minutes to reach the island. If you need more information, call Washington State Ferries at (360) 464–6400 or the statewide toll-free number at (800) 843–3779.

Living on an island is somewhat different from living on the mainland. For example, when the locals leave the island they often say, "We're going shopping over in America."

Note from the islanders: Do not under any circumstances try to crowd your automobile into the ferry line—you will incur the wrath of not only the islanders but also everyone else in line.

Washington State Ferries: (360) 464–6400, www.wsdot.wa.gov/ferries

Highway 525, which becomes Highway 20 north of Keystone, runs down the center of the island, carrying most through traffic. You can also take the meandering local roads that follow the shoreline for better views and less traffic.

Langley, on Saratoga Passage, is a favorite island community to visit. To get there, turn right on Langley Road off Highway 525 and follow signs into town.

On the way, stop to visit **Whidbey Island Vineyard and Winery** (5237 South Langley Road; 360–221–2040; www.whidbeyislandwinery.com), where you can taste samples of its rhubarb, pinot noir, and siegerrebe varieties, as well as others. The tasting room is closed on Tuesday during July and August.

Langley has many antiques and art galleries and you can sample two of them, **Gaskill/Olson Gallery** located at 302 First Street (360–221–2978; www.gaskillolson.com) and **Blackfish Gallery** at 111 Anthes Street (360–221–1274). Although a busy tourist town during summer weekends, Langley is always pleasant, with plenty of spots to sit and view the nautical scenery on Saratoga Passage. On First Street you can join the bronze statue of a sea-gazing boy leaning over the railing above Saratoga Passage, with his dog lying at his side. From here a wooden staircase leads down to the beach, where you can stroll along a grassy walkway or descend farther to the pebbly shore, below a bulkhead sculpted with images of salmon and whales.

You'll find cafes, restaurants, espresso bars, and bistros to suit every taste on First and Second Streets. For a Mediterranean treat, try **Cafe Langley** at 113 First Street (360–221–3090). The **Braeburn Cafe,** at 197 Second Avenue (360–221–3211), is one of the locals' favorite breakfast hangouts.

Find the splendid **P. S. Bakery Cafe** at 221 Second Street (360–221–9434) by following the brick walkway to the rear of the courtyard. Peter, a chocolatier formerly from Aspen, Colorado, bakes up the finest of pastries, including delicious liqueur cakes. Try **Whidbey's Coffee Company** at 224 First Street (360–221–8676) for excellent coffee, espresso, and pastries. It's open to 5:00 P.M. weekdays and to 7:30 P.M. Friday and Saturday. For fine dining locals suggest **Star Bistro** at 201 First Street (360–221–2627; see Northwest seafood and pasta fare menu listed at www.whidbeynet.net/starbistro) and **Trattoria Giuseppe Italian Restaurant** (360–341–3454; see www.trattoriagiuseppe.com for current menu and evening entertainment schedule), located at the corner of Langley Road and Highway 525. It's open Monday through Friday for lunch from 11:30 A.M. to 2:30 P.M. and for dinner daily at 5:00 P.M.

For a spin on live theater, plan to attend the **Langley Mystery Weekend** sponsored by the Chamber of Commerce (360–221–6765; www.whidbey.com/langley/lc/mystery) and held during the last full weekend of February. Mystery buffs meet over coffee in local cafes and coffee shops to pore over clues in order to nab the character that did the nefarious deed. Previous mysteries, all locally written, have included *A Taste for Murder, Much Ado about Kitties or The Cat's Revenge,* and *A Murder of Crows.* It's great fun with locals dressed in vintage garb and helping with the special effects. You can also arrange for tickets to attend plays and musicals by the **Island Theatre Players** at Whidbey Island Center for the Arts located at 565 Camano Avenue in Langley (360–221–8268; www.whidbey.net/wica). Recent offerings included the backstage farce *Moon over Buffalo* and the musical thriller *Little Shop of Horrors.*

To stay overnight in the Langley area, call the innkeepers at **Country Cottage of Langley Bed & Breakfast,** located at 215 Sixth Street (360–221–8709; www.acountrycottage.com) and one of the first vintage homes to be remodeled for bed-and-breakfast travelers. Innkeepers Jerry and Joanne Lechner offer fine hospitality at **Eagles Nest Inn Bed & Breakfast,** a contemporary octagonal-shaped home situated with a fine view of Saratoga Passage at 4680 Saratoga Road (360–221–5331; www.eaglesnestinn.com). You can also find amenable lodgings in and close to Langley at **The Potting Shed Cottage,** 3557 Saratoga Road (360–221–5494 or 800–637–4436; www.dovehouse.com); at

Boatyard Inn Suites and Lofts, 200 Wharf Street (360–221–5120, www.boatyardinn.com); at *Garden Path Inn,* 111 First Street (360–221–5121; www.whidbey.com/gp/); and *Victoria's Bed & Breakfast,* 117 Sixth Street (360–221–5979 or 360–221–3898; www.victorias bandb.com).

The rhododendron, Washington's state flower, is especially prolific on Whidbey Island. If these pique your interest, you'll want to visit *Meerkerk Rhododendron Gardens* at 3531 South Meerkerk Lane, Greenbank 98253 (360–678–1912; www.meerkerkgardens.org). The rhododendron blooms are usually at their peak the last two weeks of April and the beginning of May, but the gardens are lovely at any time. Featuring more than 800 mature rhododendron and companion plants, the forested landscape includes ponds, forest, and waterside nature trails. To get there, turn east off Highway 525 on Resort Road, 1½ miles south of Greenbank, or follow the scenic Honeymoon Bay Road for 5 miles north from Freeland along Holmes Harbor.

You could check to see if the charming log cottages are available at *Guest House Log Cottages* (24371 State Route 525, Greenbank 98253; 360–678–3115; www.guesthouselogcottages.com). If these cottages are not available, you could try *Farmhouse Bed & Breakfast,* 2740 East Sunshine Lane in Clinton (360–321–6288; www.farmhousebb.com) or *Thistle Cottage* and *Blackberry Cottage* at Spring Hill Inn at 24811 State Route 525 (360–678–5210; www.springhillinn.com). Or call innkeeper Peggy Moore to ask about the romantic *Seacliff Cottage,* 727 Windmill Drive in Freeland (360–331–1566; www.cliffhouse.net/cottage/).

Hillsides covered with vines at the historic *Whidbey's Greenbank Berry Farm & Winery* (360–678–7700; www.greenbankfarm.com) are a pleasant setting for a picnic, and visitors are welcome to tour the farm where loganberries (a raspberry/blackberry cross) are distilled into a popular liqueur, Whidbey's Loganberry Liqueur. The gift shop sells snacks for your picnic basket in addition to a selection of Washington State wines. The farm, on Wonn Road off Highway 525, ¼ mile north of Greenbank, is open daily from 10:00 A.M. to 4:30 P.M.

For good eats and tasty take-out entrees, try the deli at *Coupe's Greenbank Store* (360–678–4326) located at the corner of Wonn Road and Highway 525.

Historic *Coupeville* is located several miles north of here, about midway up the island on scenic Penn Cove. Saratoga Passage lies to the east, and Admiralty Inlet lies to the west. Look for a gaggle of mussel rafts floating out on Penn Cove where the famous Penn Cove mussels are grown and harvested. The annual *Mussel Festival,* with much eating of local seafood and deliciously prepared mussels, takes place the first weekend in March.

To learn about Coupeville's Native American, pioneer, maritime, and sailing history and to pick up a walking tour guide, visit the *Island County Historical Museum,* at 902 Northwest Alexander Street (360–678–3310) at the end of Front Street by the wharf. The museum is open Tuesday through Sunday from 11:00 A.M. to 5:00 P.M.

After browsing the museum go across the street to the wharf, which overlooks Penn Cove and the floating mussel-growing rafts. Poke into the *Gallery at the Wharf* and also the *Coupeville Harbor Store* (360–678–3625) for local art, gifts and souvenirs, Asian and deli food, ice cream, and kayak rentals. Walk along Front Street and up Main Street to see more historic buildings, then stop at *Miriam's Espresso & Videos,* 101 South Main Street (360–678–3777), if you're ready for steaming lattes or cups of Tully's freshly brewed coffee. Or detour into *Mariti Chocolate Company,* 12 Northwest Front Street (360–678–5811), for locally made fudge and chocolates. If you are in the area on Saturday, take in the *Coupeville Farmers' Market* (from April through October; 360–678–5434) on the corner of Main and Eighth Streets to mingle with friendly locals and load up on fresh berries, flowers, and vegetables. For fabulous freshly baked cinnamon rolls, soups, and salads, stop at *Knead & Feed Restaurant* on Front and Main Streets (360–678–5431), a former storehouse and laundry built in 1871 and nestled one level down the bluff facing Penn Cove under the Tartan and Tweed Store. Its original post-and-beam structure adds to the ambience of this pleasant, waterside spot. Local folks swear by the steamed mussels and garlic bread at *Toby's Tavern* (360–678–4222).

To stay overnight in the Coupeville area, contact *Anchorage Inn Bed and Breakfast,* 807 North Main Street (360–678–5581 or 877–230–1313; www.anchorage-inn.com), where children over ten are welcome; *The Compass Rose Bed and Breakfast,* 508 South Main Street (360–678–5318; www.compassrosebandb.com); *The Colonel Crockett Farm Bed and Breakfast,* located a short distance from downtown out near Fort Casey State Park, 1012 South Fort Casey Road (360–678–3711; www.crocketfarm.com), where children over twelve are welcome; and the ten renovated historic officers' houses at *Fort Casey Inn,* 1124 South Engle Road (360–678–8792 or 866–661–6604; www.fortcasey

inn.com). For evening dining in Coupeville, ask about local restaurants that do great things with mussels, seafood, and steaks including *The Oystercatcher* (360–678–0683), *Christopher's* (360–678–5480), and *Rosi's* (360–678–3989). Another pleasant lodging alternative is the circa 1907 *Captain Whidbey Inn* (2072 West Whidbey Island Inn Road, Coupeville 98239; 360–678–4097; www.captainwhidbeyinn.com) situated on the west shore of Penn Cove. The lodge, built of madrona logs, has comfortable rooms, good food, a cozy beachstone fireplace, and a restaurant. Cabins and cottages are also available.

You'll find the impressive *Admiralty Head Lighthouse* interpretive center located near the Keystone ferry landing at *Fort Casey State Park;* call the staff at (360) 678–7391 for seasonal tours. The park (360–678–4519) is open year-round for camping on a first-come, first-served arrangement. There are old forts to explore, long stretches of undeveloped public beaches to walk, and major tracts of protected forest and farmland to see in the area, which includes *Ebey's Landing National Historical Reserve.*

Before continuing north to scenic Deception Pass at Whidbey Island's north end, an awesome sight in practically any kind of weather, you can find pleasant eateries in the community of Oak Harbor. Or replenish your cooler, put together an impromptu picnic, and continue north to *Deception Pass State Park.* Pull into any large grocery outlet for supplies, or stop at *Deli by the Bay* (705 Southeast Pioneer Way; 360–240–0203); *Chocolates for Breakfast* (321 Southeast Pioneer Way, 360–675–2141); *Solid Ground Coffee Shop* (275 Southeast Cabot Street; 360–679–3014); and *Dairy Valley Old Fashioned Ice Cream Parlor* (296 Northeast Kettle Street; 360–675–5300).

Trivia
The Washington State ferry Klickitat, *which runs between Whidbey Island (from Keystone ferry landing west of Coupeville) and Port Townsend, was built in San Francisco in 1927. The vessel is 256 feet long and carries seventy-five cars and 800 passengers. The ferry trip across Admiralty Inlet at a running speed of 12 knots takes about twenty minutes.*

One of the best ways to see Deception Pass is from the water. *Mosquito Fleet Enterprise* (800–325–6722; www.whale watching.com) offers scenic day cruises and day-long whale-watching excursions from Everett up Saratoga Passage through the steep canyon walls of Deception Pass, and on through the San Juan Islands. The boat carries 150 passengers and offers snacks to purchase from an onboard galley; you can also bring your own snacks in nonglass containers. Also bring cameras, film, and binoculars.

Northern Sound

Just across the Deception Pass bridge from Whidbey Island, travelers reach Fidalgo Island. For a bird's-eye view of this island, turn west from Highway 20 just south of Pass Lake and follow Rosario Road as it forks right, away from Burrows Bay. At the Lake Erie Grocery take an acute left onto Heart Lake Road, then turn right to enter **Mount Erie Park.** The steep road (not recommended for trailers or RVs) has several trails and observation points along the way, and the wide-angle views of northern Puget Sound and its islands from the 1,300-foot summit is spectacular. Continue right on Heart Lake Road to reach the town of **Anacortes,** the main gateway to the San Juan Islands. But before you head for the large ferry terminal, take time to explore this eclectic community. Anacortes also makes a great base camp where you can leave your bags and car to board the ferry for a day trip to Friday Harbor on San Juan Island.

During your walking tour, you'll meander past the **Burlington Northern Railway Station** at Seventh Street and R Avenue. The revitalized station houses an arts center. **The Depot Gallery** (360–293–3663) is open from mid-May to mid-October Tuesday through Friday and Sunday from 1:00 to 4:00 P.M. and on Saturday from 10:00 A.M. to 4:00 P.M.

You'll encounter a bevy of shopping opportunities in downtown Anacortes, including **Bunnies by the Bay** at 3115 V Place (360–293–8037). You can tour the facility where the charming stuffed bunnies are made Monday through Friday at 10:00 A.M. and 2:00 P.M.

Located nearby and a local favorite, **Gere-a-Deli** (502 Commercial Avenue; 360–293–7383) offers tasty clam chowder, salads, and sandwiches from 8:00 A.M. to 5:00 P.M. Monday through Saturday. **Calico Cupboard Cafe and Bakery** at 901 Commercial Avenue (360–293–7315) offers tasty lunch fare, and **La Vie En Rose** at 418 Commercial Avenue (360–299–9546) is well known for its French pastries, cookies, scones, and espresso as well as salads, sandwiches, and pizza. **Randy's Pier 61** located at 209 T Avenue (360–293–5108) offers waterfront dining with great views of Guemes Channel; it's open daily for lunch and dinner and Sunday for brunch. **Rock Fish Grill & Anacortes Brewery** at 320 Commercial Avenue (360–588–1720) is a local favorite for microbrews and ales, seafood, and pizza done in a wood-fired oven.

One of the best-kept secrets in Anacortes is **SeaBear Specialty Seafoods** (605 Thirtieth Street; 360–293–4661). Here you'll discover alderwood-smoked salmon, soups, chowders, and barbequed salmon sandwiches.

The warehouse store is in an industrial complex just east of Commerical Avenue and off Thirtieth at T Street.

You'll find the older neighborhoods just west of Commercial Avenue on Sixth through Twelfth Streets. *Causland World War I Memorial Park,* on Eighth Street between M and N Avenues, is a pleasant green hideaway surrounded by mosaic walls made of white quartz and red argillite swirling in brown-and-gray sandstone. Across the street you can review the history of Fidalgo Island at the *Anacortes History Museum* (1305 Eighth Street), once the town's Carnegie Library. Several blocks west is the *Blue Rose Bed and Breakfast* (1811 Ninth Street, Anacortes 98221; 360–293–5175), a country-style bungalow

Anacortes Mural Project

*A*nacortes resident Bill Mitchell initiated the idea for the life-size cutouts and life-size townsfolk figures that appear all over town. His goal is to create one hundred such murals that represent one hundred years of the community's history. Enjoy some eighty-two of them with a map and numbered list from the Anacortes Visitors Information Center (819 Commercial Avenue; 360– 293–3832, www.anacortes.org). Here are some favorites:

Edna Whitney, tandem bicycle & friends, circa 1910 (#3, on Commercial Avenue near Second Street)

Toulouse-Lautrec poster lady, Paris, France, 1895 (#5, corner of Commercial Avenue and Third Street)

Skagit Saloon window, 1891 (#6, corner of Commercial Avenue and Third Street)

Dancing flapper by John Held Jr., 1920s cartoonist (#10, on Third Street)

Ann Bessner and Guemes Island girls in a north Beach canoe, 1934 (#13, on Third Street)

Rainier Bar bartender with two puppies, circa 1908 (#17, on Fifth Street and Commercial Avenue)

Hubert Crosby, Empire Theater assistant manager, 1925 to 1928 (#29, on Seventh Street)

Guemes Island ferry with 16-piece band, July 4, 1919 (#38, on Commercial Avenue between Eighth and Ninth streets)

1947 Harley Davidson, two-sided (#53, on Eighteenth Street)

Cecil Weyrich, Black Ball Line & Washington State ferries, 1928 to 1972 (#74, at the ferry dock)

Bill Mitchell, self-portrait with 1954 Autoette electric cart & wheelchair (#75, between Fifth and Sixth Streets)

First train in town, 1890 (#80, on R Avenue below Seventh Street)

built in 1910 and featuring delicious breakfasts and a splendid perennial garden. You could also call the friendly Anacortes innkeepers at *Nantucket Inn Bed & Breakfast,* close to downtown at 3402 Commercial Avenue, Anacortes 98221 (360–293–6007 or 888–293–6007; www.whidbey.com/nantucket); *Old Brook Inn Bed & Breakfast,* offering island hospitality just outside of town at 7270 Old Brook Lane (360–293–4768 or 800–503–4768; www.oldbrookinn.com); and *Sunset Beach Bed & Breakfast* with expansive water views west of downtown at 100 Sunset Beach Drive (360–293–5428 or 800–359–3448; www.whidbey.com/sunsetbeach).

For a pleasant drive or bicycle ride, take Twelfth Avenue westward past the ferry exit. Follow Sunset Avenue onto Loop Road around *Washington Park,* where you'll find access to several public beaches. At Fidalgo Head stop at the viewpoint on a high promontory overlooking Burrows Island and Bay. When you can tear yourself away from the great views, circle back to Sunset Drive.

Heading north from Anacortes via Interstate 5, the Skagit and Nooksack Valleys are flat, fertile, and filled with traditional family farms that flank the communities of La Conner and Mount Vernon. During April some 1,100 acres are carpeted with blooming tulips and daffodils, which thrive in the rich loamy soil of the Lower Skagit Valley. On clear days views of snowcapped Mount Baker in the distance frame the colorful scene. Tulips and bulbs are sold at roadside stands, and you can tour some of the fields. Check (360) 428–5959 and www.tulipfestival.org for information on the annual Skagit Valley Tulip Festival in April. *Note:* Visit mid-week to avoid busy weekends, when the narrow farm roads are often clogged with traffic.

The White Swan Guest House (1388 Moore Road, Mount Vernon 98273; 360–445–6805; www.thewhiteswan.com) offers cozy accommodations on pastoral Fir Island, just a few miles from La Conner. The restored 1890s Victorian farmhouse offers three guest rooms on the second floor, a big porch, a wood stove, and colorful perennial gardens. For greater privacy try the Garden Cottage, ideal for families with children or for a romantic retreat.

Just north of Fir Island at 1935 Chillberg Road is *Pleasant Ridge Pottery and Gallery* (360–466–4592), a charming haven of locally produced pottery, jewelry, clothing, and woodwork. Then follow Chillberg Road west to *La Conner,* which sits on the bank of the Swinomish Channel, which carries a parade of small boats between Padilla Bay to the north and Skagit Bay to the south. Once a quiet village serving local

Blueberry-Lemon Muffins

Blueberry-Lemon Muffins from The White Swan Guest House Bed & Breakast (360–445–6805) near La Conner and Mount Vernon.

Dry ingredients:

2 cups flour

¹/₂ cup sugar

1 teaspoon baking soda

2 teaspoons baking powder

1 teaspoon salt

1 cup fresh or frozen blueberries

Wet ingredients:

1 egg, beaten

1 8-oz. container fat-free lemon yogurt

2 tablespoons milk

¹/₂ cup vegetable oil

Preheat oven to 400 degrees. Fold wet ingredients into flour mixture until just mixed and lumpy. Spoon into lined muffin cups in muffin pan. Sprinkle sugar on top. Bake for 18 to 20 minutes until golden brown on top.

"These muffins are a favorite of guests," says innkeeper Peter Goldfarb, "just next to my chocolate chip cookies!"

farmers and fishermen, La Conner is now a popular tourist destination, with restaurants, antiques shops, and boutiques clustered along First Street. Be sure to climb the hill to the *Skagit County Historical Museum* at 501 Fourth Street (360–466–3365), which includes exhibits on the area's history, industries, and fashions. The museum is open from 1:00 to 5:00 P.M. Wednesday through Sunday and charges a small admission fee. Also, don't miss visiting the *La Conner Quilt Museum* located in the circa 1891 Gaches Mansion at 703 South Second Street (360–466–4288; www.laconnerquilts.com). The museum houses a wonderful collection of quilts from the Northwest and also offers ongoing exhibits of quilts and fiber art throughout the year. Afterwards, you can pause for a bite to eat at *Calico Cupboard Cafe & Bakery* (720 South First Street; 360–466–4451), at *Hungry Moon Cafe* (110 North First Street; 360–466–1602), and *Whiskers Waterfront Cafe* (128 South First Street; 360–466–1008), or order take-out snacks at *La Conner Landing Deli & Espresso* (101 North First Street; 360–466–2950).

Head north from La Conner on Whitney–La Conner Road and cross Highway 20 onto Bayview Edison Road, which offers views of the off-shore islands and marine wildlife of *Padilla Bay.* If you have time, walk

A Moveable Winter Feast

During February on the tidal flats and fields of Fir Island, visitors can marvel at some 30,000 Arctic snow geese, 1,500 trumpeter swans, and hundreds of tundra swans in addition to more than twenty species of ducks who pause to munch and rest while winging it along the Pacific Flyway. For maps and directions to best viewing spots, contact La Conner Visitors Information Center, 413 Morris Street, P.O. Box 1610, La Conner 98257; (360) 466–4778 or (888) 642–9284; www. laconnerchamber.com.

or bicycle along the 2¼-mile Padilla Bay Shore Trail. You'll pass Bay View State Park, Padilla Bay National Estuarine Research Reserve, and **Breazeale–Padilla Bay Interpretive Center** located at 1043 Bay View–Edison Road (360–428–1558). In addition to fish tanks and displays of local birds and mammals, the kids can enjoy environmental games and hands-on activities. Because of its fertile waters, Padilla Bay is a major stop for migrating birds. Breazeale is open year-round from 10:00 A.M. to 5:00 P.M. Wednesday through Sunday.

Small, comfortable inns entice travelers to pause in the Skagit Valley area, and among them are the romantic **Skagit Bay Hideaway Bed & Breakfast** at 17430 Goldenview Avenue, La Conner 98257 (360–466–2262; www.skagitbay.com); family-friendly **Arts Place Guesthouse** at 511 Talbot Street, La Conner 98257 (360–466–3033); **Benson Farmstead Bed & Breakfast** at 10113 Avon–Allen Road, Bow 98232 (360–757–0578; www.bbhost.com/bensonbnb); and **Alice Bay Bed & Breakfast** for intimate waterside views at 11794 Scott Road on Samish Island, Bow 98232 (360–766–6396 or 800–652–0223; www. alicebay.com).

Chuckanut Drive (Highway 11) is one of those scenic drives that everyone should experience. Continuing north from Padilla and Samish Bays for about 20 miles, the winding road skirts high bluffs, offers distant views of the San Juan Islands, and brings you into the Bellingham environs. Bellingham Bay, Fairhaven Park and Rose Gardens, and Fairhaven Historic District come into view soon after passing Larrabee State Park. Many of Bellingham's old commercial and residential buildings have been renovated to their nineteenth-century grandeur, especially in the **Fairhaven District** and downtown Bellingham. To reach Fairhaven from I–5 take exit 250 and follow Highway 11 west to Twelfth Street. From Old Fairhaven Parkway you can access and stroll along the **Interurban Trail;** its route follows a section of the 1920s electric trolley line. You can also take a passenger shuttle express (360–671–1137), near Marine Park, for a day trip over to bustling **Friday Harbor** on San Juan Island. Or, just west of downtown follow signs to the **Lummi Island** ferry landing, take the eight-minute ferry ride, and enjoy a leisurely drive on this scenic little island. While exploring the eclectic

Fairhaven District near Bellingham's waterfront, pause at **Colophon Cafe,** 1208 Eleventh Street (360–647–0092), with its funky cow memorabilia and bovine decor, or at **Skylark's Cafe,** 1308-B Eleventh Street (360–715–3642), for courtyard dining. On Wednesday afternoons browse **Fairhaven Farmers' Market** at Eleventh and Mill Streets for fresh seafood, veggies, fruits, baked goodies, and crafts. Visit splendid **Sehome Hill Arboretum,** also located nearby at Western Washington University, and plan to take in a university **Summer Stock Theater** production (360–650–3876 for performance dates). To stay overnight in the area inquire at **Fairhaven Bed & Breakfast,** Terry and Kitty Todd's historic home located at 1714 Twelfth Street, Bellingham 98225; (360–734–7243 or 888–734–7243; www.fairhavenbandb.com).

The **Whatcom Museum of History and Art** (360–676–6981), in the Old City Hall at Prospect Street, is a good place to pick up a walking map of downtown Bellingham and the Fairhaven Historic District. The museum is open noon to 5:00 P.M. Tuesday through Sunday, and admission is free. **Allied Arts of Whatcom County** operates a bright, friendly gallery at 1418 Cornwall Street. Also check out **The American Museum of Radio** located at 1312 Bay Street (360–738–3886; www.antique-radio.org). From 11:00 A.M. to 5:00 P.M. Wednesday through Saturday, history buffs can browse the museum's collection of more than 1,000 radios and broadcasting memorabilia dating from the early 1940s. The museum will also house an FM station that will broadcast locally radio shows from the World War II era. For dining in the Bellingham area, innkeepers and locals suggest finding great Italian dishes at **Mannino's** (130 East Champion Street; 360–671–7955); avant garde decor and wood-fired pizza at **La Faimma** (200 East Chestnut; 360–767–0060);

Historic Fairhaven's Dirty Dan Harris

*H*e sported the customary beard, mustache, and longish hair worn in the 1880s. It's said that he was a sailor, trader, and rumrunner. He wore a shabby frock coat over a red undershirt. A dusty black plug hat was jammed on his head. On his feet he wore a pair of dirty boots. He didn't bother to lace them. He also didn't bathe very often. But the man, Dirty Dan, or Daniel Harris, in 1883 filed the original plat to create the community of Fairhaven. Dirty Dan is memorialized at 1211 Eleventh Street at Dirty Dan Harris' Steakhouse (360–676–1011). The place opens daily at 5:00 P.M. and offers slow-cooked prime rib, seafood, steaks, fine wines, and spirits. Wear clean shoes and call for reservations.

pasta, seafood, and great desserts at **Pastazza** (2945 Newmarket Street; 360–714–1168; www.pastazza.com); fresh Northwest fare at **Wild Garlic** (114 Prospect Street; 360–671–1955); and delicious Asian and Northwest cuisine at **Pacific Cafe** (100 North Commercial Street; 360–647–0800). **Chocolate Necessities,** located just off Meridian Street and Horton Road (360–676–0589 or 800–804–0589), offers fine chocolates and decadent chocolate truffles. At **Schnauzer Crossing Bed & Breakfast** (4421 Lakeway Drive, Bellingham 98227; 360–733–0055 or 800–562–2808) longtime innkeepers Donna and Vermont McAllister offer one guest room, one large suite, and a cottage—two of the rooms are handicapped-accessible. Guests also enjoy saying hello to the two resident standard schnauzers, Marika and Klipsun. At **Stratford Manor Bed & Breakfast** (4566 Anderson Way, Bellingham 98227; 360–715–8441), innkeepers Leslie and Jim Lohse offer comfortable lodging in an English Tudor–style home with a large pond and perennial garden. You could also contact innkeeper Jan Simmons at **Big Trees Bed & Breakfast** (4840 Fremont Street, Bellingham 98227; 800–647–2850), where two of the three guest rooms offer views of Lake Whatcom.

Another fun and unusual attraction worth a visit is **Big Rock Garden City Park** (360–676–6985) located just outside the Bellingham area at 2900 Sylvan Street. This large Japanese garden features Northwest and Oriental garden art. Grab a seat on the deck or patio, relax, and enjoy the lush surroundings. Open March through November.

The small community of **Ferndale** is a great place to explore both history and nature. Two blocks south of Main Street on First Avenue you'll find **Historic Pioneer Park** (360–384–0792), home to the largest collection of nineteenth-century log structures in the state. You and the kids can tour these sturdy buildings, hewn from giant cedars, from noon to 5:00 P.M. May 1 through September 30.

Housed in the restored turn-of-the-century Nielsen Farmhouse, the **Tennant Lake Natural History Interpretive Center** (360–384–3064) provides information about the wetland environment surrounding Tennant Lake. Next to the circa 1906 farmhouse and its beds brimming with summer perennials, stroll the paths of the splendid fragrance garden. Touch and smell the leaves of curry, gingermint, chamomile, lavender, sage, or woolly thyme. The garden is wheelchair accessible, and braille signs are posted on the inside of the handrails. Then follow the path out past the viewing tower and toward the lake. Walk along the half-mile system of boardwalks to see a wide variety of wetlands vegetation along with raptors and waterfowl, including large flocks of trumpeter swans in winter. To get to the nature center, follow the signs from downtown Ferndale.

Find another historic destination by following the marked, half-mile road from Tennant Lake to **Hovander Homestead Park** (5299 Nielsen Road; 360–384–3444). The restored family farmhouse was built in 1896 by Hakan Hovander, a Swedish architect who helped rebuild Chicago after the Great Fire of 1871. Volunteers in period clothing will show you through the elegant rooms from noon to 4:30 P.M. on Saturday and Sunday in May and Thursday through Sunday from June through Labor Day. There are farm animals on the grounds in summer and antique farm equipment at the big red barn, as well as a demonstration garden. On the park's 200 acres you'll find hayfields, orchards, walking trails, river views, playground equipment, and picnic tables. You can also experience traditional Scottish fun when the park hosts the **Bellingham Highland Games** in June.

Slater Heritage House Bed and Breakfast, located a mile east of Ferndale at 1371 West Axton Road (360–384–4273), offers a warm, tranquil respite from modern times in a comfortable Victorian farmhouse. Or you could head east into the Cascade Mountain foothills on Highway 542 and follow the road for glorious views of 10,778-foot Mount Baker. At Glacier, near milepost 38, stop at the USDA Forest Service/National Park Service Visitors Center (360–499–2714 or 360–856–5700) for current information on scenic hiking trails and campgrounds in the North Cascades. From here it's an easy summer drive up to the Shuksan Picnic Area, Heather Meadows, and on to **Artist Point Viewpoint** at road's end, 58 miles from Bellingham, at a brisk elevation of 5,140 feet. The nearby **Mount Baker Ski Area** is open during the winter; call (360) 671–0211 for ski reports.

You'd rather retreat from these imposing mountain vistas to sea level, you say? Well, not to worry; just beat a path to **Birch Bay** just northwest of Ferndale (exit 270 from I–5) and close to the U.S.–Canadian border. Plan your visit for Thursday through Monday between mid-June and Labor Day so that you can stop at **The C Shop** (4825 Alderson Road and Birch Bay Drive; 360–371–2070), a combination bakery, candy shop, and hometown cafe. After munching sticky buns, cinnamon rolls, pizza (available after 5:00 P.M.), and handmade chocolates, take a brisk walk along the beach at **Birch Bay State Park and Campground** (360–371–2800). Here you'll see seabirds and shorebirds, beachcombers, and wide water views of Birch Bay, Georgia Strait, and the San Juan Islands; see www.birchbay.net for current tide tables, annual events, and other helpful information about this friendly seaside community. For overnight stays inquire with Charlotte Beck at **Beck and Call Bed & Breakfast,** 7413 Jackson Road, Birch Bay 98230; (360) 371–0268.

Lynden, a friendly community with a proud Dutch heritage, is located in the fertile Nooksack Valley farmlands east of Birch Bay. Stroll down Front Street, bedecked with flowers and quaint Dutch decor, and stop in for fresh pastries at **Lynden Dutch Bakery** or authentic European cuisine at **Dutch Mothers Restaurant** (360–354–2174).

At **Lynden Pioneer Museum,** 217 Front Street (360–354–3675), you can stroll through a re-created turn-of-the-century main street, with stores, cafe, doctor and dentist offices, school, church, and train station. Then take a look at the collection of early automobiles, more than forty restored horse buggies and wagons, and antique farm machinery. In midsummer you'll see the steam tractors and threshing machines get fired up at the Puget Sound Antique Tractor and Machinery Association's Threshing Bee.

From here you can continue north via I–5 to Blaine, Peace Arch State Park, and U.S.–Canadian Customs for entering British Columbia. But first, before departing into Canada, backtrack to Mount Vernon so that you can access those scenic **San Juan Islands** that you have spied from distant viewpoints on the mainland ever since leaving Whidbey Island. From Mount Vernon head west to Anacortes and follow the signs to the Washington State Ferry Terminal.

All four islands with regular ferry service—Lopez, Shaw, Orcas, and San Juan—offer plenty to explore. Lopez and Shaw Islands are the most off the beaten path. Shaw, the smallest San Juan island accessible by public ferry, offers a pleasant step back in time. Franciscan Sisters run the ferry dock and the adjacent **Little Portion General Store.** This is the only place on Shaw to buy provisions, so stock up there for a picnic. The charming old store also features gift items handmade by various religious orders, including herb vinegars, sachets, and spices prepared by the Shaw Island Franciscan Service. Old baskets, fruit boxes, and nautical paraphernalia decorate the walls.

The **Shaw Island Public Library,** in the center of the island on Blind Bay Road, is a sunny little building, open 2:00 to 4:00 P.M. Tuesday and Saturday, and 10:00 A.M. to noon on Thursday. Inside, the smell of cedar fills the air as you sit back in a cozy spot with a good book and a view of the surrounding forest. The children's corner is full of old favorites and new storybooks arranged around a colorful rug peppered with pillows and child-size chairs. Opposite the library you can see the old red schoolhouse, more than one hundred years old. A new school was built in the 1980s for the island's small number of elementary-age students.

Head south along Hoffman Cove Road, then left on Squaw Bay Road past secluded Squaw Bay. Past the bay is the turnoff to **South Beach County Park,** with several campsites overlooking the bay. The small beach provides a quiet picnic spot with ample supplies of driftwood logs for rustic benches in the sand. From here follow Squaw Bay Road through a scenic valley back to Blind Bay and the ferry dock.

Lopez Island is larger and more developed than Shaw but still offers many opportunities for quiet and seclusion. Located 4 miles from the ferry landing, Lopez Village, with a museum, store, and several restaurants, is the island's commercial center. The *Lopez Historical Museum* (360–468–2049), full of island history and lore, is worth a stop. The museum is open Friday to Sunday, noon to 4:00 P.M. For good

Lummi Island

*L*ummi Island, near Bellingham and a six-minute ferry ride from Gooseberry Point across Hale Passage, is one of the smaller San Juan isles. It's about 9 miles long and 2 miles wide, but it offers a few surprises. For one, during the month of August, you can watch the ancient fishing technique of reef-netting from boats at Legoe Bay on the west side of the island. Riley Starks and Judy Olsen, owners of **Nettles Organic Farm** and of **The Willows Bed & Breakfast and Cafe** (360–758–2620; www.willows-inn.com), employ workers who reef-net for wild salmon that later appear in gourmet entrees at the inn's cafe Thursday through Sunday. Call for lunch or dinner reservations and for cozy rooms. At **West Shore Farm Bed & Breakfast** (360–758–2600), Carl and Polly Hanson offer comfortable rooms in their octagonal home overlooking Rosario Strait. For a special treat, guests can also ask Carl to play his Scottish bagpipes. You can also call Sandy and Howard McCandles at scenic **Cottage by the Sea Bed & Breakfast** (360–758–7144). Near the ferry landing meet Gwendolyn Bass at **Well! Latte Dah Cafe** (360–758–2569), and enjoy espressos, soups, pasta, chicken, and potato salad. Also at the landing, **Beach Store Cafe** (360–758–2233) offers hamburgers and casual fare, and **Islander General Store** (360–758–2190) carries beverages and grocery supplies. On Memorial Day or Labor Day weekend, attend the annual Artist Tours to see splendid watercolors, oils, sculpture, jewelry, glass, pottery, and fiber arts for sale at artists' studios around the island.

eateries in Lopez Village, try *Love Dog Cafe* (360–468–2150), *Holly B's Bakery* (360–468–2133), *Cafe Verdi* (360–468–2257), *Isabel's Espresso* (360–468–4114), and *Lopez Old Fashioned Soda Fountain* (360–468–4511) located in the pharmacy. *Bay Cafe* at 9 Old Post Road (360–468–3700) is an island favorite for fine dining and offers breakfast on weekends. At scenic Fisherman Bay try *The Galley* (360–468–2713) for the best water views along with tasty fish-and-chips, juicy hamburgers, and good Mexican dishes.

For a comfortable overnight stay in Lopez Village, call the friendly folks at *Edenwild Inn Bed & Breakfast* (360–468–3238 or 800–606–0662; www.edenwildinn.com), who offer eight guest rooms, cozy fireplaces, and delicious country breakfasts. At *MacKaye Harbor Inn Bed & Breakfast* (circa 1904), 949 MacKaye Harbor Road (360–468–2253 or 888–314–6140; www.mackayeharborinn.com), Mike and Robin Bergstrom offer five guest rooms, bountiful breakfasts, and great water views along with kayak rentals and the use of the inn's mountain bikes during your stay. For doing your own thing, try *Fisherman Bay Guest House* (360–468–2884), which offers a kitchen and deck with bay views and colorful sunsets. Or tucked into the woods, you might welcome eagles and ravens for neighbors, along with two pleasant resident cats, at *Ravens Rook Guest Cabin,* located off Shark Reef Road (360–468–2838 or 877–321–2493; www.rock island.com/~ravensrook/) and done in rustic Northwest post-and-beam style. From here a short walk through adjacent Shark Reef Sanctuary takes you to the rocky beach, which offers large tide pools filled with intriguing sea creatures.

Public beaches on Lopez Island include the west side of *Fisherman Bay* off Bay Shore Road, *Shark Reef Park* (good tide pools here but rocky) at the end of Shark Reef Road on the island's southwest tip, and *Agate Beach* off Mackaye Harbor Road at the island's south end. *Spencer Spit State Park and Campground* (360–468–2251) on the island's east shore is a scenic spot with hiking trails and nearby rocky beach areas to beachcomb. *Odlin County Park* (360–378–8420) is closer to the water and offers camping and RV spaces (no hookups) about 4 miles from Lopez Village.

The next ferry stop in this watery region of some 175 islands is *Orcas Island.* By now any stressed city dwellers are beginning to relax into island time. The salt water and crisp breezes open to wider and wider vistas of small islands covered with tall, red-barked madrone, low-lying manzanita, and weathered rocks covered with myriad algae in soft hues of cream, yellow, and green. The wide green-and-white ferry lumbers to the dock at Orcas Island, bumping against tall wooden pilings and lurching to a stop. Crew members attach the huge lines and ready the debarkation process. Those departing onto Orcas are in their vehicles and ready to motor carefully from their section of the ferry's lower and midlevels.

You can easily spend two or three days on Orcas exploring its nooks and crannies. Drive over to **Moran State Park and Campground** (360–376–2326), hike its many trails, and then drive up to nearby Mount Constitution. One of the grandest views of the islands is from atop the tower here, especially fine at sunset. Poke into small communities of Deer Harbor, Eastsound, Westsound, Olga, and Doe Bay. Have a picnic by the water. Visit art galleries and artists' studios.

Hopefully, you have called well in advance to make overnight reservations at one of the welcoming bed-and-breakfast inns on Orcas Island: Not far from the ferry landing, **Turtleback Farm Inn** (Crow Valley Road; 360–376–4914; www.turtlebackinn.com) offers guests pastoral views and excellent cuisine along with resident sheep, chickens, and geese. At **Kingfish Inn Bed & Breakfast** and **West Sound Store & Cafe** (360–376–4440), located 3 miles from the Orcas ferry landing at the intersection of Deer Harbor and Crow Valley Roads, Lori and Mike Breslauer offer four light and airy guest rooms with water views on the second floor of a historic building they restored in 1997. Your night's

Orca Whales 101

*I*t's no wonder that Free Willy *was filmed in the San Juans, as three pods of orca whales make their home in these waters. You can whale-watch by sea, by land, and by air in the San Juans, and you might see one without even trying. Here are some facts you can use to embellish your own whale tales:*

- *Males average 29 feet in length, females average 24 feet. Females outnumber males four to one and can live to age eighty. The average male lives to about thirty.*

- *Males weigh up to 16,000 pounds, females up to 12,000 pounds.*

- *Whales give birth to one calf at two- to six-year intervals.*

- *Typical diet is fish, squid, sea lions, seals, and other whales. Orcas eat from 100 to 300 pounds of food a day.*

- *The whales "talk" to each other with a dialect unique to the pod.*

- *Orcas navigate the waters at about 2 to 6 mph.*

The Pig War

In 1859 on San Juan Island, a longstanding border dispute between British and American residents nearly resulted in an all-out war. The catalyst and only casualty, however, was an Englishman's pig. An American shot the pig when he found the errant animal rummaging in his potato patch. The resulting "Pig War" lasted until 1872, when the island's ownership was awarded to the United States.

Today you can visit American Camp at the south end of the island, where the American troops were stationed, and British Camp, on Garrison Bay at the north end, where the Royal Marines of Britain were posted. Both offer interpretive displays, hiking trails, and scenic beaches.

stay includes the option of a breakfast basket delivered to your room or, better yet, tasty morning fare served in the couple's pleasant cafe (open 9:00 A.M. to 3:00 P.M.) on the first floor along with great views of the small marina, the water, and islands beyond. For those who like getting farther away from it all, contact the innkeepers at *Otters Pond Bed & Breakfast,* located beyond Eastsound and near Moran State Park (360–376–8844; www.otterspond.com). Even farther off the beaten path, call *Spring Bay Inn* near Olga (360–376–5531; www.springbayinn.com). Here the innkeeper takes guests kayaking before breakfast.

If you're interested in private cottages available by the day or week on Orcas Island, call *Buckhorn Farm Bungalow* located at 17 Jensen Road (360–376–2298; www.buckhornfarm.com). The bungalow is close to the beach, sleeps four, and comes with a woodstove, cozy sitting areas, and a cheerful kitchen. At *The Old Trout Bed & Breakfast* located at 4272 Orcas Road (360–376–7474; www.oldtroutinn.com), ask about the *Water's Edge Cottage,* where a couple can snuggle up with a view of the pond.

For fine dining in and near Eastsound, the largest community on Orcas, try *Bilbo's Festivo* (360–376–4728) for regional Mexican, *Christina's* (360–376–4904) for Northwest seafood, and *Sean Paul's* (360–376–7030) for serious gourmet cuisine. For morning, midday, or takeout, locals suggest *Sunflower Cafe* (360–376–2335), *Rose's Bread & Specialties* (360–376–5805), and *Comet Cafe* (360–376–4220). Enjoy a scenic drive past Rosario Resort and beyond Moran State Park and Campground to try *Cafe Olga at Artworks* (360–376–5098) for an international flair or *Olga's* nearby (360–376–5862) for tasty regional fare (plus food to go for your picnic basket) and great views from its deck overlooking the bay. For a comfortable overnight stay right in the village of Eastsound, contact *Kangaroo House Bed & Breakfast* (360–376–2175 or 888–371–2175; www.kangaroohouse.com).

Getting off the island takes a bit of planning. Double-check the ferry departure you want, and plan to arrive at the ferry landing a couple of hours early, particularly during the busy summer season. Vehicles line up in a first-come, first-served arrangement. From Orcas you can either ferry back to Anacortes on the mainland or continue on to San Juan Island and, even farther, on to Vancouver Island, British Columbia (U.S. and Canadian Customs personnel meet the ferries at the Sidney, B.C., ferry terminal). Check the current ferry schedule for the international sailings (206–464–6400; www.wsdot.wa.gov/ferries).

Bustling Friday Harbor is the largest town on *San Juan Island,* which is the largest of the inhabited islands in the San Juans. Folks find a busy marina, the ferry landing, and a plethora of shops and eateries. For mornings and mid-day try *San Juan Coffee Roasting Co.* at the Cannery Landing (360–378–4443), *Garden Path Cafe* on Second Street (360–378–6255), and *Felicitations Bakery* on Nichols Street (360–378–1198). For casual and fine dining in Friday Harbor, check with *The Place Bar & Grill* on Spring Street next to the ferry landing (360–378–8707), *Haley's Bait Shop & Grill* on Spring Street near the local movie theater (360–378–4434), *Vinny's Italian* on West Street (360–378–1934), *Angie's Cannery House Restaurant* on First Street overlooking the ferry landing and harbor (360–378–2500), and *Friday Harbor House* on West Street overlooking the harbor and marina (360–378–8455). For fine dining away from town, try the much-loved *Duck Soup Inn* on Roche Harbor Road (360–378–4878) and, at *Roche Harbor Resort* at the northwest tip of the island, *Madrona Grill* or *McMillan's Dining Room* (360–378–5757). *Note:* Some island eateries close during the winter months.

For bedding down on lively San Juan Island, call well ahead for information and reservations. On the water at the marina, you can arrange accommodations on *Wharfside Bed & Breakfast* aboard the *Slow Season* (360–378–5661; www.slowseason.com). There are two cozy staterooms aboard the 60-foot ketch-rigged sailboat. You tend to get seasick sleeping aboard? Well, not to worry; for other spots on dry land in Friday Harbor, check with the Schutte family at *Panacea Bed & Breakfast,* 595 Park Street (360–378–3757; www.panacea-inn.com) or with *Harrison House Suites* at 235 C Street (360–378–3587; www.san-juan-lodging.com). Outside of Friday Harbor try *Highland Inn Bed & Breakfast* near

Native American Terms

The ferries that sail from Anacortes to Shaw, Lopez, Orcas, and San Juan Islands are named after Native American terms. The most well-known and best-loved island ferries:

Elwha, *meaning "elk"*

Illahee, *meaning "land, place, or location"*

Kaleetan, *meaning "arrow"*

Washington State Ferry information: www.wsdot.wa.gov/ferries or (360) 464–6400.

Lime Kiln Whale Watch Park (360–378–9450; www.highlandinn.com); *Oak Ridge Bed & Breakfast* at 141 Glen Oak Lane (360–378–6184; www.oak-ridge.net) on the way out to Cattle Point; and *Lakedale Resort Log Cabins,* 4313 Roche Harbor Road (360–378–2350; www. lakedale.com). You can also find scenic camping and RV sites on the island by checking with the Visitors Information Center in Friday Harbor (360–378–5240; www.sanjuanisland.org) and with www.guideto sanjuans.com. For those who like the hinterlands, call the friendly innkeepers at *Olympic Lights Bed & Breakfast,* located several miles from Friday Harbor (360–378–3186; www.san-juan.net/olympiclights). The renovated 1895 farmhouse sits in a wide meadow near the bluff that overlooks the Strait of Juan de Fuca. From here you can walk to the site of *American Camp* and enjoy scenic walks at 4th of July Beach. Check out *British Camp* and its historic displays about the infamous Pig War. Don't miss a visit to the *Whale Museum* in Friday Harbor at 62 First Street (360–378–4710; www.whalemuseum.com). *Note:* The public is encouraged to report any signs of stranded marine mammals (800–562–8832).

A tiny peninsula situated just below the 49th parallel, south of British Columbia, *Point Roberts* became U.S. territory in the late 1840s. Finding Point Roberts is easy. First proceed through Canadian Customs at the U.S.–Canadian border at Blaine, some 20 miles north of Bellingham. While the driver waits in the customs line, members of your party can walk alongside and through the gorgeous gardens of *Peach Arch Park.* Continue north into British Columbia and follow the signs to Tsawwassen, about 23 miles. Here follow signs to Point Roberts and proceed through a small U.S. Customs station to reenter the United States and this small resort community, population about 860. *Note:* Heightened security will cause longer lines at the U.S.–Canadian border at Blaine. Carry current voter registration card or passport; your driver's license is not proof of citizenship but can be used for photo I.D. For pets you will need proof of up-to-date rabies vaccination.

For wide water views stop at *Lighthouse Marine Park* (811 Marine Drive, 360–945–4911) at the peninsula's southwest corner. The windswept park has camping and picnic sites adjacent to the beach. A 30-foot wooden tower above the boardwalk offers great views of Georgia Strait.

At *Point Roberts Marina* (360–945–2255), at the south end of Tyee Drive, you can inspect a flotilla of sailboats and motor craft, then stop for a snack at the *Dockside Cafe* (360–945–1206). A fine place to have dinner while still taking in the splendid views is *South Beach House* (360–945–0717) east of the marina at 725 South Beach Road. They serve Wednesday through Sunday from 5:30 P.M.

Call ahead to arrange a room at *Maple Meadow Bed and Breakfast,* located at 101 Goodman Road, Point Roberts 98281 (360–945–5536; www.travel-wise.com/maple/index.html). Innkeepers Terrie and Keith LaPorte welcome visitors to their comfortable circa 1910 Victorian farmhouse near Boundary Bay. "Just forty minutes north of us is Vancouver, British Columbia," says Terrie. Large old-fashioned maples shade the grounds and lawn areas. Folks can also arrange to stay in The Old Pumphouse, a secluded and romantic getaway separate from the main house.

PLACES TO STAY ON PUGET SOUND

ANACORTES
Fidalgo Bay Resort RV Park
1107 Fidalgo Bay Road
Anacortes 98221
(360) 293–5353
or (800) 727–5478

Sunset Beach Bed &
Breakfast
100 Sunset Beach Drive
Anacortes 98221
(360) 293–5428

ANDERSON ISLAND
Inn at Burgs Landing Bed
and Breakfast
8808 Villa Beach Road
Anderson Island 98303
(253) 884–9185

ASHFORD
Mountain Meadows Inn
28912 State Route 706 E
Ashford 98304
(360) 569–2788

BELLINGHAM
Big Trees Bed & Breakfast
4840 Fremont Street
Bellingham 98227
(800) 647–2850

Ramada Motor Inn
215 Samish Way
Bellingham 98226
(360) 734–8830

Schnauzer Crossing Bed
& Breakfast
4421 Lakeway Drive
Bellingham 98227
(360) 733–0055

BIRCH BAY
Birch Bay Beachside RV
Park
7630 Birch Bay Drive
Birch Bay 98230
(800) 596–9586

BOW
Benson Farmstead Bed
& Breakfast
10113 Avon-Allen Road
Bow 98232
(360) 757–0578

GIG HARBOR
Fountains Bed & Breakfast
926–120th Street NW
Gig Harbor 98332
(253) 851–6262

Gig Harbor RV Resort
9515 Burnham Drive
Gig Harbor 98332
(800) 626–8311

Peacock Hill Guest House
9520 Peacock Hill Avenue
Gig Harbor 98332
(800) 863–2318

LOPEZ ISLAND
Fisherman Bay
Guest House
Fisherman Bay,
P.O. Box 271
Lopez 98261
(360) 468–2884

Raven's Rook Cabin
58 Wildrose Lane
Lopez 98261
(360) 468–2838

LUMMI ISLAND
West Shore Farm Bed &
Breakfast
2781 West Shore Drive
Lummi Island 98262
(360) 758–2600

MOUNT VERNON
The White Swan Guest
House
1388 Moore Road
Mount Vernon 98273
(360) 445–6805

OLYMPIA
Swantown Inn Bed &
Breakfast
1431 Eleventh Avenue SE
Olympia 98501
(360) 753–9123

ORCAS ISLAND
Bay Side Cottages
65 Willis Lane
Olga 98279
(360) 376–4330

Buckhorn Farm Bungalow
17 Jensen Road
Eastsound 98245
(360) 376–2298

Cayou Cove Cottages
P.O. Box 310
Deer Harbor 98243
(360) 376–3199

POINT ROBERTS
Maple Meadow Bed
& Breakfast
101 Goodman Road
Point Roberts 98281
(360) 945–5536

PORT ORCHARD
Reflections Bed
and Breakfast
3878 Reflection Lane E
Port Orchard 98366
(360) 871–5582

PORT TOWNSEND
Ann Starrett Mansion
Victorian Bed and Breakfast
744 Clay Street
Port Townsend 98368
(800) 321–0644

Ravenscroft Bed &
Breakfast
533 Quincy Street
Port Townsend 98368
(360) 385–2784

POULSBO
Foxbridge Bed & Breakfast
30680 Highway 3 NE
Poulsbo 98370
(360) 598–5599

SAN JUAN ISLAND
Harrison House Suites
235 C Street
Friday Harbor 98250
(360) 378–3587

Lakedale Resort
Log Cabins
4313 Roche Harbor Road
Friday Harbor 98250
(360) 378–2350

Tucker House Cottages
206 B Street
Friday Harbor 98250
(360) 378–2783

SNOQUALMIE
The Honey Farm Bed &
Breakfast
9050–384th Avenue SE
Snoqualmie 98065
(425) 888–9399

TACOMA
Chinaberry Hill Bed &
Breakfast
302 Tacoma Avenue North
Tacoma 98403
(253) 272–1282

DeVoe Mansion Bed &
Breakfast
208 East 133rd Street
Tacoma 98445
(253) 539–3991

VASHON ISLAND
Betty MacDonald Farm
Bed & Breakfast
12000 Ninety-ninth
Avenue SW
Vashon Island 98070
(206) 567–4227

WHIDBEY ISLAND
Anchorage Inn Bed &
Breakfast
807 North Main Street
Coupeville 98239
(360) 678–5581

Country Cottage of Langley
Bed & Breakfast
215 Sixth Street
Langley 98206
(360) 221–8709

Guest House Log Cottages
24371 State Route 525
Greenbank 98253
(360) 678–3115

PLACES TO EAT ON
PUGET SOUND

ANACORTES
Gere-a-Deli
502 Commercial Avenue
Anacortes 98221
(360) 293–7383

BELLINGHAM
Colophon Cafe & Deli
1208 Eleventh Street
Bellingham 98227
(360) 647–0092

Mannino's Italian
Restaurant
130 East Champion Street
Bellingham 98227
(360) 671–7955

Skylark's Fairhaven Cafe
1308-B Eleventh Street
Bellingham 98227
(360) 715–3642

BIRCH BAY
The C Shop Bakery & Cafe
4825 Alderson Road
Birch Bay 98230
(360) 371–2070

Edric's Restaurant
8394 Harborview Road
Blaine 98230
(360) 371–3838

ISSAQUAH
Boehm's Candies at
Gilman Village
255 Northeast Gilman
Boulevard
Issaquah 98027
(425) 392–6652

LOPEZ ISLAND
The Galley Cafe
Fisherman Bay
Lopez 98261
(360) 468–2713

Holly B's Bakery
Lopez Village Plaza
Lopez 98261
(360) 468–2133

LUMMI ISLAND
Well! Latte Dah Cafe
Lummi Island
Ferry Landing
Lummi Island 98262
(360) 758–2569

Willows Inn Restaurant
2479 West Shore Drive
Lummi Island 98262
(360) 758–2620

LYNDEN
Lynden Dutch Bakery
421 Front Street
Lynden 98264
(360) 354–3911

OLYMPIA
Budd Bay Cafe
525 Columbia Street NW
Olympia 98501
(360) 357–6963

Tugboat Anniees
2100 West Bay Drive, #3
Olympia 98502
(360) 943–1850

ORCAS ISLAND
Bilbo's Festivo
Eastsound 98245
(360) 376–4728

Olga's Waterfront Cafe
Olga 98279
(360) 376–5862

West Sound Cafe
4362 Crow Valley Road
Eastsound 98245
(360) 376–4440

POINT ROBERTS
The Breakers Bar & Grill
531 Marine Drive
Point Roberts 98281
(360) 945–2300

Helpful Web Sites in the Puget Sound Region

Seattle
www.seeseattle.org

Tacoma–Pierce County
www.tpctourism.org

Mount Rainier National Park
www.mount.rainier.national-park.com

Port Townsend Area
www.ptguide.com

Bellingham & Whatcom County
www.whatcom.kulshan.com

Ferry Information
www.wsdot.wa.gov/ferries

San Juan Islands
www.guidetosanjuans.com

Whidbey Island
www.whidbey.net/islandco

PORT HADLOCK
Ajax Cafe
271 Water Street
Port Hadlock 98339
(360) 385-3450

PORT TOWNSEND
Fountain Cafe
920 Washington Street
Port Townsend 98368
(360) 385-1044

Nifty Fifties Cafe
817 Water Street
Port Townsend 98368
(360) 385-1931

Port Townsend Fudge
& Espresso
1046 Water Street
Port Townsend 98368
(360) 385-9955

POULSBO
Shelia's Bay Cafe
18779 Front Street
Poulsbo 98370
(360) 779-2997

That's-A-Some Italian
Ristorante
18881 Front Street
Poulsbo 98370
(360) 779-2266

SAN JUAN ISLAND
Garden Path Cafe
Second Street
Friday Harbor 98250
(360) 378-6255

Haley's Bait Shop & Grill
Spring Street
Friday Harbor 98250
(360) 378-4434

San Juan Coffee
Roasting Co.
Cannery Landing
Friday Harbor 98250
(360) 378-4443

SEATTLE
Pike Place Public Market
Pike Street to Virginia
Street
Seattle 98101
(206) 682-7453

SNOQUALMIE
Snoqualmie Falls Candy
Factory & Cafe
8102 Railroad Avenue SE
Snoqualmie 98065
(425) 888-0439

STEILACOOM
The Bair Restaurant
1617 Lafayette Street
Steilacoom 98388
(253) 588-9668

TACOMA
Engine House #9 Power-
house
611 North Pine Street
Tacoma 98402
(253) 272-3435

Lobster Shop South
Restaurant
4013 Ruston Way
Tacoma 98402
(253) 759-2165

Over the Moon Cafe
709 Opera Alley Court C
Tacoma 98402
(253) 284-3722

VASHON ISLAND
Sound Food Café & Bakery
20312 Vashon Highway SW
Vashon 98070
(206) 463-0888

Stray Dog Cafe
17530 Vashon Highway N
Vashon 98070
(206) 463-7833

WHIDBEY ISLAND
The Braeburn Cafe
197 Second Avenue
Langley 98206
(360) 221-3211

Knead & Feed Cafe
Front Street
Coupeville 98239
(360) 678-5431

P. S. Bakery & Cafe
221 Second Street
Langley 98206
(360) 221-9434

ALSO WORTH SEEING

Pacific Rim Bonsai
Collection
Weyerhaeuser Campus,
Federal Way
(253) 924-5206

Underground Tour, Seattle
(206) 682-4646

Selected Visitor Information Centers

Tacoma–Pierce County Visitor & Convention Bureau
1001 Pacific Avenue, Suite 400, Tacoma 98402
(253) 627-2836 or (800) 272-2662

Kitsap Peninsula Visitors and Convention Bureau
P.O. Box 270, Port Gamble 98364
(360) 297-8200

North Cascades and North Central Washington

The forces of nature raised huge chunks of granite thousands of feet into the air to form the far north section of the Cascade mountain range. We're talking *big* mountains that reach some 8,000 and more feet into the sky. We're talking craggy snow-covered peaks that fill the horizon from left to right, that cause tingles up the spine, and that also awaken a bit of fear and wonder in the heart and soul.

Abundant water, rich volcanic soil, and hot summers make the Okanogan, Chelan, and Wenatchee river valleys on the east side of the Cascades ideal for fruit growing. Many visitors leave with cases of fruits and vegetables to preserve. Depending on the season you'll find ripe and juicy cherries, apples, pears, peaches, corn, and field-ripened vegetables.

Farther east, the landscape mellows into dry, tan hills covered either with sagebrush and bitterbrush or pine and manzanita. You can explore back roads, ghost towns, and a scattering of small lakeside fishing resorts. Okanogan and North Cascades national forests offer thousands of miles of trails, making it easy to hike, cross-country ski, trail ride, or mountain bike your way off the beaten path.

North Cascades

The North Cascades are high, craggy mountains, covered with green forests and cut by dozens of rivers, waterfalls, and lakes. If you're approaching from the west, you'll see lush forests of western red cedar, Douglas fir, and western hemlock along with those towering summits often clothed in snow until July.

At the timberline between 4,500 and 5,500 feet elevation, alpine meadows carpeted with brightly colored wildflowers and rugged outcroppings sprout stands of mountain hemlock and alpine fir. Crossing over the passes to the eastern side of the Cascades, you'll see how the

North Cascades and North Central Washington

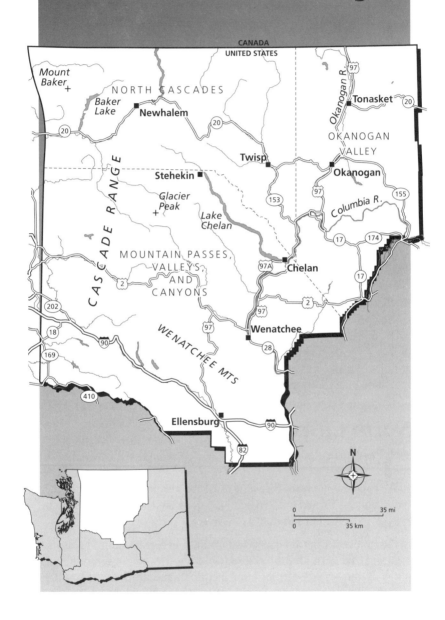

CANADA
UNITED STATES

Mount Baker +

NORTH CASCADES

Baker Lake

Newhalem

20

20

Twisp

Stehekin

Glacier Peak +

Lake Chelan

153

97

Okanogan R.

97

Tonasket

20

OKANOGAN VALLEY

Okanogan

Columbia R.

155

CASCADE RANGE

MOUNTAIN PASSES, VALLEYS, AND CANYONS

2

97A

Chelan

17

174

17

2

202

18

169

90

97

97

WENATCHEE MTS

Wenatchee

28

410

Ellensburg

90

82

N

0   35 mi
0   35 km

wrung-out clouds leave the hills and canyons to drought-tolerant species of lodgepole, western white pine, and ponderosa pine.

Highway 20, Washington's only paved road across this northern wilderness, was completed in 1972. The highway closes with the first heavy snowfall, usually around Thanksgiving. It normally opens again for the fishing season in April. Call Washington State Department of Transportation at (800) 695–7623 for road condition information. Late spring or early fall are the best times to view displays of colorful spring flowers or gorgeous autumn leaves. The USDA Forest Service and **North Cascades National Park** office complex located at 810 State Route 20 in Sedro Woolley 98284 (360–856–5700) is a good place to stop for information as you approach from the west. The office is open Saturday through Thursday from 8:00 A.M. to 4:30 P.M. from Memorial Day weekend through mid-October and Monday through Friday (same hours) during the rest of the year.

The **North Cascades Institute,** also in the same office complex, offers yearly seminars that delve into the natural, cultural, and aesthetic diversity of the North Cascades, its wilderness areas, and the Skagit Valley. The institute offers classes and field experiences taught by enthusiastic

FAVORITE ATTRACTIONS

*North Cascades
National Park*

The Methow Valley

Lake Chelan

*Lower Yakima River
Canyon, Highway 821*

*Sinlahekin Valley and
Wildlife Area*

experts. You and the kids can learn about butterflies, wildflowers, Native carving, naturalist journals, wilderness poetry, photography, alpine ecology, and more. For the current program guide, contact North Cascades Institute, 810 State Route 20, Sedro-Woolley 98284-9394; (360) 856–5700; www.ncascades.org.

Many visitors to northcentral Washington enjoy river-rafting adventures. More than a dozen rivers from Rockport to Wenatchee are popular for rafting, ranging from a relaxing Class I to suicidal Class VI rapids. Several professional rafting companies supply the equipment, information, and confidence beginners need to tackle a river. Most guided rafting trips concentrate on Class III and IV rivers; that is, rivers that have enough riffles, rapids, and white water to guarantee a great adventure. Some easy float trips are scheduled to observe eagles and osprey. For current information contact the North Cascades Visitor Information Center in Newhalem (206–386–4495; www.fs.fed.us/r6/mbs and www.cascadeloop.com).

Traveling east on Highway 20 from Sedro-Woolley, you'll follow the winding Skagit River, a designated National Wild and Scenic River, colored blue-green with glacial meltwaters. Take the turnoff north on Baker Lake Road if you wish to visit *Baker Lake,* a lovely mountain reservoir with campsites, trails, and lake access. You'll enjoy spectacular views of Mount Baker, due north, known to the local Nooksack Tribe as Koma Kulshan, "the steep white mountain." *Shadow of the Sentinels,* on your right just past the Koma Kulshan Guard Station at Baker Lake's south end, is a pleasant half-mile, wheelchair-accessible trail and interpretive hike through old-growth forest. For information about forest and lakeside campgrounds in the North Cascades, contact the Visitors Information Center in Newhalem (206–386–4495). Inquire about water sources because in some instances campers need to pack in freshwater.

Located about 23 miles east of Interstate 5, the town of *Concrete* is worth a stop before you continue traveling east on Highway 20. The Superior Portland Cement plant here was once the largest in the state, producing nearly half the cement used to build the Grand Coulee Dam and supplying plenty more for construction of the local dams on Diablo and Ross Lakes. The plant closed in 1968, and Concrete now serves as a jumping-off point for recreation in the Skagit Valley and North Cascades. The 1916 concrete bridge that spans the Baker River at the town's east end is listed in the National Register of Historic Places. Today, a jaunt across the bridge leads to East Shannon Road and an overlook to

Baker Dam. *Shannon Lake,* the reservoir behind the dam, is the site of the largest nesting osprey colony in the state.

There are a couple of places to bed down in the Concrete-Birdsview area, making this a good jumping-off spot for exploring the scenic North Cascades Highway and mountainous regions to the east. At *Ovenell's Heritage Inn Bed & Breakfast,* located at 46276 Concrete Sauk Valley Road, Concrete 98237 (360–853–8494; www.ovenells-inn. com), travelers are greeted by a noisy but friendly welcoming committee—a gaggle of ducks, geese, and farm animals, including several resident dogs and cats, four ponies, two quarter horses, and about 180 head of cattle. There are four comfortable guest rooms in the main house and two self-contained suites in a separate guest house. The best view is from the morning deck; this is especially fine on sunny mornings when breakfast can be served outdoors. At the second bed-and-breakfast, *Cascade Mountain Inn* (40418 Pioneer Lane, Concrete 98237; 360–826–4333; www.cascade-mtn-inn.com), the environment is a bit more quiet and sedate although just as welcoming. John and Sally Brummett enjoy sharing their corner of the North Cascades with travelers. Guests find five comfortable rooms on the second floor of the large home, each with country-style decor and views of Sauk Mountain, South Twin Mountain, or of nearby pastures and meadows.

You'll see snowcapped peaks as you continue east on Highway 20. For a strenuous hike that leads to even more spectacular views, turn north off the highway at milepost 97 onto steep and winding Sauk Mountain Road. In 7 miles turn onto the first road to your right. In a quarter mile this road ends at the trailhead to *Sauk Mountain Trail.* Three miles and twenty-six switchbacks later, you'll have attained a panoramic view of the North Cascades, with vistas on clear days that stretch back to Puget Sound and Mount Rainier. *Sauk Springs Trail,* just north of the highway at *Rockport State Park,* provides an easier hike on a barrier-free path. Five miles of trails surround the park's old-growth Douglas fir trees, which are more than 300 years old.

The *Bald Eagle Interpretive Center* (open weekends from mid-December to mid-February) is

Claim to Fame

Concrete was the setting, and also the filming location, for selected scenes in the autobiographical novel This Boy's Life, by one-time Concrete resident and author Tobias Wolff. The novel was made into a film in 1993 starring Leonardo DiCaprio as a troubled teen whose alienation compounds when his mother, played by Ellen Barkin, remarries and moves the family to a remote Cascade Mountain town. The movie, also starring Robert DeNiro, was a sleeper, but it is well worth renting for a glimpse of Concrete scenery and an admirable performance by DiCaprio long before his rise to stardom.

Bald Eagle Vital Statistics

Weight: *Up to 13.9 pounds*

Length: *Up to 3 feet*

Wingspan: *Nearly 6 feet*

Breeding season, Pacific Northwest: *April to August*

Number of eggs: *1 to 3*

Incubation period: *About 35 days*

Fledging period: *70 to 92 days*

Breeding interval: *1 year*

Typical diet: *Mainly fish and seabirds*

Lifespan: *25 years in the wild; about 45 years in captivity*

For more information: Bald Eagle Interpretive Center, Rockport: (360) 853–7009

located in Rockport, 1 block south of Highway 20 on Alfred Street in the Rockport Fire Hall (360–853–7009). Contact the center in January for information about the early February Upper Skagit Bald Eagle Festival and about guided float trips to see the eagles during this yearly event. Home to one of the largest wintering Bald Eagle populations in the continental United States, some 350 eagles are counted here annually, with January and February the best times to see the majestic birds in the Skagit River area.

About 3 miles east on Highway 20, just past the town of Rockport, is the ***Skagit River Bald Eagle Natural Area*** with its viewpoints and interpretive signs overlooking the river. Designated sites such as this are the best places to watch eagles without disturbing them. The great birds flock here in autumn from as far away as Alaska to feast on chum salmon that are exhausted and dying after navigating miles and miles upstream from the Pacific Ocean.

At milepost 101 you'll find the ***Cascadian Farm Organic Market*** (55749 Highway 20, Rockport 98283; 360–855–8173), a roadside stand that sells the Cascade Farm company's outstanding organically grown products. Cascade Farm organic foods are shipped all over the country. At this busy little stand, you can taste delicious berry shortcakes, low-sodium pickles and sauerkraut, fresh salads, sweet corn, all-fruit sorbets, and espresso. There are shaded picnic tables and self-guided tours of the experimental gardens. The market is open June through mid-September from 10:00 A.M. to about 6:00 P.M. weekdays and to 9:00 P.M. on weekends.

Another cozy spot for an overnight stay, you ask? Close to the wilderness and sans television? Not to worry, Dave and Andrea Daniels welcome folks to ***A Cab in the Woods,*** located at 9303 Dandy Place, Rockport 98283—between Rockport and Marblemount at milepost 103.3. Look for the bright yellow vintage taxi cab on display as you turn into the driveway. On five forested acres, guests find five cedar log cabins complete with kitchens, gas-log fireplaces, and no TV. Bring your bags of groceries and cook up a great steak or stew, curl up with a good novel, and enjoy the peace and quiet. Outside, you can try your hand at croquet or badminton, or you can explore nearby hiking trails that skirt the creek. Contact the innkeepers at (360) 873–4106, or browse the Web site at www.cabinwoods.com.

Or you could call the Clark family at *Skagit River Resort & Clark's Eatery,* located at 58468 Clark Cabin Road, Rockport 98283; (360) 873–2250. The resort offers pleasant overnight accommodations—cabins and a number of RV sites, tent sites, and laundry facilities. The owners seem to love rabbits; there are some 175 of the furry critters living in the woods and on the grounds of the resort. In the small cafe find such tasty fare as pumpkin pancakes, homemade apple syrup, and homemade soups.

Near the confluence of the Skagit and Cascade Rivers, the town of Marblemount has been the last-chance stop for food, fuel, and news for travelers heading into the high wilderness ever since miners trekked through these rugged mountains in the 1880s. *Buffalo Run Restaurant* at 60084 Highway 20 (360–873–2461) features buffalo steaks and burgers as well as venison and elk. Open daily for breakfast, lunch, and dinner during the summer months and on weekends during the winter. The *Marblemount Wilderness Information Center* has North Cascades National Park information and backcountry permits (360–873–4500).

Cascade River Road is a 25-mile gravel spur road heading southeast from Highway 20 at Marblemount, passing subalpine meadows on its way to the *Cascade Pass Trailhead.* This 3.7-mile trail leads to spectacular views of the North Cascades. As with all mountain trails, stay on the path to avoid damage to native vegetation. Volunteers have carefully transplanted the area with fragile, high-elevation plants grown in Marblemount to help restore damage caused by overuse.

The Skagit River's aqua color deepens as it churns through billowing rapids in the increasingly narrow valley. Just west of the Goodell Creek Campground, you'll find the rough, winding gravel road that goes 4.7 miles to the *Thornton Lakes Trailhead.* From there, the steep 5-mile trail rewards hikers with superb views of alpine lakes with those ever-present mountains beyond.

The Skagit River Valley widens at *Newhalem,* a company town just off Highway 20. There you'll find picnic sites next to an old steam locomotive, a general store with souvenirs and supplies, gentle trails, and the *Seattle City Light Visitors Center* (206–684–3030). The center has information about dam tours (mid-June through early September), which include scenic boat trips on Diablo Lake, rides 560 feet up the side of Sourdough Mountain on an antique incline railway (the last of its kind in the United States), and all-you-can-eat chicken dinners with homemade desserts at the Diablo Cookhouse. *Note:* Because of heightened security measures, the tour schedule may at times be interrupted or cancelled, so for current information check the Web site at www.city ofseattle.net/light/tours/skagit.

At the end of Newhalem's Main Street you can stroll along the **Trail of the Cedars.** This self-guided loop nature trail, a third of a mile long, crosses a suspension bridge into the forest on the Skagit's south bank. **Ladder Creek Falls,** behind the Gorge Powerhouse, snakes its way through a landscaped garden of native plants and quiet pools, lit up at night with river-generated power. The open-grate bridge at the **Gorge Creek Scenic Lookout,** between mileposts 123 and 124 on Highway 20, provides breathtaking views of the 242-foot gorge below. The big parking lot makes this spot easily accessible to highway travelers.

To get farther from the crowds and thoroughly enjoy yourself in the process, stay at the floating **Ross Lake Resort.** This unique isolated resort is not accessible by road; you must either hike on a 2-mile mountain trail from Highway 20 or enjoy a three-part journey that begins with a tugboat ride from the Ross Lake Resort parking lot on Diablo Lake at 8:30 A.M. or 3:00 P.M. Piles of food (visitors must bring their own since there is no store or restaurant at the resort), ice chests, baggage, and people all jumble together in the small, bobbing tugboat as it chugs past rocky islands and into a narrow passageway between steep canyon walls. Near the foot of Ross Dam, resort staff meet travelers at the dock. With gear and everyone safely loaded onto open trucks, it's a short but bumpy ride up switchbacks through the forest to Ross Lake. Speedboats from the resort ferry guests across the lake to the cluster of twelve comfortable wood cabins floating on huge cedar logs off the northwestern shore.

The cabins, built in the 1930s for logging crews, have been modernized with kitchens, plumbing, and electricity. Canoes and small motorboats are available for fishing or exploring the area's high-country terrain. Hikers can arrange water-taxi service to trailheads for backcountry adventures. The resort is open from mid-June through the end of October and gets especially busy when fishing season starts in early July. *Note:* Boat rental is required for cabins on weekends; no pets, no telephones, no restaurant or grocery store. Rental options include 14-foot boats with outboard motors, 17-foot aluminum canoes, 17-foot single kayaks, 20-foot double kayaks, and fishing rods and reels for rainbow trout. Instruction is provided for all equipment. Check the Web site, www.rosslakeresort.com, for photos of the cabins and other helpful information. For reservations, write to Ross Lake Resort, Rockport 98283, or call (206) 386–4437.

Ross Lake Resort

Back on Highway 20 heading east, you can stop for sweeping views of Diablo Lake and the hanging glaciers of Colonial and Pyramid peaks beyond from the overlook at milepost 131.8. A few miles farther, the *Happy Creek Forest Walk,* south of the highway, provides a barrier-free boardwalk a third of a mile long past huge fallen and standing old-growth trees. Interpretive signs tell the forest's story to the sounds of the bubbling creek. Ross Lake stretches before you from the ***Ross Lake Overlook,*** north of the highway. There is trail access to the dam from here. A few miles farther east, at the ***East Bank Trailhead,*** a quarter-mile hike will take you to Ruby Creek, an important spawning area for native trout (no fishing allowed). In 3 miles on the trail, you can reach the shore of Ross Lake and, in 28 miles, the Canadian border. ***Canyon Creek Trailhead,*** where Highway 20 veers southeast, marks the beginning of a short walk over a bridge to a turn-of-the-century mining site. About 2 miles up the trail, you'll see Rowley's Chasm, a 200-foot cleft in the rocky hillside.

The roadside scenery gets even more spectacular as you approach the high mountain passes. Creeks cascade down avalanche chutes—vertical alpine meadows are dotted with purple fireweed and red Indian paintbrush in the summer. There are several places to pull off the road to enjoy the views, such as the ***Whistler Basin Overlook*** at milepost 160, the barrier-free ***Rainy Lake Trail,*** or the point at which the 2,600-mile ***Pacific Crest National Scenic Trail*** from Mexico to Canada crosses the highway at Rainy Pass. Cast your gaze on Liberty Bell Mountain, a jagged-edged precipice that looms above **Washington Pass Overlook** (milepost 162.2), a spot with wide-angle views perched 700 feet above the highway. The wheelchair-accessible loop path to the overlook offers close-up views of alpine plants and geology, from spiral-grained trees to smooth, glacier-carved stones. At an elevation of 5,477 feet above sea level, Washington Pass is the North Cascades Highway's uppermost point. From here the highway winds down a steep U-shaped valley into the drier terrain below Liberty Bell.

A semiarid landscape is dominated by tall cinnamon-barked ponderosa pine on the Cascade Mountains' eastern slopes as you descend into the **Methow Valley.** There are pleasant, streamside campgrounds along the way at **Klipchuck** and **Early Winters.** A National Park Service Visitors Center and Ranger Station (206–386–4495) open daily, June 19 through Labor Day, from 10:00 A.M. to 4:00 P.M., in Newhalem, provides helpful maps and campground information for the North Cascades. Some 45 miles farther east, the tiny village of **Mazama** is located a quarter mile north of the highway at the upper end of the scenic Methow Valley. At first glance, Mazama's country store, gas station, and post office appear to be all that is left of this once-booming mining town. Look just beyond the village center to discover the **Mazama Country Inn** (HCR74, Box B-9, Mazama 98833; 509–996–2681; www.mazamacountryinn.com), an all-season retreat nestled in the forest between mountains. Located at the edge of the **Pasayten Wilderness,** the inn's fourteen-room wood lodge and comfortable rooms open onto miles of hiking and mountain bike trails. In the winter, you can cross-country ski out your door on the second-largest groomed trail system in the United States. The inn's restaurant is open to travelers as well as overnight guests. In Mazama other eateries include **Heenan's Burnt Finger Bar-B-Q Co. & Steakhouse** (509–996–2481) for Texas-style ribs, chili, steaks, and vegetarian options and **Freestone Inn Dining Room** (31 Early Winters Drive; 509–996–3906) for Northwest gourmet fare. During the winter when Highway 20 is closed, Mazama is accessible only from Highways 97 and 153 from Wenatchee to the southeast.

There's lots to do in this area during all four seasons. **Rendezvous Outfitters** (P.O. Box 728, Winthrop 98862; 509–996–8100; www.methow. com/huts) offers backcountry hut-to-hut ski touring on the **Methow Valley Winter Trail System** in the Okanogan National Forest for a combination of daytime adventure and overnight comfort. If you've ever wanted to experience the excitement of winter dogsledding, contact Roy and Sue Fuller at **Malamute Express** (Route 2, Box 422, Twisp 98856; 509–997–6402; www.malamute-express.com). You will be given

Ten Essentials for Every Hiker

1. Flashlight, spare batteries

2. Map of your hiking area

3. Compass and GPS (global positioning system) device

4. Extra food, water

5. Extra clothing

6. Sunglasses and sunscreen

7. First aid supplies, medications

8. Pocketknife

9. Matches in waterproof container

10. Fire starter

Avid Pacific Northwest Orienteering groups offer outdoor workshops in how to find your way in all types of terrain and weather. Locate regional activities on the organization's informative Web site, www.pnwo.org. Ask about the essentials for hikers when you call or visit regional USDA Forest Service Ranger Stations on your travels. The Mount Baker–Snoqualmie National Forest headquarters in Sedro-Woolley (360–856–5700; www.fs.fed.us/r6/mbs) provides helpful maps, information, and advice for camping and hiking in the North Cascades.

instruction in the athletic art of mushing through the snowscapes of the Methow Valley, pulled by AKC–registered Alaskan malamutes, the "classic freighters" among sled dogs. Call well ahead; their winter schedule fills quickly. If scenic horseback riding adventures are your style, consider a summer or fall wilderness pack trip or cowboy wagon dinner ride with *Early Winters Outfitting & Saddle Co.,* located nearby. Contact Aaron Lee or Judy Burkhart (HCR 74 Box 6B, Mazama 98833; 800–737–8750; www.earlywintersoutfitting.com). Scenic horseback rides are also available for guests staying at *Freestone Inn at Wilson Ranch,* 31 Early Winters Drive, Mazama 98833 (800–639–3809; www. freestoneinn.com) and at *Sun Mountain Lodge,* Patterson Lake Road, Winthrop 98862 (800–572–0493; www.sunmountainlodge.com).

Hikers and mountain bikers can obtain current information for all types of trails from the Methow Valley Ranger District (509–996–4000) and from *Methow Valley Sports Trails Association* (509–996–3287; www. mvsta.com). For fly-fishing information and guide service, contact *Mazama Troutfitters,* 50 Lost River Road, Mazama 98833 (509–996–3674). Those interested in guided river-rafting trips can contact *Osprey River Adventures* in Twisp at (509) 997–4116.

Even if you're not camping, the *Methow River KOA Campground* (509–996–2258) is worth a detour from Highway 20 for a look at its display of license plates from around the world collected by local resident Mike Meyers.

Highway 20 traffic slows as it winds through the small town of *Winthrop,* an early 1900s trading post now spruced up with a touristy Western theme. The *Schafer Museum,* in a historic log home on the hill 1 block above town, is worth a visit to glimpse some of the town's early history. The museum is open from 10:00 A.M. to 5:00 P.M. daily from Memorial Day to Labor Day. Also, stop and say hello to Carol and D.J. Stull at *Winthrop Blacksmith Shop* located at 236 Riverside Avenue (509–996–2703). You can often see D.J. working at his small gas-fired forge, and you can also browse their gallery of hand-forged gifts and home accessories.

Good eateries along Winthrop's main street, Riverside Avenue (Highway 20), include *Boulder Creek Deli* (509–996–3990) for great specialty sandwiches; *Grubstake & Co.* for gourmet pizza (509–996–2375); *Sheri's Sweet Shoppe* (509–996–3834) for freshly made fudge, chocolates, cinnamon rolls, and handmade ice cream; *Three Fingered Jack's Saloon* (509–996–2411) for Old West saloon atmosphere, big-screen TV, and family dining; *Winthrop Brewing Company* (509–996–3183) for fine handcrafted ales and tasty pub fare; and *Duck Brand Cantina* (509–996–2192) for superb Mexican fare along with daily gourmet pasta, chicken, and fish specials and a fine wine list. For gourmet eats at a crisp altitude of 2,850 feet with wide-angle views of the Methow Valley 1,000 feet below, try the elegant dining room at *Sun Mountain Lodge Resort* (509–996–2211), some 10 miles from town via Twin Lakes and Patterson Lake Roads.

Comfortable places to bed down in the scenic Winthrop area include small but cozy rooms at the *Duck Brand Hotel* (800–996–2192; www.methownet.com/duck) located above the cantina; the friendly, family-oriented *Wolf Ridge Resort* (509–996–2828; www.wolfridgeresort.com); and casually elegant *Chewuch Inn Bed & Breakfast* (509–996–3107 or 800–747–3107; www.chewuchinn.com).

Those who hanker to learn the art of catch-and-release fly-fishing can find an able teacher near Winthrop. On a private pond at *Fly Road Ranch,* located at 494 Rendezvous Road (509–996–2784), Ben Dennis teaches the art of fly-casting. If golf's your passion call the Court family at *Bear Creek Golf Course* (509–996–2284) to set up a tee time. Located out Eastside County Road from Winthrop about 3 miles, the scenic and somewhat hilly course offers nonstop views of Mount Gardner and Studhorse Mountain as well as the distant Sawtooth Range and Pasayten Wilderness. On your round of golf, you'll likely hear birds twittering along Bear Creek or spy evidence of local wildlife such as deer, moose, bear, and coyotes.

The Eastside Winthrop-Twisp Road is a pleasant, less-traveled route to the small community of Twisp. On the way, about 5 miles east of Winthrop, you can explore the world of firefighting at the **North Cascades Smokejumpers Base** operated by the U.S. Forest Service. Contact the Base (Route 1, P.O. Box 180, Winthrop 98862; 509–997–2031) Monday through Friday, 7:45 A.M. to 4:30 P.M., for tour information. The Twisp Ranger Station (509–997–2131) offers maps and information for backcountry hikes in the Twisp River Valley region.

Pause for espresso drinks, pastries, or tasty gourmet meals in the Twisp area at **Michaelisa's Coffee Stand** on Highway 20; at **Cinnamon Twisp Bakery,** located at 116 Glover Street (509–997–5030); or at **Fiddlehead Bistro,** 201 Glover Street (509–997–0343). For an overnight stay here in the scenic Twisp Valley, call the Larson family at **Methow Valley Inn Bed & Breakfast,** 234 Second Avenue, Twisp 98856 (509–997–2253; www.methowvalleyinn.com). You could also ask about what's currently playing at **The Merc Playhouse,** located in the historic Twisp Mercantile building at 101 Glover Street (509–997–2306).

A couple miles past Twisp, the highway forks. Highway 20 continues east to Okanogan. Highway 153 proceeds southeast along the Methow River as it winds and bubbles over its pebbly bed to Pateros. On this route you'll pass the pleasant community of Methow then plunge into orchard country as the river gorge deepens before its confluence with the Columbia River.

Okanogan Valley

The Okanogan Valley stretches from the British Columbia border at Oroville south to the Columbia River. Much of the land along the river is planted with fruit orchards. The area above the river valley is drier, covered with rolling grass and sagebrush meadows dotted with occasional stands of ponderosa pine, glacially deposited boulders, and lakes. *Okanogan* is the Kalispel word for "rendezvous," or "gathering place."

Highway 20 merges with Highway 97 in the city of Okanogan. You can visit the **Okanogan County Historical Museum,** located on the Highway 97 business alternate between Okanogan and Omak, open daily from 11:00 A.M. to 5:00 P.M. Fine displays cover local geography and history of Indian and pioneer life. Outside, poke into a collection of log buildings, including a settlers' cabin, a blacksmith's shop, and a saloon.

If time allows linger in Okanogan so you can visit **The Rusty Shovel** (111 Second Avenue South, 509–422–0558) and **The Jackass Butte Trading Company** (509–422–2349) located on the second floor of the same building. The owners offer all kinds of Western-style gifts and rustic handmade treasures for homes and gardens. Locals and folks as far away as Oroville say they wouldn't miss stopping here.

The **Breadline Cafe** (509–826–5836), a few miles north at 102 South Ash Street in Omak, offers good food and live entertainment.

Also in Omak, stop by **Novel Delights Inc.** at 19 North Main Street (509–826–1113) for tasty espressos, bagels and cream cheese, or delicious cookies homemade by owner Jody Daubert. Among the locals' favorites are her spicy ginger molasses and cranraisin–white chocolate cookies. You can also browse the large selection of used books that are arranged by categories such as gardening, travel, and mystery. **Magoo's Restaurant** at 24 North Main Street (509–826–2325) is a good choice for breakfast and lunch amid colorful Disney decor. Locals suggest **Rancho Chico's** at 22 North Main Street (509–826–4757) for excellent Mexican fare.

Heading north again on Highway 97, stop at the small town of Riverside on any day except Saturday. Pull up and park at **Historic Detro's Western Store,** hunkered down on Main Street (509–826–2200), but remember that it's open every other day but closed on Saturdays. You'll see a gaggle of hats, boots, jeans, shirts, belts, jewelry, and all sorts of Western wear for cowboys, cowgirls, and kids too. You can inspect all kinds of tack supplies like ropes, bridles, bits, and saddles. You might even meet a real cowboy or cowgirl. Ask the Detro's staff if the rustic saloon in town is a good spot to eat and sip a brew.

Conconully Jail, Sam's Story

*A*lthough it was built for impenetrability, the Conconully jail became the butt of many a local joke for the frequent prisoner escapes it endured between 1891 and 1915. Perhaps the most amusing is the story of Sam Albright, who found out that two of his friends were guests of the hoosegow and went with another man to pay them a visit. Finding the jailer absent, he and his partner unlatched the window and climbed through. The four friends proceeded to engage in a lively poker game, after which Sam and his friend left candy and books for the inmates, then exited back through the window, latching it behind them.

For a pleasant overnight campout, head north and west of Omak a few miles to **Shady Pines Resort Cabins and RV Park,** located at 125 West Fort Salmon Creek Road (800–552–2287) on the shores of 350-acre Conconully Reservoir. Steve and Dena Byl and their son Jake offer small cabins that sleep four and a log cabin duplex that sleeps six, all shaded from summer's heat by tall pines. All cabins come with full kitchens, queen beds, and cozy sitting areas. Beachfront RV sites offer full hookups, and a few tent sites are also available. You can bring your own motorboat, or you can rent rowboats to fish for rainbow trout or go for a relaxing paddle around the scenic lake. Inquire about fishing regulations.

For tasty regional fare in Conconully, try **Tamarack Historic Saloon** at 316 North Main Street (509–846–8137) for good hamburgers, ales, and pub fare; **Silver Lode Restaurant** at 215 North Main Street (509–826–2573) for hearty breakfasts and lunches; and **Sit'N Bull's** at 308 North Main Street (509–826–2947) for steaks and hamburgers.

For more area information, check the Web site www.visitokanogan country. com, or call the Okanogan Tourism Council at (509) 826–5107.

East of Tonasket on Highway 20, the tiny community of **Wauconda** offers a great introduction to the open beauty of the Okanogan high desert. You'll pass a scattered collection of homes, old homestead cabins, and barns set on the 3,000-foot-high desert plateau. The **Wauconda Store and Cafe** (509–486–4010), a one-stop store/gas station/cafe/sawshop/gallery/meeting place at 2360 East Highway 20 is worth a stop. The wood-paneled cafe, decorated with local art and historical photos, offers great views of the rolling valley, and the staff serves up delicious pies and other home-baked treats.

Bonaparte Lake Resort located at 695 Bonaparte Lake Road (509–486–2828) has cabins (with kitchens), camping, gas, and a lodge with a small store and cafe famous for its great hamburgers. To get there, turn north about 3 miles west of Wauconda off Highway 20 onto a 6-mile country road that winds along Bonaparte Creek through meadows and forests. The Okanogan National Forest also has several campgrounds in the area. **Lost Lake Campground** to the north (turn left off Bonaparte Creek Road onto Myers Creek Road) offers several fine hiking trails, including the easy Big Tree Trail where you can see 600-year-old western larches, and the Strawberry Mountain Trail, offering panoramic views from hillsides covered with wild strawberries. The Tonasket Ranger Station is located at 1 West Winesap, Tonasket 98855, (509) 486–2186; www.fs.fed.us/r6/oka.

Located about 20 miles east and north of Oroville, Molson's two historical museums are worth seeing. The **Molson School,** open daily from 10:00 A.M. to 5:00 P.M. Memorial Day weekend through Labor Day, offers three floors of well-organized displays highlighting local history. After browsing through the classrooms and library upstairs, the vintage clothing and furniture on the main floor, or the huge tool collection downstairs, you can enjoy homemade treats and lemonade provided by museum volunteers in a breezy main-floor classroom. The **Old Molson Outdoor Museum** (509–485–3292), open during daylight hours for self-guided tours from April through December, exudes an Old West feeling with its nineteenth-century cabins, shingle mill, mining and farm tools, and storefronts. Both museums are free, but donations are requested. **Sidley Lake** and **Molson Lake,** just north of town, are popular with travelers who like to fish. Birdwatchers also delight in the array of waterfowl, from blue-billed ruddy ducks to long-necked canvasbacks, feeding amid reeds and islands in the tiny lakes. From Molson retrace your route back to Oroville and Highway 97.

Oro, the Spanish word for "gold," bespeaks this town's early history as a miner's mecca. Oroville's original Great Northern Depot has been restored as a museum and community hall on the corner of Twelfth and Ironwood Streets, 1 block west of Main Street. The **Oroville Depot Museum** (509–476–2303), open Tuesday and Thursday from 1:00 to 4:00 P.M., provides insight into the town's history as a railroad, mining, and agricultural center buffeted by changing times.

For good eats in Oroville try **Fat Boy's Diner** at 1518 Main Street (509–476–4100) for hamburgers, malts, and shakes amid nostalgic 1950s decor; **Espressions Espresso** at 817 Apple Way (509–476–2970) for light sandwiches, baked goods, and soft ice cream; **Home Town Pizza** at 1315 Main Street (509–476–2410) for made-from-scratch pizza, Italian pastas, and gourmet desserts to die for; and **The Old Peerless Restaurant** at 1401 Main Street (509–476–4585) for dining amid early 1900s decor. At nearby **Osoyoos State Park,** stop at the McDaniel's open-air stand for their twelve varieties of fabulous homemade breads and soups along with German hot dogs. Eat at picnic tables with outstanding views of Osoyos Lake, then enjoy the 3-mile **River Park Walkabout** loop trail that takes in more great views of the lake and the mouth of the Okanogan River.

Chopaka Lodge, located at 1995 Loomis Oroville Highway (509–223–3131) at the lake's north end, is a lovely spot with three log cabins on a bluff overlooking Palmer Lake and surrounded by fruit trees. Follow

Old Molson Outdoor Museum

the lakeshore southeast past hillside orchards and lakeside cabins and homes to reach **Split Rock Park** at the lake's south end. A great stop for a picnic, the sandy beach is surrounded by willows and punctuated by a big piece of rock cut sharply in two. The park is maintained by local residents (you can help by packing out your own trash) who flock here to swim, boat, or play from the shallow south shore.

Continue southwest to **Loomis,** traversing dry hillsides above the green Sinlahekin Valley. Loomis is another quiet village that boomed during the gold rush of the 1890s and busted soon after. You'd never know from the orchards, old houses, and 1-block main street that this was once the largest city in the county. South from Loomis you can take a primitive but scenic road through the **Sinlahekin Valley and Wildlife Area** back to Conconully.

East from Loomis on the Loomis-Oroville Road is narrow Spectacle Lake, rimmed with cattails, dry hills, and remnants of an old wooden irrigation flume. There are several rustic resorts along this roadside lake, but the best one is hidden away to the north on secluded Wannacut Lake. Watch for the sign on your left, past Spectacle Lake, for **Sun Cove Resort and Guest Ranch,** located at 93 East Wannocut Lane (Route 2, Box 1294), Oroville 98844; (509) 476–2223. You can also get there directly from Oroville on a 10-mile, partially gravel road by following signs on Twelfth Avenue west of the Oroville Depot. *Note:* Before heading into the hinterlands by car, have a full tank of gasoline; check the water and oil; and always pack water, beverages, and healthful snacks. The log cabins and larger cottages are comfortable and offer splendid lake views. Besides excellent fishing opportunities, including plenty

**TOP ANNUAL EVENTS IN
NORTH CENTRAL WASHINGTON**

Skagit Eagle Festival,
Rockport, early February

'49er Days, Winthrop, May;
(888) 463–8469

Manly Man Festival, Roslyn,
June

Cowboy Poetry Gathering,
Omak, August

Ellensburg Rodeo,
Ellensburg, late August–early
September

of rainbow and Lahonton Cutthroat trout, the wooded grounds provide plenty of fun activities for both children and adults, including hiking trails, a swimming pool, playground, and sports equipment. The Bear's Den (the resort office and meeting area) offers snacks, groceries, and reading and laundry facilities. The resort is open from April through November.

If you don't take the turnoff to Sun Cove, you can continue straight on the Loomis-Oroville Road past Whitestone Lake and merge right onto the Tonasket-Oroville Westside Road. This less-traveled route traverses the hills west of the Okanogan River, parallel to Highway 97. During summer, keep an eye out for fresh-fruit stands along the way to refill your picnic hamper with locally grown apples, pears, peaches, cherries, and apricots. You can cross the river to Highway 97 at Tonasket, but before heading south toward Lake Chelan, pause for refreshments at *Shannon's Ice Cream Parlor & Cafe* at 626 South Whitcomb Avenue (509–486–2259). You'll find delicious ice cream in a gaggle of flavors plus tasty sandwiches, soups, salads, and desserts in this welcoming oasis. An option for hearty meals is *Whistler's Family Restaurant,* located at 616 South Whitcomb Avenue.

If you are in the area during the winter ski season, the Tonasket Ranger District located at 1 West Winesap (509–486–2186; www.fs.fed.us/r6/oka) can provide information about *Sitzmark Ski Area* and Highland Cross Country Snow Park and about nearby snowmobile trails.

Mountain Passes, Valleys, and Canyons

You don't mind being surrounded on three sides by 8,000-foot high craggy mountain peaks, dense alpine forests, and miles of hiking trails? You don't mind a four-hour boat ride to the end of a 55-mile-long lake that reaches deep into the *Lake Chelan Recreation Area* and the *Sawtooth Wilderness?* You love the idea of winter moonlight snowshoe treks? And you like the idea of staying overnight in rustic tent-cabins or cozy lodge rooms without TVs, telephones, daily newspapers, or Internet access? If so, this qualifies you for an extraordinary outdoor adventure to *Stehekin* and the scenic Stehekin Valley, one of the most isolated outposts in the central Washington Cascades. The good news is that Stehekin also offers a small restaurant (in the lodge), a bakery, and mountain bike rentals and shuttle van rides up-valley to trailheads—but that's about it. We're talking small here; we're talking low key and down-home friendly. This is way too much wilderness or too much lakeside scenery, you say? Not to worry; you can go back to Chelan for your overnight stay as long as you catch the boat for the return trip.

Two passenger ferries sail daily between the town of Chelan and Ste-hekin. The *Lady of the Lake* takes four hours to travel each way. The *Lady Express* does the same trip in a little over two hours. If time allows take the slower trip, which provides more time to enjoy the fine views. During the trip, Forest Service rangers offer presentations on local natural history and the mountain wilderness environment. For schedules, contact Lake Chelan Boat Company, (509) 682–4584 and www.ladyofthelake.com. Chelan Airways (509–682–5065) offers float-plane trips from Chelan to Stehekin.

If you're interested in camping and hiking, in the Stehekin Valley area, first call the National Park Service/USDA Forest Service Visitors Infor-mation Center located in Stehekin, (360) 856–4700, extension 340, then extension 14—this is a satellite telephone so callers will need to be patient; on-line information is available at www.nps.gov/noca. Park rangers can help with trail maps, weather conditions, campgrounds and camping sites, other lodging in Stehekin, equipment lists, guide services, and permits for backcountry excursions. The center is open daily from 8:00 A.M. to 4:30 P.M. from mid-May through mid-October. There is also an information center in Chelan at 428 West Woodin Avenue (509–682–2549). *Note:* Do not hike into wilderness areas without being fully equipped and fully informed about the areas you plan to explore. See "Ten Essentials for Every Hiker" in the North Cascades section.

For a gentler outdoor adventure, try the **Stehekin Valley Ranch** (P.O. Box 36, Stehekin 98852; 509–682–4677), which is open from mid-June to the last week of September. Located 9 miles up-valley from the boat land-ing, the Courtney family offers rustic one-room tent-cabins—a few of them come with electricity and baths. In the open-air dining lodge, guests hunker down at huge log slab tables to enjoy steaming cups of coffee and hearty meals cooked by ranch staff. There are no water views here, but you can arrange for scenic horseback rides and rafting trips.

Folks can also contact **North Cascades Stehekin Lodge** (509–682–4494; www.stehekin.com) to bed down in Stehekin. The lodge offers a restau-rant and small convenience store. **Silver Bay Inn,** located at 10 Silver Bay

Skiing Washington

Alpine and Cross-Country Ski Areas:

Individual Web sites offer specific information about downhill runs; extent of cross-country trail systems; snowboarding areas; snowshoeing; day lodge amenities; directions, weather, snow conditions, and Sno-Park fees; and overnight accommodations in the area.

Hurricane Ridge—Located 18 miles south of Port Angeles in Olympic National Park (360–417–4555; www.hurricaneridge.net)

Stevens Pass—Located between Seattle and Leavenworth via Highway 2 (206–812–4510; www.stevenspass.com)

Snoqualmie Pass—Located 45 miles east of Seattle via Interstate 90 (425–434–7669; www.summit-at-snoqualmie.com)

Mount Baker—Located 56 miles east of Bellingham via Highway 542 (360–734–6771; www.mtbakerskiarea.com)

White Pass—Located 90 miles southeast of Olympia and near Mount Rainier National Park via Interstate 5 and Highway 12 (509–672–3100; www.skiwhitepass.com)

Methow Valley Winter Trail System—Located north of Wenatchee and near Mazama, Winthrop, and Twisp via Highways 97, 153, and 20 (509–996–3287; www.mvsta.com and www.methow.com/huts)

Mission Ridge—Located 12 miles from Wenatchee (509–663–6543; www.missionridge.com)

Loup Loup Ski Area—Located between Okanogan and Twisp off Highway 20 (509–826–2720; www.skitheloup.com)

Sitzmark Ski Area—Located 17 miles northeast of Tonasket off Highway 97 (509–485–3323; www.skiresortsguide.com/stats.cfm/wa09.htm)

Mount Spokane Ski Area—Located 23 miles north of Spokane (509–238–2220; www.mtspokane.com)

49 Degrees North Ski Area—Located 42 miles north of Spokane via Highway 395 (509–935–6649; www.ski49n.com)

Further information:
www.skiwashington.com
(October through March)

Road (509–682–2212; www.silverbayinn.com), offers cozy and self-contained accommodations in the Lake Cabin (sleeps four), the Bay Cabin (sleeps six), the River View Room (sleeps two), and the most recent Lakeview House. The latter sleeps six and comes with two bedrooms, two baths, and a full kitchen. The property offers panoramic views of Lake Chelan and those 8,000-foot-high craggy mountains.

Bring sturdy walking shoes and bottles of water so you can enjoy the easy 3$\frac{1}{2}$-mile hike up-valley from Stehekin to view **Rainbow Falls.**

Just a short walk from the main road brings you to a good viewpoint to see some 312 feet of cascading water. For a taste of history, explore the old one-room Stehekin School down the road from the falls, then walk a short distance to the Buckner orchard and early 1900s homestead. On your return walk, stop at the **Stehekin Bakery** for delicious, fresh-baked treats (open May 15 through October 15). If you can hold off munching everything, carry your snack the 2 miles back to Stehekin, and enjoy your luscious pastries with grand views of the lake at one of the picnic tables on the large deck near the boat landing.

The Columbia River is tamed in the center of the state by the Rocky Reach, Rock Island, Wanapum, and Priest Rapids dams, which create long, narrow reservoirs, generate electricity, and provide irrigation for the Wenatchee Valley region. Like the Okanogan Valley to the north, nearly all available plots of land along the east side of the Columbia River and several smaller valleys to the west toward Cashmere are planted in orchards, making this one of the nation's prime sources of apples, pears, peaches, and apricots. Boating, swimming, fishing, and bicycling are popular during the long, sunny summers; skiing and snowshoeing are popular in winter.

The town of **Chelan,** set on the southeast shore of 55-mile-long Lake Chelan, is a popular tourist destination. The downtown area is a pleasant place for strolling, shopping, and leisurely eating. **Chelan Riverwalk Park** offers a shoreline walking trail and a pavilion where outdoor concerts are scheduled during the summer. Situated on a hill just above town, **A Quail's Roost Inn** (121 East Highland Avenue, Chelan 98816; 800–681–2892 or 509–682–2892) offers cozy bed-and-breakfast accommodations in a circa 1902 Queen Anne Victorian painted in soft yellow with white and lavender trim. "It's one of those wonderful old painted ladies," says innkeeper and artist Marilee Stolzenburg. The house is also on the National Register of Historic Places. Guest rooms on the second floor command great views of Lake Chelan to the west. Among the many good eateries in the area, try the historic **Campbell House** in downtown Chelan (104 West Woodin; 509–682–2561) with a full-service dining room on the main floor, but the best place to eat is in the pub on the second floor, which offers outdoor seating on its veranda along with superb views of the lake. For excellent deli sandwiches and tasty Thai fare, find **The Hungry Belly** in Lake Chelan Plaza at 246 West Manson Road (509–682–8630); for good take-out pizza try **Local Myth Pizza** at 514 East Woodin (509–682–2914); and for giant cinnamon rolls, bagel sandwiches, salads, and specialty espressos, find **Latte Da Coffee Stop Cafe** at 303 East Wapato Avenue (509–682–4196).

Apples, Apples, Apples

Nearly 10,000 acres of the Chelan Valley are devoted to growing apples, with smaller crops of other luscious fruit such as cherries, pears, apricots, and peaches. Year-round apple varieties that folks love to munch include

- *Red Delicious*

- *Golden Delicious*

- *Granny Smith*

- *Gala*

- *Fuji*

- *Jonagold (available September through March)*

- *Braeburn (available October through July)*

Look for fruit stands throughout the valley on your travels.

In the Manson area on the north lakeshore a few miles from Chelan, try *Laura's Restaurant & Pies* at 70 West Wapato Way (509–687–6105) for espresso and coffee drinks and freshly baked pies and pastries, along with lunch and dinner specials, and *Morrison's Dock at the Bay* at 45 Wapato Way (509–687–0356) for healthful breakfast and lunch fare; and for Italian pastas, garden salads, fresh baked subs, and burgers, head out to *Uncle Tim's Pizzeria & Pasta House/Sports Bar* at 76 West Wapato Way also in Manson (509–687–9273). If you have a deli picnic, follow the signs to scenic *Willow Point Park* near Manson. While the city parks can get lively and noisy with kids and families, this small shoreside park offers a quiet alternative and great views of the lake. If you're in the area on a Monday between late June and the end of September, you could drive about 4 miles from Manson to *Banjo Creek Farms* (509–687–0708; www.banjocreekfarms.com) for the weekly Renaissance Farmers Market from 9:30 A.M. to 12:30 P.M. Here you find local fresh vegetables and fruits, cut flowers, and a gaggle of homemade cinnamon rolls, pies, and breads along with homemade jams and jellies, quilts and crafts, a cowboy barbecue lunch, and live musical entertainment.

If you head east on Highway 2 from the Columbia River, about 25 miles south of Chelan (via Highway 151), you'll climb through wheat-covered rolling hills to the town of Waterville. The *Douglas County Historical Museum* on Highway 2 on the west side of town has interesting displays, including an extensive rock collection. In front of the museum, you can see a large metal bucket that was once part of an overhead conveyor system that in the early 1900s carried wheat 2,400 feet down to the river where it was loaded on grain barges. Waterville is a pleasant community with many old houses and a fine county courthouse. Directly across from the museum at 102 East Park Street, the circa 1903 *Waterville Historic Hotel* (888–509–8180; www.watervillehotel.com) is in the process of being restored by owner Dave Lundgren. One large suite and ten comfortable rooms (some with private baths and with claw-footed tubs) are now open for travelers. You'll see some of the original oak and leather Mission-style furnishings on the main floor in the cozy lobby and tearoom area, where a light continental breakfast is served to guests. Ask Dave about The Nifty Vaudeville Theater in town, which screens old movies and offers occasional melodramas. It's a short hop from here to Wenatchee, Leavenworth, and Chelan.

Heading south on Highway 97A from the Chelan area and away from the dense forests of the North Cascades, the Columbia River is on your left as you drive toward **Wenatchee.** Tan-colored hills looming on your right (west) are now clothed in sagebrush, bitterbrush, and aromatic juniper. But across the river to the east, you see compact orchards that are lush and green from irrigation.

Author's Note

At 2,640 feet, Waterville boasts the distinction of being the town with the highest altitude in the state.

Detour at **Rocky Reach Dam** (509–663–8121) and enjoy a rest stop and perhaps an impromptu picnic amid a splendid perennial garden, hanging baskets of summer flowers, and a children's playground. With camera in hand, climb the steps to the top of the children's slide and snap a picture of the large floral U.S. flag, Old Glory Garden, planted in red, white, and blue annuals in the lawn. More than 5,000 annuals bloom on Petunia Island surrounding the fish ladders.

Just prior to reaching Wenatchee, look for the sign to **Ohme Gardens** and detour to 3327 Ohme Road (509–662–5785; www.ohmegardens. com) to visit this lush and cool alpine wonderland. Beginning in 1929 Herman and Ruth Ohme developed the family gardens on their barren hilltop 600 feet above the Columbia River. Ten years later, friends and community members urged the Ohmes to allow public visits to their splendid garden. Travelers still flock to this nine-acre alpine garden atop the bluff that allows wide views of the Columbia River, Cascade

Recreation & Picnicking in the Lake Chelan Area

Lake Chelan Mural Walk—*Over a dozen murals in and around the downtown area, each containing an apple in some form. Pick up a mural map from the Visitor Information Center (509–682–3503).*

Chelan Riverwalk Park—*Scenic 1-mile shoreline trail along the Chelan River near downtown.*

Chelan Falls Park—*Picnic area,* *swimming beach, boat ramp, and docks about 5 miles north of Chelan.*

Willow Point—*Scenic and quiet lakeside spot near Manson.*

Old Mill Park—*Picnic sites, boat launch, short-term moorage, and marine wastewater station located in the Manson area about 10 miles up the north lakeshore. For information, call (509) 687–9635.*

Mountains, and Wenatchee Valley. Irregular stepping stones and narrow flagstone pathways meander up and down and around shaded fern-lined pools, next to large ponds, and around immense boulders. You'll see many varieties of sedum along with creeping thyme, creeping phlox, alyssum, and dianthus. Tall western red cedar, mountain hemlock, grand fir, Douglas fir, and alpine fir grow around the garden's perimeter. The garden is open from April 15 to October 15, 9:00 A.M. to 6:00 P.M. There's a nominal admission fee. *Note:* The upper garden is handicapped accessible. Wear sturdy walking shoes here.

For other things to see and do in the Wenatchee area, stop by the Visitors Information Center at 116 North Wenatchee Avenue, Wenatchee 98801; (800) 572–7753. Browse the Web sites www.wenatcheevalley.org and www.appleblossom.com for additional information. A pleasant overnight option is *Apple Country Bed & Breakfast,* located at 524 Okanogan Avenue, Wenatchee 98801; (509) 664–0400; www.apple countryinn.com. Innkeepers Jerry and Sandi Anderson welcome guests to their circa 1920 Craftsman-style home with its deep and inviting porch. Guest rooms in the main house are named for the apples that grow in the valley—Gala, Fuji, Red Delicious, and Golden Delicious. A separate Carriage House offers a cozy and private haven. Located about 4 miles from downtown and toward *Mission Ridge Ski Area,* Dave and Mary Cook welcome guests to their three spacious guest rooms at *Rimrock Inn Bed & Breakfast,* located at 1354 Pitcher Canyon Road (509–664–5113 or 888–664–5113; www.rimrockinn.com).

For good eats in the Wenatchee area, try *Jeeper's It's Bagels* at 619 South Mission Street (509–663–4594) in the Victorian Village; *The Cellar Cafe* in a vintage house at 249 North Mission Street (509-662–1722); *Coffee Sensations Cafe* at 26 North Wenatchee Avenue (509–662–5808); *McGlinn's Public House* at 111 Orondo Street (509–663–9073) for pastas, gourmet pizza, homemade desserts, and live jazz; and *The Windmill* at 1501 North Wenatchee Avenue (509–665–9529) for legendary steaks and freshly baked pies to die for. Then enjoy walking off the calories on a scenic section of the 11-mile *Apple Capital Recreation Loop Trail* that skirts the Columbia River. Find parking and trail access at Riverfront Park at the end of Fifth Street in downtown Wenatchee or at Walla Walla Park off Walla Walla Avenue at the north end of town. The path is wheelchair accessible.

Heading west on Highway 2 from Wenatchee toward Leavenworth, detour first at the small town of Cashmere to tour the Liberty Orchards *Aplet & Cotlet Candy Factory,* located at 117 Mission Avenue (509–782–4088). The tour includes samples of the delicious fruit and nut confections. If time allows plan an hour or so to tour the *Pioneer Village and Museum,* located at 600 Cottage Avenue (509–782–3230; nominal admission fee). Volunteers in pioneer dress encourage you and the kids to snoop into some twenty pioneer structures dating from the 1800s that are outfitted with vintage furniture, linens, dishes, kitchenware, clothing, and accessories of those earlier times. Browse the well-stocked Wine and Gift Shop, which offers a selection of wines from Wenatchee Valley wineries.

Once upon a time the town of *Leavenworth* was dying. But that was back in the 1960s when it was a tired and worn-out 1920s-style railroad and lumber town. Now, with years of revitalization by enthusiastic townsfolk, Leavenworth is a vibrant Bavarian-style village with a bit of Austria and Switzerland thrown in for good measure. And it sits smack in the middle of the Central Washington Cascades, where the craggy mountains look very much like the Alps. The village is good for walking because it is small and compact. Carved window boxes and hanging baskets spill over with bright flowers and greenery; shop signs are hand-painted in old Germanic script; building exteriors show lots of gingerbread detailing and rich carving; and tiers of second- and third-floor exterior decks and dormers are also done in the carved and richly appointed Bavarian style.

Enjoy strolling and poking into shops like *Die Musik Box* at 933 Front Street (509–548–6152), where you'll find more than 3,000 music boxes from around the world; *Der Sportsmann* at 837 Front Street (509–548–5623) for clothing related to hiking, biking, fishing, climbing, and skiing as well as bike rental and ski rental/repair; *Rocky Mountain Chocolate Factory* at 636 Front Street (509–548–6525) for fine chocolates, fudge, and caramel apples; *The Cuckoo Clock* at 725 Front Street for a large selection of cuckoo and other kinds of clocks; *Kris Kringl* at 907 Front Street (509–548–6867) for European ornaments, Pipka Santas, and Slavic treasures; *Sweet Dreams* at 220 Ninth Street (509–548–5144) for Teuscher fine chocolates from Switzerland and Howard Miller grandfather clocks; and *Nussknacker Haus* at 735 Front Street (509–548–4708) for a large selection of nutcrackers and smokers.

After all this ogling and shopping, you'll be ready to enjoy coffee and eats. Your alpine-influenced choices include *Alpine Coffee Roasters* at 894 Highway 2 in the Clocktower Building (509–548–3313); *Andreas Keller,* downstairs at 829 Front Street (509–548–6000), for rotisserie-cooked chicken, German potato salad, sausages, sauerkraut, beer, and wine; *The Gingerbread Factory* at 828 Commercial Street (509–548–6592) for freshly baked cookies, cakes, turnovers, and espresso;

Rumpelstilzchens at 1133 Highway 2 (509–548–4663), a good family place for Reuben sandwiches and Bavarian-style dishes; and *Lorraine's Edel Haus* at 320 Ninth Street (800–487–3335) for romantic torch-lit patio dining featuring Northwest and German dishes with fresh fish, pastas, and wild game. *Note:* Plan to eat early, as most eateries in town close before 9:00 P.M.

For a comfortable overnight stay in the Leavenworth area, consider these friendly bed-and-breakfast inns: *Abendblume* at 12570 Ranger Road (800–669–7634) offers gourmet breakfasts, a Grecian spa, and luxury suites. *Tumwater Mountain Bed & Breakfast* at 106 Center Street (509–548–2072; www.tumwatermtn.com) offers three cheerful guest rooms and bountiful breakfasts along with close-up views of Tumwater and Wedge Mountains. *Bosch Garten Bed & Breakfast,* located at 9846 Dye Road (800–535–0069), offers three guest rooms, a well-stocked library, and a hot tub in an enclosed Japanese teahouse in the garden. *Run of the River Bed & Breakfast,* a log-style inn located at 9308 East Leavenworth Road (800–288–6491), offers mountain hospitality and elegant amenities in six guest rooms with decks overlooking the Icicle River. *Pine River Ranch,* located at 19668 Highway 207 (509–763–3959 or 800–699–3877; www.prranch.com) and close to both *Lake Wenatchee* and *Kahler Glen Golf Course,* offers suites with river-rock fireplaces, whirlpool tubs, and gourmet breakfasts—French toast stuffed with chocolate and nuts and topped with brandied cherries is one of the tasty entrees.

For additional information about the Leavenworth area, check the Visitor Information Web site, www.leavenworth.org, or call the Visitor Information Center at (509) 548–5807. Less-crowded annual events and activities include *Bavarian Cross-Country Ski Pursuit* in early February, *International Folk Dance Performance* in late May, *Bavarian Bike & Brew Mountain Bike Race* in early June, *International Accordion Celebration* in late June, Icicle Creek Music Center's *Chamber Music Festival* on weekends in July, and the *Leavenworth Outdoor Summer Theater* from July through Labor Day. See www.leavenworth summertheater.org for the current schedule, which usually includes the musical *The Sound of Music.*

Highway 2 west up to *Stevens Pass* is spectacular, but not nearly as dramatic as it must have been for travelers in the late nineteenth century, when the first railroad line crossed the Cascade Mountains here. The original route included 13 miles of switchbacks cut into the mountainside that required the train to stop on spur tracks, change the track switch, then reverse up the next leg. Folks now drive the mountainous route with ease including a trip through the 8-mile Cascade Tunnel, currently the longest railroad tunnel in use in North America. For one more summertime adventure, this one on the **Iron Goat Trail** (206–283–1440; www.irongoat.org and www.fs.fed.us/r6/mbs) built by volunteers on the old Great Northern Railroad bed, detour from Highway 2 at milepost 55, which is 9 miles west of Stevens Pass summit, and follow the signs to Martin Creek Trailhead and parking area. For great mountain views, waves of blooming wildflowers, and interpretive signs, do the 2.4-mile round-trip hike along the lower grade to the Twin Tunnels and back. The trail is wheelchair accessible. From here continue west on Highway 2 through the small towns of Skykomish (there's a Forest Service Ranger Station here), Index, Gold Bar, and Startup toward Snohomish and Everett to the north. Or you can veer to the south toward Edmonds, Bellevue, Seattle, and the greater King County and Puget Sound environs.

Heading south from Leavenworth, Highway 97 takes you through the southeastern section of the Wenatchee National Forest and toward Cle Elum, Roslyn, Thorp, and Ellensburg. The current route over Swauk Pass is scenic enough, but for a special treat take the old winding highway over **Blewett Pass.** Except for occasional logging trucks, you're likely to have the road to yourself. It's also a popular route with bicyclists. For an alternate adventure take Liberty Road 2 miles east from Highway 97 to the town of **Liberty,** the oldest mining town site in Washington State. Originally established as Williams in 1880, then renamed Meaghersville in 1897, it finally became Liberty in 1912 when the post office was moved from another community of that name. It's a secluded, one-street community consisting of several modest homes, many of them log cabins, and the Liberty Gift Shop, where you can enjoy ice cream or a hot drink, depending on the season.

The Kittitas Valley pushes into the eastern slope of the Cascade Mountains in the center of the state, and here you'll find the old coal-mining town of **Roslyn,** settling back into relative quiet after its starring role as Cicely, Alaska, on the *Northern Exposure* television series. The entire town is on the National Register of Historic Places.

Trivia

The town of Roslyn was so fiercely proud of its mining prowess, that it shipped a twenty-two-ton lump of coal to the 1893 Chicago World's Fair as an exhibit.

Railroad buffs will enjoy a pilgrimage to South Cle Elum's **Iron Horse Inn Bed and Breakfast** at 526 Marie Avenue, Cle Elum 98922 (509–674–5939). The renovated railroad workers' bunkhouse offers cozy rooms, and on the grounds two comfortable cabooses can accommodate up to five guests each. Ask about the newest acquisition,

Iron Horse Inn Bed and Breakfast

a 1928 wood-sided caboose that sleeps two in a cozy love nest. Railroad memorabilia at the pleasant inn include tools, switch lights, toy trains, and conductors' uniforms. Ask the innkeepers about progress on the renovation of the Milwaukee Rail Depot and grounds located behind the inn (see www.milwelectric.org for updates and details about the community effort).

Iron Horse Trail State Park, a 25-mile section of the John Wayne Trail system, runs adjacent to the inn. Here you can ride mountain bikes, enjoy pleasant riverside walks, or try cross-country skiing. In Cle Elum you can visit the circa 1914 Craftsman-style *Carpenter House Museum* and *High Country Artists* on the corner of Third and Billings (509–674–9766), open weekends from noon to 4:00 P.M. Ask about the *Telephone Museum* interpretive exhibit, located at 221 East First Street (509–674–5702), and the *Roslyn Historic Mining Museum* at 203 Pennsylvania Avenue (509–964–9640)—both not far from the Carpenter House. Find good Italian fare at *Mama Vallone's Pasta & Steak House* (509–674–5174) and an extensive specialty menu at *Spacone's* (509–674–9609), both located in Cle Elum's small downtown area. Or, at *Wildflower Cottage,* 841 McDonald Road (509–674–9798), you can reserve a spot for a four- or eight-course afternoon tea, which may include such tasty Scottish and Irish fare as potato and leek soup, ham and cheese toasties, white chocolate scones, lemon curd tarts, and butterscotch meringue pie.

For a bit of history restored, turn off I–90 at the Thorp exit (milepost 101), then travel west 3 miles through the village of Thorp, past the schools, to reach the *Thorp Gristmill.* The mill operated from 1883 until

1946, initially powered by a waterwheel. Local citizens have worked to preserve all three stories of the sprawling structure and its fifteen well-crafted antique machines. The mill is open for tours on weekends from the end of May to the end of September and by appointment the rest of the year. Call (509) 964–9640 or write P.O. Box 7, Thorp 98946, before you go.

The city of **Ellensburg** has a unique downtown historic district that is ideal for strolling. Contact the Ellensburg Visitor Information Center (436 North Sprague Street, Ellensburg 98926; 509–925–3137) for a walking-tour guide. Along the walk you'll discover more than two dozen ornate brick buildings constructed between the 1880s and 1910, most of which have been renovated and now house small businesses and shops. The **Clymer Museum and Gallery,** in the 1901 Ramsey Building at 416 North Pearl, highlights Western art, especially the work of local historical painter John Clymer. You'll also see fanciful public art along the streets of Ellensburg, including a life-size bronze bull relaxing on a downtown bench.

Central Washington University's Chimpanzee and Human Communication Institute offers unique seminars called **Chimposiums** at its pleasant downtown campus. These one-hour, educational workshops explore scientists' personal observations of world-renowned signing chimps and discuss chimpanzee culture and conversations. Tuition is $10.00 for adults and $7.50 for students. The workshops are offered Saturday morning and Sunday afternoon. Call (509) 963–2244 for reservations (which are recommended) and more information.

Within walking distance of historic downtown areas and the Central Washington University campus, travelers can enjoy warm and hospitable accommodations at **Wren's Nest Bed & Breakfast,** located at 300 East Manitoba Avenue, Ellensburg 98926; (509) 925–9061; www.wrensnest.com. Innkeeper Marcia Williams offers guest rooms with antique beds, sumptuous coverlets, and fresh flowers from her perennial gardens. She also kept the rich wood floors and woodwork in the circa 1912 Craftsman-style home. Other welcoming inns in the Ellensburg area include **Meadowlark Farm Guest House** (606 North Main Street; 509–962–3706), where innkeeper Sara Ames offers two sumptuous suites on the second floor; **Pure West Guest House** (7626 Manastash Road; 509–962–2125), where innkeeper Missy Montana likes to give her guests a Western welcome; **Westside Loft** (4500 Hanson Road; 509–925–6734) with skylights and cozy built-in beds; and **Wilson Creek Ranch,** a circa 1940s ranch house (5321 Wilson Creek Road; 509–933–2527) where innkeeper Samantha "Sam" King welcomes travelers—especially those who might bring their horses to go on trail rides in the area. Good eats in Ellensburg can be found at **Pearl's on Pearl** (311 North Pearl Street; 509–962–8899), at **Valley Cafe** (104 West Third Street; 509–925–3050), and at **Yellow Church Cafe** (111 South Pearl Street; 509–933–2233). For pastries, coffee, espresso, and fresh-roasted beans, stop at **D & M Coffee Cafe,** 301 North Pine Street (509–962–6333). Then plan a brisk walk or bike ride on a section of **The John Wayne Pioneer Trail** (see www.parks.wa.gov/activites), which follows the former roadbed of the Chicago-Milwaukee-St. Paul-Pacific Railroad two-thirds of the way across the state. From downtown Ellensburg you can access the lightly graveled trail on North Water Street or just off Chestnut Street near the Kittitas County Fairgrounds complex.

The old road between Ellensburg and Yakima, Highway 821, follows the scenic **Lower Yakima River Canyon** for approximately 25 miles. The drive offers outstanding views of the wide valley nestled between sheer basalt cliffs and the river. A variety of raptors and songbirds live in the canyon, as well as herds of bighorn sheep. The river is famous among anglers as a Blue Ribbon catch-and-release trout stream.

The **Vantage Highway** from Ellensburg east to the Columbia River is a great alternative route that misses the traffic of I–90 and offers views of rich farmlands that give way to rolling sagebrush meadows. The highway passes by the **Quilomene Wildlife Area,** a 45,000-acre preserve popular with hunters. Watch for **Gingko Petrified Forest State Park** to your left as you descend to the Columbia River. The park has two short trails highlighting exposed "trees of stone." This area is rich with wildlife, including mammals, reptiles, and songbirds. Fifteen to twenty million years ago this land was moist and lush, covered with tropical swamps and thick forests. When layers of lava from volcanic eruptions covered the area, many logs that had sunk to the bottom of shallow lakes were entombed and eventually turned to stone, after minerals replaced organic materials.

Brochures along the trailhead will help you identify the petrified gingko, spruce, and fir logs scattered along the path. The park also has rock carvings of early peoples dated from 200 to 10,000 years old. You'll find drinking fountains, picnic tables, rest rooms, and ample parking here. **The Gingko Petrified Forest Interpretive Center** (P.O. Box 1203, Vantage 98950; 509–856–2700) is open from 10:00 A.M. to 6:00 P.M. daily from May through Labor Day and is well worth a visit. It's best to call ahead for hours if you're visiting September through April. Admission is $1.00. The center features more than 200 petrified wood displays as well as a twelve-minute film that tells the petrification story.

The highway ends at Vantage, where you'll cross the wide Columbia River. Take the 5-mile detour south on Highway 243 to the ***Wanapum Dam Visitors Center,*** open April through October, where you can visit a museum describing the area's history. The museum offers a detailed description of the Native people who inhabited the region for thousands of years and explains the impacts of white culture on this tribe. Although the dam itself flooded the tribe's historic village site and ended the traditional livelihood of salmon fishing, the Wanapum people have continued to exist and are working to create a viable future for their community.

From here you can continue east toward Spokane and the Palouse region, or head south to the Tri-Cities (Richland, Pasco, Kennewick) and west on Highway 14 or on I–84 (the faster route on the Oregon side of the river) and into the scenic Columbia River Gorge region.

PLACES TO STAY IN NORTH CENTRAL WASHINGTON

CHELAN
Best Western Lakeside Motor Lodge
2312 West Woodin Avenue
Chelan 98816
(800) 468–2781

A Quail's Roost Inn Bed and Breakfast
121 Highland Avenue
Chelan 98816
(800) 681–2892
or (509) 682–2892

CLE ELUM
Hidden Valley Guest Ranch
3942 Hidden Valley Road
Cle Elum 98922
(800) 526–9269 or
(509) 857–2322

The Iron Horse Inn Bed and Breakfast
526 Marie Street
Cle Elum 98922
(800) 22–TWAIN
or (509) 674–5939

CONCRETE
Cascade Mountain Inn Bed & Breakfast
40418 Pioneer Lane
Concrete 98237
(360) 826–4333

North Cascade Motor Inn
44618 Route 20
Concrete 98237
(360) 853–8870

ELLENSBURG
Meadowlark Farm Guest House
606 North Main Street
Ellensburg 98926
(509) 962–3706

Wren's Nest Bed & Breakfast
300 East Manitoba Avenue
Ellensburg 98926
(509) 925–9061

Selected Visitor Information Centers

North Cascades National Park
810 Highway 20, Sedro-Woolley 98284
(360) 856–5700

Winthrop
202 Riverside Avenue, Winthrop 98862
(509) 996–2125

Lake Chelan
102 East Johnson, Chelan 98816
(800) 424–3526
www.chelan.org

Ellensburg
609 North Main, Ellensburg 98926
(509) 925–3137 or (888) 925–2204
www.ellensburg-chamber.com

LEAVENWORTH
Icide River RV Resort
7305 Icide Road
Leavenworth 98826
(509) 548–5420

Pine River Ranch Bed and
Breakfast
19668 Highway 207
Leavenworth 98826
(509) 763–3959 or
(800) 669–3877

Run of the River Bed
and Breakfast
9308 East Leavenworth
Road
Leavenworth 98826
(800) 288–6491

LOOMIS
Chopaka Lodge
1995 Loomis-Oroville
Highway
Loomis 98827
(509) 223–3131

MAZAMA
Mazama Country Inn
42 Lost River Road
Mazama 98833
(509) 996–2681

OMAK
Shady Pines Cabins,
RV Park
125 West Fort Salmon
Creek Road
Conconully 98819
(800) 552–2287

OROVILLE
Sun Cove Resort
and Guest Ranch
Route 2 Box 1294
Oroville 98844
(509) 476–2223

PATEROS
Lake Pateros Motor Inn
115 Lake Shore Drive
Pateros 98846
(800) 444–1985

ROCKPORT
A Cab in the Woods Cabins
9303 Dandy Place
Rockport 98283
(360) 873–4106

Ross Lake Resort
Rockport 98283
(206) 386–4437

Skagit River Resort
RV Park
58468 Clark Cabin Road
Rockport 98283
(360) 873–2250

ROSLYN
Huckleberry House
Bed & Breakfast
301 Pennsylvania Avenue E
Roslyn 98941
(509) 649–2900

STEHEKIN
North Cascades Stehekin
Lodge
Stehekin 98853
(509) 682–4494

Silver Bay Inn
10 Silver Bay Road
Stehekin 98852
(800) 555–7781
or (509) 682–2212

THORP
Circle H Holiday Ranch
810 Watt Canyon Road
Thorp 98946
(509) 964–2000

TONASKET
Bonaparte Lake Resort
695 Bonaparte Lake Road
Tonasket 98855
(509) 486–2828

TWISP
Riverbend RV Park
19961 Highway 20
Twisp 98856
(800) 686–4498

WATERVILLE
Waterville Historic Hotel
102 East Park Street
Waterville 98858
(509) 745–8695

WENATCHEE
Apple Country
Bed & Breakfast
524 Okanogan Avenue
Wenatchee 98801
(509) 664–0400

La Quinta Inn
1905 North
Wenatchee Avenue
Wenatchee 98801
(800) 531–5900

WINTHROP
Best Western Cascade Inn
960 Highway 20
Winthrop 98862
(509) 996–3100

**PLACES TO EAT IN NORTH
CENTRAL WASHINGTON**

CHELAN
Campbell House
104 West Woodin
Chelan 98816
(509) 682–2561

Latte Da Coffee Stop Shop
303 East Wapato Avenue
Chelan 98816
(509) 682–4196

CLE ELUM
Cottage Cafe
911 East First Street
Cle Elum 98922
(509) 674–2922

Mama Vallone's Pasta &
Steak House
302 West First Street
Cle Elum 98922
(509) 674–5174

Twin Pines Drive-in
Highway 97
Cle Elum 98922
(509) 674–4362

CONCRETE
North Cascade Inn
4284 Highway 20
Concrete 98237
(360) 853–8771

ELLENSBURG
D&M Coffee Cafe
301 North Pine Street
Ellensburg 98926
(509) 962–6333

Pearl's on Pearl
311 North Pearl Street
Ellensburg 98926
(509) 462–8899

Vinman's Bakery
700 East Eighth Avenue
Ellensburg 98926
(509) 933–1850

Yellow Church Cafe
111 South Pearl Street
Ellensburg 98926
(509) 933–2233

LEAVENWORTH
Alpine Coffee Roasters Cafe
894 Highway 2,
Clocktower Building
Leavenworth 98826
(509) 548–3313

Helpful Web Sites in North Central Washington

Cascade Loop Association
www.cascadeloop.com

Mount Baker–Snoqualmie National Forest
www.fs.fed.us/r6/mbs

Welcome to Okanogan County
www.okanogancountry.com

Lake Chelan
www.lakechelan.com/

Wenatchee Valley
www.wenatcheevalley.org

Road Reports, Washington State
Department of Transportation
www.wsdot.wa.gov

Leavenworth Brewery
626 Front Street
Leavenworth 98826
(509) 548–4545

Reiner's Gasthaus
829 Front Street
Leavenworth 98826
(509) 548–5111

MARBLEMOUNT
Buffalo Run Cafe
60084 Highway 20
Marblemount 98267
(360) 873–2461

OMAK
The Breadline Cafe
102 South Ash Street
Omak 98841
(509) 826–5836

OROVILLE
Fat Boy's Diner
1518 Main Street
Oroville 98844
(509) 476–4100

Trino's Mexican Cafe
1918 Main Street
Oroville 98844
(509) 476–9151

ROSLYN
Roslyn Cafe
201 Pennsylvania Avenue
Roslyn 98941
(509) 649–2763

TONASKET
Shannon's Cafe & Ice
Cream Parlor
626 South Whitcomb
Avenue
Tonasket 98855
(509) 486–2259

TWISP
Cinnamon Twisp Bakery
116 Glover Street
Twisp 98856
(509) 997–5030

Fiddlehead Bistro
201 Glover Street
Twisp 98856
(509) 997–0343

WATERVILLE
Waterville Cafe & Lounge
104 West Locust Street
Waterville 98858
(509) 745–8319

WAUCONDA
The Wauconda Store
and Cafe
2432 Highway 20
Wauconda 98859
(509) 486–4010

WENATCHEE
Jeeper's It's Bagels Cafe
619 South Mission Street
Wenatchee 98801
(509) 663–4594

McGlinn's Public House
111 Orondo Street
Wenatchee 98801
(509) 663–9073

WINTHROP
Boulder Creek Deli
Riverside Avenue
(Highway 20)
Winthrop 98862
(509) 996–3990

Duck Brand Cantina
248 Riverside Avenue
Winthrop 98862
(509) 996–2192

Winthrop Brewing
Company
155 Riverside Avenue
Winthrop 98862
(509) 996–3183

ALSO WORTH SEEING

Olmstead Place State Park
Heritage Area (and
gardens), Ellensburg

South Central Washington

The south central section of Washington State sports impressive statistics and offers everything from apples to windsurfing, from two snowcapped mountains each over 11,000 feet high to waterfalls that drop from basalt ledges with one narrow ribbon of water falling over 600 feet. On the high plateau above the river that stretches north to Yakima, farmers tend vast orchards of apples, apricots, peaches, and cherries. Vintners tend hundreds of acres of grapes including pinot noir, Chardonnay, and Riesling. Washington State shares the awesome scenery of the *Columbia River Gorge* with its neighbor Oregon. The wide river forms a natural boundary with Washington to the north and the Beaver State to the south. Snowy *Mount Adams,* at 12,307 feet high, guards the Washington side and snowy *Mount Hood,* at 11,235 feet high, overlooks the Oregon side. The watery border extends roughly 300 miles from the eastern end of the gorge at the Tri-Cities (Kennewick, Pasco, and Richland) to the Pacific Ocean at the Long Beach Peninsula. Travelers can trek back and forth across the river on substantial bridges that span the waters at Long Beach/Astoria, Longview/Rainier, Vancouver/Portland, Stevenson/Cascade Locks, White Salmon/Hood River, Goldendale/The Dalles, and Tri-Cities/Umatilla.

The native Indian tribes who lived in the region weren't so lucky; they had to use canoes or rafts to cross the swift-flowing river as did the first French and American trappers, British Hudson's Bay Company explorers, American explorers and road surveyors, and the folks who traveled from the east on the Oregon Trail. One of those early groups of explorers sent by the U.S. government, the Lewis & Clark Corps of Discovery, trekked along the north side of the Columbia River in the fall of 1805, reaching the Pacific Ocean around November 15. The party numbered thirty-three and included Captain Clark's slave, York, and Captain Lewis's Newfoundland dog, Seaman.

Where it may take today's travelers a day or so to complete the same journey from the Tri-Cities to the Pacific Ocean by automobile, it took Lewis and Clark and their corps about one month to cover this leg of their

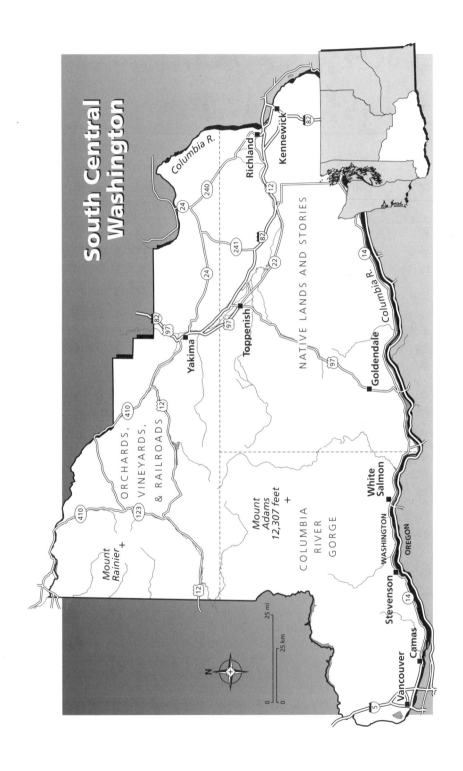

SOUTH CENTRAL WASHINGTON'S TOP HITS

Fort Vancouver National Historic Site, Vancouver

Hulda Klager Lilac Gardens, Woodland

Beacon Rock State Park, North Bonneville

Columbia Gorge Interpretive Center, Stevenson

Whistle Punk Forest Trail, Carson

Yakama Nation Mount Adams Recreation Area, Trout Lake

Conboy Lake National Wildlife Refuge, Glenwood

Maryhill Museum, Goldendale

Goldendale Observatory State Park, Goldendale

Timberframe Country Inn Bed & Breakfast, Goldendale

Sacajawea State Park, Kennewick

Liberty Theatre, Toppenish

Yakima Valley Rail and Steam Museum, Toppenish

Yakama Nation Cultural Heritage Center, Toppenish

Fort Simcoe State Park Heritage Site, White Swan

The Real Yakama Fruit and Produce Stand, Yakima

El Ranchito Restaurant, Zillah

Central Washington Agricultural Museum, Union Gap

Yakima Greenway

North Front Street Historic Distirict, Yakima

Orchard Inn Bed and Breakfast, Yakima

Indian Painted Rocks, Yakima

journey mainly by water. At **Sacajawea State Park,** located near the Tri-Cities, you can visit an interpretive center devoted to the expedition and the role of Sacajawea, the Shoshoni Indian woman who served as guide and interpreter. During the 200th anniversary of the **Lewis & Clark Expedition** from 2002 through 2006, you can also see exhibits, pictorial displays, interpretive material, and wide-angle views of the gorge and river at these sites: **Hat Rock State Park** near Umatilla; **Horsethief Lake State Park** near The Dalles; the **Columbia Gorge Interpretive Center** near Stevenson; **Beacon Rock State Park** west of Stevenson and the Bridge of the Gods; **Lewis & Clark State Park** near Troutdale and Portland; and **Fort Canby State Park** and the **Lewis & Clark Interpretive Center** near Long Beach. You can also visit the living-history program at **Fort Clatsop National Memorial,** the expedition's 1805–6 winter headquarters near Astoria.

Columbia River Gorge

When the British came to the Oregon Country in the early 1800s, among the many trading forts they established was Fort Vancouver. This fort was situated near the Columbia River and near what is now the city of **Vancouver.** The Interstate Bridge links

Vancouver to both Hayden Island and to Portland on the Oregon side of the river. On the island travelers find several service stations, a large, well-stocked grocery store, two large motor inns that overlook the water, a number of good restaurants, and dozens of large chain stores and shops, along with condominiums, houseboats, marinas, and pleasure boats of all kinds. The island is a good place to pause and stock up on groceries and beverages for a trip north from Vancouver toward Seattle or for a trip east on Highway 14 heading into the Columbia Gorge area. If time allows, have breakfast, lunch, or dinner at one of the oldest eateries on the island, *Waddles Restaurant,* located adjacent to the large grocery store. Notice the wonderful old camperdown elm that grows next to the entry door. Inside the restaurant look for the vintage

Lewis & Clark Expedition Bicentennial 2003–6

*E*arly in the nation's history, from 1803 through 1806, Thomas Jefferson undertook planning, recruiting, and dispatching a corps of men for a discovery expedition to the Pacific Ocean. It is said that Jefferson made the right choice in selecting Meriwether Lewis and William Clark to lead the expedition. Jefferson felt the two men, although different in their personalities, possessed qualities important for exploring uncharted wilderness: youth, intelligence, resourcefulness, courage, and a sense of adventure. Both men were experienced woodsmen and frontiersmen as well as seasoned army officers. From 1804 to 1806 the party of thirty-three folks traveled more than 8,000 miles on foot, horseback, and dugout canoe. The record shows the precise time frame as two years, four months, and ten days. Their route encompassed sections of Illinois, Missouri, Kansas, Nebraska, Iowa, South Dakota, North Dakota, Montana, Idaho, Washington, and Oregon. To plan your own bicentennial travels over the route, check these sites

for events and activities that range from 2002 through 2006:

Lewis & Clark Bicentennial (www.lewisandclark200.org)— Official national Web site listing Signature Events, activities, and other happenings for the eleven states encompassing the journey, plus other states involved in preparation for the journey; first Signature Event scheduled for January 18, 2003, at Monticello, Thomas Jefferson's home in Virginia (www.monticello.org).

Discovering Lewis & Clark (www.lewis-clark.org)—A multimedia site incorporating the entire route from east to west.

Lewis & Clark Trail Heritage Foundation (www.lewisandclark.org)— Information, preservation efforts, and maps of the trail.

Fort Clatsop National Memorial (www.nps.gov/focl)—Living-history programs mid-June through Labor Day at the 1805–6 winter headquarters site near Astoria, Oregon.

SOUTH CENTRAL WASHINGTON

FAVORITE ATTRACTIONS

Beacon Rock State Park
Goldendale Observatory
Yakama Nation Cultural Heritage Center

black-and-white photographs that picture Hayden Island during the 1940s and 1950s. You might spot a photo of the old amusement park, Jantzen Beach, which featured an enormous roller coaster, other rides, park and picnic areas, a large indoor dance pavilion, and two outdoor Olympic-size swimming pools. But the amusement park was razed in the mid-1960s, and in its place now is the large shopping complex that takes up much of the west side of the island.

Located just east of Vancouver's downtown area, **Fort Vancouver National Historic Site** is well worth a stop. The National Park Service operates the large complex. First stroll through the informative museum and visitor information area at the upper section of the complex, then walk down the grassy lawn area to find the fort and the fully restored **Fort Vancouver British Gardens.** In the 1840s grapevines trailed over greenhouses for shade and the garden yielded such produce as Thomas Laxton peas, English broad beans, and yellow pear tomatoes. The flower garden section contains a walk-through arbor of hop vines, large clumps of scented lavender, old-fashioned climbing roses, and vintage perennials in large beds. You can also see the remnants of the extensive fruit orchard on the grounds.

Then pay a small admission fee and gain entrance to the restored fort inside the re-created stockade walls. Watch living-history vignettes in the trading house, the blacksmith shop, the bakery cabin, and the kitchen—staff and volunteers in period dress offer youngsters and oldsters alike an authentic look at life in the early 1800s. You learn that both early settlers and members of local native Indian tribes often visited the fort to socialize and trade for tobacco, candles, beads, blankets, and cotton cloth as well as vegetables, grains, and other supplies. Dr. John McLoughlin, the fort's chief factor for many years, lived in the large house that stands next to the kitchen. Visitors can tour the house, which contains furnishings and memorabilia from the McLoughlin family's time here. Fort Vancouver is located at 1501 East Evergreen Boulevard, Vancouver 98660; (360) 696–7655. Visit the fort and its living history programs from 9:00 A.M. to 4:00 P.M. during winter and 9:00 A.M. to 5:00 P.M. during summer. The gardens are open until dusk.

You'll notice **Officer's Row,** the stately Victorian-style homes that sit in a tidy row along the boulevard just north of the park. These functioned as housing quarters for various military officers during World War II. The lovely houses are now preserved and open to the public during part of the year. Watch Vancouver's Heritage Players reenact tales from the

Ghosts Galore

It is said that ghosts and spirits hang around at times other than Halloween, perhaps to startle and amuse visitors. Folks claim they've "heard" or "seen" them in old theaters and hotels, vintage bed-and-breakfast inns, Victorian houses, ghost towns, and other places appropriate for denizens of the otherworld. Here are a few places to look for friendly ghosts on your travels in Washington state:

Marshall House, Officer's Row National Historic District, Vancouver (360–696–8297)

Capitol Theatre, Yakima (Yakima Valley Visitor Info Center; 800–221–0751)

Monaghan Hall (circa 1898) at Gonzaga University, Spokane (Spokane Visitor Info Center; 800–248–3230)

Blackman House Museum (circa 1878) and also at one of the town's taverns (the ghost's name is Henry), Snohomish (Snohomish County Visitor Info Center; 888–338–0976)

past, including ghost stories around Halloween, in several of the parlors and on several of the wide verandahs. It is said that Grant's House boasts its own resident ghost. For more information about the theatrical events and other public events on Officer's Row during the year, call (360) 696–8297.

Vintage airplane buffs can also visit the **Pearson Air Museum,** located just east of Fort Vancouver at 1115 East Fifth Street (360–694–7026; www.pearsonairmuseum.org). Located at circa 1905 Pearson Field, the oldest continuously operating airfield on the West Coast, the museum is housed in the Jack Murdock Aviation Center. The center includes two aircraft hangars, a theater, a hands-on activity center for the kids, and a vintage airplane restoration section. Pearson Field offers a fascinating history that dates to World War II. The grounds are open from 10:00 A.M. to 5:00 P.M. Tuesday through Sunday. Nominal admission fee.

Travelers can head north from Vancouver for about 20 miles to Woodland to visit an early garden, the **Hulda Klager Lilac Gardens,** located at 115 South Pekin Road (360–225–8996; www.lilacgardens.com). It may seem old-fashioned to like lilacs, but thanks to Hulda's work during most of the ninety-six years of her life, garden lovers can enjoy some 250 different hybrid varieties and colors of lilacs and their frothy blooms. Hulda's family settled in this area in 1877, immigrating from Germany first to Wisconsin in 1865. Hulda received many honors throughout the years, including one from an arboretum in Cambridge, Massachusetts, for her work as a leading hybridizer of lilacs. As you walk around the small farmhouse, now restored as a museum, you first see the lawn areas bordered by lush roses and other perennial plantings. To the rear, garden volunteers have restored the old woodshed, water tower, picturesque windmill, and carriage house. The latter houses a small gift shop. The apple tree and lilac collections grow in the arboretum section at the back of the four and one-half acres;

included are sixty-four lilacs listed in the National Registry. The grounds are open daily from dawn to dusk. The house is open selected times in April and May, when members of the Hulda Klager Lilac Garden Society don period dresses and greet visitors during the annual open house; lilac starts and plants are offered for sale during this time as well. The arboretum is wheelchair accessible.

The *Cedar Creek Grist Mill National Historic Site,* built in 1876, is located 9 miles east and north of Woodland (360–225–5832). Although rough-hewn and unpretentious, the mill was for generations the center of local industry and also the site of dances, parties, and musical shows. The mill was restored in the early 1980s and is now a working museum, with a water-powered stone flour mill and machine shop on the ground floor. On the second floor you can visit the small museum with photos and artifacts from the mill's history.

The mill is open Saturday from 1:00 to 4:00 P.M. and Sunday from 2:00 to 4:00 P.M. Admission is free, and you may even be able to take home a small bag of fresh-milled flour, but donations are always appreciated. To reach the mill, take I–5 exit 21 at Woodland, turn right at the first stoplight, and proceed east across the Lewis River toward Amboy. Bear left onto Northeast Hayes Road, which becomes Cedar Creek Road. Turn left after 9 miles onto Grist Mill Road and continue 1 mile to the covered bridge that spans Cedar Creek. The mill is on the far bank.

Continue on to Amboy, then turn south on Highway 503 through green fields and forests. In 7 miles turn left (east) on Northeast Lucia Falls Road and go 4$^1/_2$ miles to visit the *Pomeroy Living History Farm* at 20902 Northeast Lucia Falls Road, Yacolt 98675 (360–686–3537). You can browse in the British specialty shop to find items such as Duerrs Scotch whiskey marmalade, Cadbury chocolates, and English teas. You can enjoy a spot of tea with scones, tea sandwiches, jellies, and desserts on Wednesday through Saturday from 11:30 A.M. to 3:00 P.M. Reservations are suggested. On the first full weekend of each month from June through September, you and the kids can see the activities of a homestead farm during the days of candles and kerosene lamps. Volunteers wear period clothing and show visitors how to grind corn and coffee, use a scrub board, feed the animals, and use a crosscut logging saw. There is a small fee for visiting the farm.

Heading east on Highway 14 from Vancouver, Washington, you'll pass the small mill towns of Camas and Washougal. Take the highway's business loop to explore the Camas downtown area. Fourth Avenue is a pleasant walking street through the main commercial district. From here the highway climbs 1,000 feet up the Columbia plateau at Cape Horn. From the top you'll enjoy an expansive view of the Columbia River Gorge. After descending back to river level, you could pause in the small community of Skamania and snoop in the *Skamania General Store* (509–427–4820), an old-style rural grocery, then continue east to *Beacon Rock State Park* (509–427–8265). Beacon Rock is an 840-foot basalt tower, the remains of a volcano core, that served as a sign to early river travelers that they had passed the difficult Cascade Rapids and faced no further obstructions to the Pacific Ocean 150 miles west. You can hike 1.2 miles through the forest to Hardy or Rodney Falls. Or for a breathtaking challenge, climb the steep and narrow trail, including a series of wood stairways with railings, to the top of Beacon Rock for panoramic views of the wide Columbia River and forested hills on both the Oregon and the Washington sides of the river.

Just past Beacon Rock in the town of *North Bonneville,* locals suggest that travelers check out *His Deli in the Gorge* (509–427–8042) for great specialty sandwiches, espresso, lattes, and blended fruit drinks. The town was moved in 1976, when an expansion of Bonneville Dam flooded its original location. The new town includes parks and miles of bike paths. Until the river was dammed in the 1930s, there were three large and challenging rapids along this wide stretch of river that made excellent salmon-fishing grounds. Native families from the coast traveled here to live for part of each year in villages and camps along the riverbank. During the mid-1850s, Fort Cascades was established just west of the rapids. You can visit the *Fort Cascades Historic Site,* which includes a 1½-mile self-guided tour. Along the way you'll see prehistoric Indian petroglyphs, the original site of Fort Cascades (which burned during an attack in 1856), and artifacts from the colonial period, when wagons and railroads were needed to portage around the rough water.

Water travel is easier now, even for the long grain and produce barges that ply the Columbia, due to the network of dams and locks that begin with the *Bonneville Dam.* Visitors can tour the dam (541–374–8820 for current info) to see the huge electrical generators and the fish-ladder system that allows salmon and steelhead to migrate over the dam and continue up the river to spawn. You can view fish through huge underwater windows as they leap and swim upriver. On the Oregon side of the river, accessed by *Bridge of the Gods* just east of here, you can also see the locks in action, raising and lowering pleasure boats, fishing boats, and grain barges.

Be sure to visit the *Columbia Gorge Interpretive Center* (990 Southwest Rock Creek Drive, P.O. Box 396, Stevenson 98648; 509–427–8211;

www.columbiagorge.org). The center is located off Highway 14 a couple of miles east of the Bridge of the Gods. This expansive, glass-walled museum highlights the river's colorful history. Witness the geological and climatic forces that formed the gorge at the Creation Theater's twelve-minute multimedia show. Learn about the region's native Indian tribes through oral histories, an interpreted pit house, and dip-net fishing displays. Examine the environmental impacts of dams on the river. Other highlights include a 37-foot-tall replica of a nineteenth-century fish-wheel, one of many that once harvested millions of pounds of fish each year. The center is open daily (except holidays) from 10:00 A.M. to 5:00 P.M. Nominal admission fee.

You can also visit nearby *Skamania Lodge* (P.O. Box 189, Stevenson 98648; 509–427–7700 or 800–221–7117), a large resort and conference center located on a bluff just above the interpretive center. The resort offers golf, swimming, mountain bike rentals, guided horseback rides, and tennis. On the main level at the lodge, you will find a well-stocked Forest Service information center (509–427–2528) and Forest Service staff who provide helpful maps and information about hiking trails, wildflower areas, and scenic drives in the gorge. Nearby *Stevenson* is a historic waterfront town and a bustling county seat for Skamania County. Many of its buildings date back to the early 1900s, with new businesses sprouting amid the old. The *River House Art Gallery and Studio,* located at 90 Southwest Second Street (Highway 14) in Stevenson (509–427–8800 or 509–427–5930; www.createworkshops.com), features Columbia Gorge images and East Coast heritage homes, original watercolors, local pottery, baskets, and pastels. Call to make sure the gallery is open.

If you have time to spare, take a trip across the Columbia to the Oregon side of the gorge for some beautiful scenery and one of the highest concentrations of waterfalls in the United States. The best route is along the Columbia Gorge Scenic Highway (Highway 30). Considered a feat of engineering when it was completed in 1910, it is now a lovely, meandering drive along which you can watch the scenery go by from the car or venture out to one of the many trailheads for a hike. Multnomah Falls is the grandest of the waterfalls; at 620 feet it is the second-highest in the United States. At Hood River, just off I–84, stop by the historic Columbia Gorge Hotel restaurant (4000 Westcliff Drive; 541–386–5566) for more eye-popping views of the Columbia River and delicious food as well.

There are a number of pleasant eateries in Stevenson with most of them easy to find along Northwest Second Street, which is Highway 14. Try *It's a Wrap* (509–427–7725), open daily to 3:00 P.M. for healthy wraps and salads; *Loafer's Bakery West* (509–427–7808), open to 8:00 P.M. Monday through Saturday and until 7:00 P.M. Sundays, for freshly baked breads, bagels, desserts, and pastries; and *Big River*

Grill (509–427–4888), open 11:30 A.M. to 9:00 P.M., for Northwest pub fare and microbrews (it's a smoke-free place). Located at 240 Southwest First Street, the **Walking Man Brewery & Public House** (509–427–5520) offers handcrafted ales and gourmet fare such as Greek salads and sautéed oysters on Wednesday through Saturday. If you're ready for an on-the-go espresso or latte, pull up at *Gotta Hava Java* (509–427–5112), serving lattes and espresso daily to 6:30 P.M. at the west end of Stevenson in the bright yellow drive-through location. For dessert stop at **Aunt Sandra's Scrumptious Shop** across the street from the Skamania County Courthouse (509–427–3600), open noon to 7:00 P.M., where friendly proprietor Sandra Warner serves espresso, cookies, fine candies, and delicious Tillamook ice cream. If time allows take a picnic to the park at the Sternwheeler dock and watch the windsurfers take off from **Bob's Beach.**

About 20 miles north of Stevenson and Carson, plan to walk the **Whistle Punk Forest Heritage Trail,** a self-guided interpretive trail in the Gifford Pinchot National Forest. Along the wheelchair-accessible trail through the second-growth Wind River Experimental Forest, you and the kids can learn Northwest logging history as well as see old logging equipment used in the area in the 1930s. The Wind River Work Center (509–427–3200), located about 10 miles north of Carson via the Wind River Highway, can provide maps and other information about summer wildflower meadows, hiking trails, and winter cross-country ski areas

Sleeping in the Trees

You'd like to do your own thing and get decidedly farther off the beaten path? It's easy— about 15 miles north of White Salmon up into the Douglas fir forest at an elevation of 2,500 feet adventurous travelers can find **Lothlorien Woods Treehouse Hide-A-Way.** Unlike the Hobbits or Hansel and Gretel, however, you'll need to take along more than bread crumbs, so stop in Hood River or White Salmon for steaks to barbecue, luscious desserts to enjoy, and breakfast provisions. Your split-level cabin in the trees, about 10 feet off the ground, is warm and snug with a comfortable sitting area, wood stove, kitchen area, and lots of windows on the main level. Up the spiral wood stairway you find a roomy sleeping suite, bath, and more windows. The treehouse comes with distant views of Mount Adams and your own hot tub on the outside deck. You can bring cross-country ski gear during winter months. Call owner Jeal Breckenridge for reservations and specific directions to this cozy treehouse hideaway, (509) 493–8733; www.lothlorien woods.com.

Catching the Wind

You're adventurous, you're hardy, and you're in excellent physical shape? The ultimate test may be learning to maneuver a windsurfing board and learning to ply the deep waves on a windy day on the mighty Columbia River near White Salmon and Hood River. To learn about the popular sport of windsurfing, contact the Columbia Gorge Windsurfing Association located at 202 Oak Street in Hood River directly south of Bingen on the Oregon side of the river (541–386– 9225; www.cgwa.net). A couple of good spots to watch and photograph the sailors are at **Port Marina Park** just west of the bridge in Hood River and farther east at **Maryhill State Park** located south of Goldendale on the Washington side of the river. Maryhill also offers picnic shelters, grassy areas, and riverfront campsites.

in the Gifford Pinchot National Forest. For fascinating facts, resources, book lists, and information about the ancient art of animal tracking, check the helpful Web site www.bear-tracker.com. Folks of all ages, including the kids, can take classes and field workshops to learn how to identify—depending on the season—tracks made in snow, mud, dirt, and sand by owls and other birds as well as beaver, deer, raccoon, fox, and even the elusive bear and bobcat.

Farther east along the Columbia is the town of *Bingen,* and just up the hill is *White Salmon.* Until recently these were quiet riverside communities of hardworking old-timers, but they have become recreation meccas, especially for windsurfers. On summer weekends the beaches along this stretch of the Columbia are crowded board-to-board with enthusiasts, and the water is alive with colorful sails. *The Inn of the White Salmon* (172 West Jewett Boulevard, White Salmon 98672; 509–493–2335), built in 1937, offers cozy, antique-decorated rooms and delicious breakfasts featuring European-style pastries, breads, and egg dishes. Just for fun, ask about the Hungarian Flavf, the Artichoke Frittata, or the tasty Chile Relleno—so much for plain toast and cereal; you're on vacation, so enjoy.

Down the street, *Klickitat Pottery Shop* (264 East Jewett Boulevard; 509–493–4456) is a fun place to browse and observe an ancient craft in action. Potter Edward Swick works in a wide-windowed studio on one side of the shop, creating high-quality earthenware pieces for sale in the shop.

For good eateries in White Salmon, check out *The Creamery* at 121 East Jewett (509–493–4007) for coffee, bagels, and desserts, open daily to 8:00 P.M., and *Elkhorn Bar & Grill* at 120 East Jewett for steaks, seafood, and pasta. In nearby Bingen try *Loafer's Old World Bakery &*

Coffee House (509–493–3100) at 213 West Steuben (Highway 14) for great breads, pastries, and espresso; *Fidel's at the Gorge* (509–493–1017) at 120 East Steuben for Mexican fare, food-to-go, and delicious margaritas; and *Big River Diner* (509–493–1414) for tasty American-style eats and a great salad bar. Or you could pop into **Wild Berry Ice Cream Shoppe,** 116 West Steuben (509–493–8655), for cool and delicious ice cream cones and desserts.

There is lots to see and do in the scenic White Salmon River Valley, which stretches from the Columbia River north to 12,307-foot-high Mount Adams. *Zoller's Outdoor Odysseys* (509–493–2641; www.zoocraft.com) will raft you down the White Salmon River. It's an exhilarating experience and is suitable for families and beginners. The standard trip lasts about three hours, including the return by road to your starting point. Call for the current river-rafting schedule and to make reservations.

Extreme Sports, Columbia Gorge

Kicking it up a notch in terms of all-season outdoor sports in the Columbia River Gorge entails a passion for the extreme. Hardy types of all ages can learn how to:

Fly stunt kites	*Skateboard*
Inline skate	*Ski*
Kiteboard	*Snowboard*
Motocross	*Surf*
Mountain bike	*Wakeboard*
Parachute	*Water-ski*
Paraglide	*Windsurf*

For training and equipment resources, get a current copy of the "Gorge Guide" from the Hood River Visitor Information Center (541–386–2000 or 800–366–3530; www.hoodriver.org).

Families can plan an overnight stay at *Llama Ranch Bed and Breakfast* (1980 Highway 141, Trout Lake 98650; 509–395–2786) 16 miles north of White Salmon. There you'll find llamas, wandering peacocks, rabbits, and the gracious hospitality of owner Jerry Stone. His homestyle rooms offer views of Mount Adams towering over green pastures and forests. After breakfast you and the kids can stroll through pine forests and past bubbling creeks and serene ponds in the company of several gentle llamas.

Or you and the kids could arrange to go horseback riding on gentle steeds at *Northwestern Lake Riding Stables,* located at 126 Little Buck Creek Road (509–493–4965) near White Salmon and Trout Lake. Hours for riding are 8:00 A.M. to sunset daily, and there are horses here for beginners as well as more experienced riders. Children under the age of six are also welcome. Riding lessons as well as day and pack trips can be arranged.

For lunch or dinner in the shadow of Mount Adams, locals suggest a favorite, *The Logs Family Restaurant* (509–493–1402), located at B Z Corner on Highway 141 about halfway between White Salmon and Trout Lake. They've been serving up great roasted chicken since the early 1930s.

Farther up Highway 141 at the base of Mount Adams, you can enjoy mountain views from the chalet cabins at *Serenity's,* located at 2291 Highway 141 (509–395–2500; www.serenity.com)1 mile south of Trout Lake. Each cabin has walls of glass highlighting forested scenery and comes equipped with kitchenette, queen-size bed, and large bathroom. A few have whirlpool tubs and lofts, and one chalet is wheelchair accessible. Chef Marcy Nordwall provides delicious dinners for guests or for dinner-only groups of ten or more, featuring such delicacies as fresh salmon, halibut, or barbequed ribs. On one Saturday each month, fine dining is also available to the public by reservation.

Folks say one of the best places to hunker down for a fresh cup of coffee, a sandwich, a slice of apple pie, and a dose of local gossip is *KJ Bear Creek Cafe,* located at 2376 State Highway 141 (509–395–2488), next to the service station in Trout Lake. If you travel by recreational vehicle, check with *Elk Meadows RV Park,* 78 Trout Lake Creek Road, Trout Lake 98650; (509) 395–2400. The RV sites come with outrageous views of Mount Adams.

For other cozy places to spend the night close to snowy Mount Adams, check out several bed-and-breakfasts in the area. At *The Farm Bed & Breakfast* (490 Sunnyside Road, Trout Lake 98650; 509–395–2488; www.thefarmbnb.com), innkeepers Dean and Rosie Hostetter offer two comfortable guest rooms decorated with antiques and quilts in their large circa 1890 farmhouse; the two rooms share a bath. When guests head outdoors they find a fine collection of scented old roses and colorful perennials like delphinium, iris, snapdragons, coneflowers, cosmos, black-eyed Susans, and sunflowers. On the expansive grounds grow four varieties of maples, along with graceful willows and tall spruce. At *Kelly's Trout Creek Inn Bed & Breakfast* (25 Mount Adams Road, Trout Lake 98650; 509–395–2769; www.kellysbnb.com), innkeepers Kelly and Marilyn Enochs offer travelers a comfortable mix of old-fashioned quilts and rustic decor in three cozy guest rooms. During warm weather you can eat outdoors on the deck next to bubbling Trout Creek and its cascades of water rushing over large rocks and low basalt ledges.

In the Mount Adams area ancient volcanoes produced numerous lava flows, caves, lava tubes, and other natural structures. Many caves in the area were once used by farmers in the days before refrigeration to store butter and cheese until they could be transported to market. These caves make the region popular with serious spelunkers (cave explorers), who approach the caverns with the same sense of challenge and caution that mountain climbers have for major peaks.

The *Ice Caves,* a series of lava tubes, are the easiest of the public caves to explore. Their name refers to columns of ice that develop naturally in the lowest chamber during the winter. A century ago the giant icicles were harvested and sold in the Oregon towns of The Dalles and Hood River. The Forest Service has constructed a ladder leading down from the main entrance. A 120-foot tube that slopes southeastward is the most accessible part of the cave. In all there are about 650 feet of passages to explore. Be sure to bring warm clothes, boots, head protection, and dependable lights. Stop at the Mount Adams Ranger Station (509–395–3400; www.fs.fed.us/gpnf), just north of Trout Lake, for more information and directions to the ice caves.

Another side of the mountain worth exploring is the *Yakama Nation Mount Adams Recreation Area.* Brilliant wildflowers cover the area in spring and peak by mid-August. Tribal rangers stock lakes in the area with trout twice during the fishing season. Road conditions can be rough at any time, so trailers more than 24 feet long and compact cars are not recommended. Camping, free firewood, drinking water, and rest rooms are available at Bench, Bird, and Mirror Lakes on a first-come, first-served basis. Sunrise Camp provides campsites only. Camping and fishing permits are issued at the site. If you plan to bring along pack animals, keep them at Mirror Lake and walk them on Trail #9. Call (509) 865–5121, extension 657, for more information.

The road east to Glenwood offers outrageous views of Mount Adams (called *Pahto* by Native people) as you pass through the rich farmlands and climb hills above the White Salmon River Valley. Watch for the turnoff on your right to *Conboy Lake National Wildlife Refuge.* A 1-mile road takes you to the entrance, where you'll find brochures describing this wetland habitat. The Willard Springs Foot Trail, a 2½-mile loop with interpretive signs, is a pleasant way to learn more about the refuge's wildlife, including porcupines and wood ducks. The area was known as Tahk (Camas) Prairie to local tribes, who relied on the abundant blue camas plants and waterfowl that thrived in this valley. Originally the valley was a wetland for much of the year, but over the past century farmers drained the lake, which decimated the wild blue camas beds and reduced the waterfowl populations. With half the area now a refuge, and cooperative management by area farmers, wild blue camas plants are again common and bird populations have increased, especially those like Canada geese that enjoy fresh marshgrass shoots encouraged by continued haying. *Note:* The white camas is poisonous.

Located just outside the small community of Glenwood, travelers find *The Flying L Ranch* at 25 Flying L Lane; (509) 364–3488; www.mt-adams.com. In the large ranch house, guests can choose from five rooms named for well-known Western figures such as Charles Russell and Sacajawea. The Lloyd family built the house in the mid-1940s, and the Lloyd sons, Darvel and Dean, further developed the property in the 1970s and 1980s. Current owners Jacquie Perry and Jeff Berend have continued to update the facilities that include, in addition to the ranch house rooms, five rooms in a separate two-story guest house and three cabins tucked into the pines. Guests enjoy a full breakfast served in the ranch cookhouse. You can also bring your own steaks for a cookout. The area around the ranch is perfect for hiking and biking as well as for cross-country skiing during winter. The place is also a good option for family reunions. Also nearby, travelers can stay at *Ann's Place Bed & Breakfast* (164 Mount Adams Highway, Glenwood 98619; 509–364–3580; www.annsplace bnb.com). Ann and Bob Beveridge offer two cozy rooms with private baths in their home, formerly one of the mountain retreats of avid outdoorsman Chief Justice William O. Douglas. If you arrive late in the day and are a bit on the hungry side, Ann also offers guests steaming bowls of homemade soup, homemade bread, and hot teas or coffee. "I have about twenty soup recipes that I like to use," she says with a grin. Her cookie jar is always filled with scrumptious homebaked cookies. Her breakfasts are simply delicious—for example, baked French toast with apples and cinnamon served with slices of ham.

Returning to Highway 14 and heading east alongside the Columbia River, consider stopping in the small community of Lyle to have brunch or dinner at *The Lyle Hotel Restaurant* (100 Seventh Street; 509–365–5953; www.lylehotel.com). Dinners are served Wednesday through Saturday beginning at 5:00 P.M. The menu changes regularly and is upscale for such an out-of-the-way location, with such tasty fare as fresh Pacific oysters, bouillabaisse, salmon and sturgeon medley, moussaka, and spanakopita. If you can stop by for brunch beginning at 10:00 A.M. on Sunday, ask about the Hangtown Fry, a delectable scrambled egg dish made with sautéed onions, bacon, and oysters. The hotel was built in 1905 to serve the town when Lyle was a major railroad center linking to major towns in the region. The boom ended, the railroad tracks were moved elsewhere, and folks moved on. But the hotel remains a nostalgic reminder of earlier times. The ten cozy guest rooms feature Early American furnishings, some have sitting areas, and most offer views of the Columbia River Gorge.

Native Lands and Stories

Some of the Columbia River Gorge's greatest wonders are now, unfortunately, flooded under the huge reservoirs behind Bonneville and The Dalles Dams. Until 1957 the Oregon side of the Columbia River cascaded over Celilo Falls. Native people had camped on this stretch of river for thousands of years, enjoying the area's abundant resources. Indians from throughout the region practiced traditional dip-net fishing from pole platforms jutting close to the swirling torrents. The area was also an important gathering place where tribes met to trade goods, enjoy festivities, and conduct peace councils. In 1805 explorer Meriwether Lewis described the Celilo Falls area as a "great emporium where all the neighboring nations assembled." Hundreds of the ancient pictographs (rock paintings) and petroglyphs (rock carvings) that once commemorated this life are now lost beneath the waters of the river.

She-Who-Watches (Tsagaglalal) is one of the most intriguing petroglyphs still visible. Legend has it that Tsagaglalal, a female chief, told Coyote, the trickster, that she wanted to guide her people to "live well

She-Who-Watches Petroglyph

and build good houses" forever. Coyote explained that the time for women chiefs would soon be over, then turned her to stone so she could watch over the river and its people unimpeded into eternity. The original petroglyph is located amid several others at **Horsethief Lake State Park,** on the Columbia River. Due to vandalism, however, the only way to see the petroglyphs is by guided tour. The tours run from the beginning of April to the end of October on Friday and Saturday at 10:00 A.M.

On the Trail in the Columbia Gorge with Lewis & Clark

*W*alking by foot, paddling dugout canoes, and sometimes riding horses, thirty-three folks including Meriwether Lewis and William Clark trekked along the north side of the Columbia River in early fall of 1805. The party included Clark's Newfoundland dog, Seaman. In mid-November they would reach their goal, the Pacific Ocean near the Long Beach Peninsula. But in October 1805 they camped at Rock Fort near The Dalles on the Oregon side of the river, a site you can visit. During the 200th anniversary of the expedition from 2002 through 2006, you can see interpretive exhibits, pictorial displays, and great views of the gorge at sites where the party stopped on the Washington side of the Columbia River in this eastern section of the gorge:

Horsethief Lake State Park— Located east of Bingen and White Salmon, the site also contains rare Indian rock paintings.

Maryhill Museum—Located west of Goldendale, the museum displays fine Indian baskets, carvings, and other Native crafts (www.maryhill museum.org).

Hat Rock State Park—Located near Umatilla.

Sacajawea State Park—Located near Kennewick, an interpretive center explores the expedition and the role of Sacajawea, the Shoshoni Indian woman who served as guide and interpreter.

Additional sources for bicentennial activities, sites, and interpretive exhibits in the Columbia Gorge area:

Columbia Gorge Interpretive Center—Located in Stevenson (509–427–8211; www.columbia gorge.org).

Columbia Gorge Discovery Center and Wasco County Historical Museum—Located in The Dalles (541–296–8600; www.gorge discovery.org).

Lewis & Clark Trail Heritage Foundation (www.lewisandclark. org)

Discovering Lewis & Clark— Multimedia site incorporating the entire route from east to west (www.lewis-clark.org).

Lewis & Clark Bicentennial— This official national Web site lists Signature Events, activities, and other happenings from 2002 to 2006 for the eleven states encompassing the journey (www.lewisandclark200.org).

Tours last about one and a half hours and must be booked at least two weeks ahead. For information about costs and reservations, contact Horsethief Lake State Park, (509) 767–1159. The park also has a sheltered bay with beaches that are great for swimming and fishing.

Fifteen miles east of Horsethief Lake via Highway 14 and near the junction with Highway 97 is *Maryhill Museum* and a reproduction of England's *Stonehenge* monument, two legacies of eccentric millionaire and road builder Sam Hill. Maryhill (open daily from 9:00 A.M. to 5:00 P.M. from mid-March through mid-November) is situated with a fine view of the Columbia River and is filled with an eclectic collection that includes Rodin sculptures and watercolors, nineteenth-century French artwork, Russian icons, regional Indian art, the Queen of Romania's royal memorabilia, and a collection of chess sets. Cafe Maryhill, in the museum, serves deli-style lunches and snacks, with outdoor seating available overlooking the river. The impressive chateau-like structure, 400 feet long, is located at 35 Maryhill Museum Drive; (509) 773–3733; www.maryhillmuseum.org. You can also check out the lively *Maryhill Saturday Market* at 65 Maryhill Highway on Saturdays, 10:00 A.M. to 5:00 P.M. from June to October. The new *Maryhill Winery* (877–627–9445), located just west of Maryhill Museum, offers an elegant tasting room and samples of the current wines produced here including pinot noir, merlot, zinfandel, and chardonnay. The intricately carved antique bar fashioned in the early 1900s of tiger oak reaches some 12 feet high with mirrors inset along its 12-foot length. Open daily from 10:00 A.M. to 6:00 P.M. with an outside patio that offers wide-angle views of the gorge.

The town of Goldendale, located 10 miles north via Highway 97, has been a commercial center for farmers since its inception. The town's well-kept homes and active downtown continue to emanate a friendly, self-sufficient atmosphere. For a historical perspective on the town, visit the *Klickitat County Historical Museum* (509–773–4303), housed in the stately Presby Mansion on Broadway Street (Highway 142) and Grant Avenue. Turn-of-the-century dolls left on the antique furniture give the impression that a child has just finished playing in the parlor, the kitchen looks as if someone is cooking dinner, the dining room table is set, and period clothing is laid out in the bedrooms. The museum is open from 9:00 A.M. to 5:00 P.M. daily, April to October, or by appointment during the off-season. There is a small admission fee.

For an exhilarating look skyward, continue down Broadway Street and turn north on Columbus, past some of Goldendale's fine old homes. Follow signs uphill to *Goldendale Observatory State Park*

(1602 Observatory Drive; 509–773–3141), where volunteer amateur astronomers share their enthusiasm for the stars. During the day, you can view the sun using a special telescope and perhaps catch sight of a solar prominence—arcs of light and energy thousands of miles high. At night, the main 26-inch telescope brings galaxies and nebulae into view. The observatory is open from 2:00 to 5:00 P.M. and 8:00 to 11:00 P.M., Wednesday through Sunday, from April 1 through September 30. From October 1 through March 31, observatory hours are Friday, 7:00 to 9:00 P.M., Saturday, 1:00 to 5:00 P.M. and 7:00 to 9:00 P.M., and Sunday 1:00 to 5:00 P.M. For more information check the helpful Web site, www.perr.com/gosp.html, which contains the evening star-watching schedule and links to Northwest astronomy clubs, NASA sites, and "This Week's Sky at a Glance."

Since you've traveled this far off the beaten path, plan to stay overnight at *Timberframe Country Inn Bed & Breakfast,* located about 4 miles north of town, up in the pine forest, at 223 Golden Pine, Goldendale 98620 (800–861–8408). Innkeeper Dorothy "Dor" Creamer offers guests the Treetop Room, complete with a whirlpool spa out on the deck for soaking one's travel-weary bones. "Folks seem to like the peace and quiet here," says Dor. Favorite breakfasts include Dor's Fruited Waffle or her Scrambled Eggs Enchilada, smoked peppered bacon, biscuits, and lots of steaming hot coffee or teas. Pleasant eateries in the Goldendale area that serve lunch or dinner include *Dine and Dash Cafe* (120 West Main Street; 509–773–4040); *Jerry's Stop & Go* (114 South Columbus Avenue; 509–773–6868); *Angelo's Pizza* (111 North Columbus Avenue; 509–773–6939); and *High Desert Dining* (123 West Main Street; 509–773–9970).

A side trip from here takes adventurous travelers east off Highway 97 onto Goldendale-Bickleton Road and 35 miles to the bucolic town of Bickleton, population 90. From mid-February to October thousands of mountain bluebirds flock to the area, earning the small town its nickname of "Bluebird Capital of the World." You can see the small handmade blue-and-white birdhouses everywhere as you drive the back roads of Bickleton; they serve as nesting boxes for the feathered couples and their chicks, gracing residential yards, farms, and roadsides.

Eateries to check out in Bickleton include *Bickleton Country Kitchen* (106 East Market Street; 509–896–2671) and *Bluebird Inn Tavern* (121 Market Street; 509–896–2273).

Prosser, located east, has more to offer than you might expect for a quiet farm town. *Hinzerling Vineyard* (509–786–2163 or 800–727–6702) is

The Bluebird Inn Tavern, Circa 1882, Elevation 3,000 Feet

*I*t's said the tavern has gone through more than fifteen owners since it opened in Bickleton in 1882. It used to double as a barbershop, and once it was a social club where hats were forbidden. For a long time the place had no telephone so the women-folk weren't able to call and check up on their card-playing menfolk. Now, the tavern sells candy to the kids and serves good food including a giant Bluebird Burger. Closed Monday, open on Tuesday at 3:00 P.M., and other days open at 10:00 A.M. Also serves breakfast on Sunday beginning at 8:00 A.M. Pull up to the small Western-style structure that looks as though it should have several horses tied up out front, just like a John Wayne movie.

located in town at the corner of Wine Country Road and Sheridan Street. Founded in 1976 by the Wallace family, this is the oldest family-owned and operated winery in the Yakima Valley. Family members share their knowledge of wine production and samples of wines, including sweet dessert wines and dry gewürztraminer. Down the road *Chinook Wines* (509–786–2725) has a friendly little tasting room in a small house just outside Prosser on Wine Country Road, a half mile east of exit 82 off I–82. Processed and aged to complement Northwest cuisine, the Chinook sauvignon blanc is a good match for the native oysters and scallops of Puget Sound; the flavorful chardonnay will heighten the richness of Pacific salmon; and the rich, red merlot is ideal with eastern Washington spring lamb.

Hogue Cellars (509–786–4557), across Wine Country Road from Chinook Wines, offers gourmet pickled vegetables in addition to a wide selection of award-winning wines, including dry, sweet, and sparkling varieties. *Pontin Del Roza* (35502 North Hinzerling Road; 509–786–4449) is located at the corner of Hinzerling and McCreadie Roads in the lovely hill district north of Prosser. You can taste the Pontin family's special Roza sunset blush and pinot gris. The *Yakima River Winery,* located at 143302 North River Road (509–786–2805), is a small operation near the Yakima River. The winery is especially proud of its barrel-aged red wines, cabernet sauvignon, and merlot. To get there take Wine Country Road northwest from Prosser, and just after you cross the Yakima River, turn left on North River Road; watch for the winery on your right in about 2 miles.

Gourmet cherries, preserves, toppings, and savories are other specialties you'll find near Prosser. The *Chukar Cherry Company* produces these along with Chocolate Chukars, a pitted, ripe, partly dried cherry dipped in dark chocolate. This is, indeed, a royal taste treat. The Chukar Cherry Company gift shop, just west of town at 320 Wine Country Road (509–786–2055; www.chukar.com) offers the best of the Yakima area's specialty foods, including dried cherries and berries and cherry sauces.

The *Benton County Historical Museum* (509–786–3842), at the Prosser City Park, is open Tuesday through Saturday from 10:00 A.M. to 4:00 P.M. and Sunday from 1:00 to 5:00 P.M. There's a little of everything, including natural history displays, an old-time general store counter, and a selection of women's clothing styles of yesteryear. One of the exhibits contains thirty hand-carved and hand-painted wooden automobiles, foot-long replicas of the real thing. While browsing and chatting with the friendly volunteers, you may hear memories of childhoods spent on farms, and stories of small-town life.

For a bite to eat in Prosser, try *The Blue Goose Restaurant* (306 Seventh Street; 509–786–1774) or *The Barn Restaurant* (490 Wine Country Road; 509–786–1131).

For a sampling of this rich farming area's home-grown bounty, stop by the *Prosser Farmer's Market* at 1230 Bennett Avenue (509–786–3600) next to City Park. There you'll find fresh Yakima Valley fruits and vegetables, delectable homemade baked goods, and crafts from local artisans. The market is open Saturdays from 8:00 A.M. to 1:00 P.M. from June through October. You can also detour at *Bushel's and Peck's* (611 Wine Country Road; 509–786–1600) to find more local fruits and vegetables.

Gourmet Dining in Yakima Valley Wine Country

*I*t is said that folks will drive from as far as 50 miles away to hunker down at **The Blue Goose Restaurant** in Prosser. They will motor down from Yakima on Fridays for owner and chef Dick Denson's clam chowder, his delectable French onion soup, or his prime rib. The chef, trained in Europe, has collected international recipes since 1963, and he offers a wide variety of gourmet dishes each weekend for international theme dinners. The beverage list offers some fifty local and regional Washington wines as well as favorite beers such as Spaten imported from Munich, Germany. Morning brings out the breakfast menu with incredible six-egg omelets, one favorite of folks who find their way to The Blue Goose's doorway, located at 306 Seventh Street in Prosser (509–786–1774). Open daily from 7:00 A.M. to 9:00 P.M.

You can reach the town of Grandview by heading northwest from Prosser on Wine Country Road. *The Dykstra House Restaurant* (114 Birch Avenue, Grandview 98930), a National Historic Site built in the 1920s, offers delicious meals. The house, restored by owner Linda Hartshorn, displays many fine antiques. The desserts are delicious, the produce is fresh, and the regional wines and ales are plentiful. The restaurant is open for lunch Tuesday through Saturday and serves dinner Friday and Saturday evenings from 6:00 to 9:00 P.M. Call (509) 882–2082 for reservations, which are required on Saturday evening.

Wine Country Road becomes Yakima Valley Highway northwest of Grandview because the community of Sunnyside, a German Baptist colony at the turn of the century, still has many residents who disapprove of wine and other alcoholic beverages.

For a pleasant spot to stay the night in this rich wine country, call innkeepers Don and Karen Vlieger at *Sunnyside Inn Bed and Breakfast* (800 East Edison Street, Sunnyside 98944; 509–839–5557; www. sunnysideinn.com). The couple offers thirteen comfortable guest rooms in their large circa 1919 home with all the usual comforts including restful colors, lovely window treatments, and country accessories. Some rooms come with four-poster beds, cozy sitting areas, fireplaces,

Top Annual Events in South Central Washington

Red Wine and Chocolate Festival,
Yakima Valley, President's Day Weekend,
February; (800) 258–7270

Rain Festival, Stevenson,
late April; (800) 989–9178

Granger Cherry Festival,
first weekend in May; (509) 854–2282

Mural-in-a-Day, Toppenish,
first weekend in June; (509) 865–3262

Festival of the Arts/Volkssport Bike and Walk, Trout Lake, mid-July;
(509) 493–3630

Columbia Gorge Bluegrass Festival,
Stevenson, late July; (509) 427–8928

Hydroplane Races, Kennewick,
late July; (509) 547–2203

Prosser Wine & Food Fair,
August; (800) 408–1517 or
(509) 786–4545

Huckleberry Festival, Bingen,
mid-September; (509) 493–3630

SausageFest, Vancouver,
mid-September; (360) 696–4407

The Great Hot Air Balloon Rally,
Prosser, late September;
(509) 786–3177

Thanksgiving in Wine Country,
Yakima Valley, Thanksgiving weekend;
(800) 258–7270

Country Christmas Lighted Farm Implement Parade, Sunnyside, first
weekend in December; (800) 457–8089

and whirlpool tubs. Families are especially welcome here. In the morning a sumptuous country breakfast is served family style in the large dining area on the main floor.

For more off-the-beaten-path adventures, continue west on Emerald-Granger Road, a scenic route that circles south of Snipes Mountain. When the road ends just outside of Granger, turn right onto Highway 223. From Granger, take Van Belle Road east for half a mile, then turn left on Beam Road and continue north 1½ miles to reach **Granger Berry Patch Farm** at 1731 Beam Road (800–346–1417 or 509–854–1413). The farm offers more than twenty varieties of U-pick berries, a petting zoo, pumpkins, and Christmas trees in season. The farm sponsors a berry festival the second and third weekends of July. Visitors are welcome to picnic on the grounds.

One Hundred Years, 1850 to 1950: The Toppenish Murals

*S*ince 1989 folks in the Toppenish Mural Society have funded more than sixty gigantic murals painted outdoors on buildings all over the downtown area, from the Western Auto building and the Reid Building to Providence Toppenish Hospital, Pow Wow Emporium, and Old Timers Plaza Park. We are not talking crayon and stick figures here. The historically accurate scenes represent the life and times of the Toppenish area from 1850 to 1950. Folks visit throughout the year and stroll downtown streets, but on the first Saturday of June you also can watch the Mural-in-a-Day come to life and join the yearly celebration. Stop by the Visitor Welcome Center at 5–A South Toppenish Avenue (509–856–3262, www.toppenish.org); pick up a Mural Map, and enjoy. Here are a few of the giant-size oil paintings of bygone days you'll see:

Rodeo Days (#13) by artist Newman Myrah of Portland, Oregon, painted on the west wall of Ferguson's Saddlery

Ruth Parton, cowgirl and trick-rider (#22) painted by Lesa Delisi of Cashmere on the United Telephone Company building

Maud Bolin, rodeo rider and early female pilot (#27) painted by artist Larry Kangas of Portland, Oregon, on the southwest wall of the Toppenish Review Newspaper building

Hop Museum Murals, a trio of painted archways open to scenes of harvesting hops (#32) painted by artist Eric Allen Grohe on two walls of the American Hop Museum

Lou Shattuck, an original booster of the Toppenish Pow Wow Rodeo (#34) painted by artist Don Gray of Flagstaff, Arizona

Western Hospitality, bordello ladies of the night (#36) painted by Betty Billups of Sandpoint, Idaho, on the second floor windows of the Logan Building

The Yakama Confederated Tribes and Bands is one of the largest self-governing Native American Nations. The Yakama Indian Reservation includes a portion of the lower Yakima Valley and much of the high desert and pine-forest–covered hills farther south. The town of **Toppenish** is located on the reservation in a wide, fertile part of the valley. In recent years, Toppenish's downtown has been renovated to emphasize Western-style false-front stores and classic turn-of-the-twentieth-century brick buildings. A walking tour of downtown reveals galleries, antiques shops, tourist cafes, and a colorful array of large outdoor murals depicting the area's history.

Pause for a look at the grand old **Liberty Theatre,** located at 211 South Toppenish Avenue (509–865–7573). Built in 1915, the theater boasted the largest stage at the time between Seattle and Spokane and hosted stars such as Lillian Gish, Raymond Navarro, and even Tex Ritter and his horse. Murals painted on the outside show wild horses running free as they did in early times.

When it's time to stop for a bite to eat in Toppenish, locals suggest **Pioneer Kitchen** at 227 South Toppenish Avenue (509–865–3201) for all-day breakfasts, cinnamon rolls, homemade soups, salad bar, hefty Rodeo Burgers, and great pies and cobblers. For good Mexican fare, try **VillaSenor** at 225 South Toppenish Avenue (509–865–4707), including piping hot appetizers, fajitas, and freshly made tortillas along with such tasty desserts as flan, sopapillas, and deep-fried ice cream. At **La Hacienda Gardens Antiques & Gallery** (207 South Toppenish Avenue; 509–865–1992), you can order specialty espresso drinks and browse folk art, old toys, old cowboy and horse gear, Indian jewelry, and pottery as well as Ranchera, Spanish Colonial, and antique painted pine furniture. At **Gibbon's Pharmacy** (117 South Toppenish Avenue; 509–865–2722), you can order something cool and tasty at the old-fashioned soda fountain.

Allow time to visit the country's only museum dedicated to the growing of hops, the **American Hop Museum,** located at 22 South B Street, 509–865–4677). The museum is open from 11:00 A.M. to 4:00 P.M. daily from May through September. You'll see the splendid murals on the front of the large building, a series of arched windows painted on either side of the entrance. The museum focuses on the hop industry that started around 1805 in New York State. In the 1850s hop growers took their perennial hop vines westward where the climate was sunnier and where there was less mildew. The sunny Yakima Valley is a prime area for growing hops, which grow on tall expanses of twine strung in long rows in the fields. In the museum you and the kids can see artifacts, memorabilia, and old photographs collected from all over the United States, including antique hop presses, tools for cultivating hops, a horse-drawn hop duster, old picking baskets, and an early picking machine. Browse in the gift shop and also learn how the hop cones are used to flavor and preserve beers and microbrews.

The *Yakima Valley Rail and Steam Museum* (509–865–1911), located on South A Street in a restored railway depot built in 1911, contains interesting rail and steam artifacts, a completely restored telegraph office, and a gift shop. In mid-August folks can attend the *Yakima Valley Rail & Transportation Show* at the depot museum held in conjunction with the *Toppenish Western Art Show* (509–865–3262) situated in nearby Railroad Park. Great art, railroad memorabilia, food booths, and live country music along with tours of the museum, engine house, and grounds make for a lively day.

You can picnic in Railroad Park, or head off to Harrah, 8 miles northwest of Toppenish, for more railroad fun. There you can catch the *Toppenish, Simcoe and Western Railroad* for a leisurly 18-mile round-trip to White Swan and back through the Simcoe Valley and with views of snowy Mount Adams. Excursions are offered Saturdays in September and October, as well as other special holiday trips. Call the Yakima Valley Rail and Steam Museum at (509) 865–1911 for current schedules and fares.

To learn more about Native American culture, visit the splendid *Yakama Nation Cultural Heritage Center,* on Highway 97 (280 Buster Road, P.O. Box 151, Toppenish 98948; 509–865–2800 or 800–874–3089). From a distance you'll spot the colorful peaked roof of the center's Winter Lodge, modeled after the ancestral A-shaped homes of the Yakama tribes. Museum exhibits and dioramas show the history and traditions of the Yakama tribes. A large, angular tule (reed) lodge at the center of the museum shows how extended families lived during the winter. Sweat lodges made from earth, branches, and animal skins illustrate sacred places of physical and spiritual purification. The museum is open Monday through Saturday from 9:00 A.M. to 5:00 P.M. and Sunday from 10:00 A.M. to 5:00 P.M. Nominal admission fee.

At the center's gift shop adjacent to the museum, you can purchase fine beadwork and other Native American art and cultural items. The center also maintains an extensive library for children and adults on First Nations history and culture. The library is open to the public Monday to Friday, 8:30 A.M. to 5:00 P.M., and Saturday, 10:30 A.M. to 5:00 P.M. The *Heritage Inn Restaurant,* also part of the tribal center, offers delicious meals, including Yakama and other First Nations

Yakama Nation RV Resort

favorites such as *Waykaanish* (salmon), buffalo stew, fry bread, and huckleberry pie. The restaurant is open for Sunday brunch from 8:00 A.M. to 2:00 P.M., and Monday to Saturday from 8:00 A.M. to 8:00 P.M. Call (509) 865–2551 for reservations.

Next door to the Heritage Center, the *Yakama Nation RV Resort* (280 Buster Road; 800–874–3087 or 509–865–2000) offers a luxury campground with ninety-five RV spaces with full hookups, a tent site, and a recreation center featuring a basketball court, hot tub, laundry room, and swimming pool. In addition to the more conventional camping facilities, you can rent a tepee with room for a whole family.

Twenty-five miles west of the Yakama Indian Tribal Center in the heart of the reservation is *Fort Simcoe State Park Heritage Site,* a lovely park with large oak trees, a lush green lawn, and a dozen restored buildings filled with period furnishings. The former military fort is located at 5150 Fort Simcoe Road (509–874–2372) near the community of White Swan and on a traditional Native village site. The ancient Mool Mool bubbling springs here have created a shady oasis of reed-filled wetlands surrounded by woods. In summer, you may catch sight of green and pink Lewis's woodpeckers, which breed in abundance in the Garry oak. The park, a popular picnic spot for local residents, features plenty of shade trees, running water, and an adventure playground. The historical buildings and interpretive center are open Wednesday through Sunday from 9:00 A.M. to 4:30 P.M. from April through September.

The Yakama Nation has developed several economic projects to enhance their cultural survival. The **Real Yakama Fruit and Produce Stand** sells quality fruits and vegetables grown on the reservation. The Yakama Nation Land Enterprise operates more than one hundred acres of apple and soft fruit orchards. The stand, open seasonally during harvest time, is off Highway 97, 20 miles northwest of Toppenish. About halfway to the produce stand, in the town of Wapato, the **Mt. Adams Furniture** facility is busy producing upholstered furniture with decorative First Nations designs, while providing employment and training to tribal members. The facility is open to the public on Wednesday from 9:00 A.M. to 4:00 P.M. To arrange a tour, call (509) 877–2191.

The **Toppenish National Wildlife Refuge** is located off Highway 97 south of Toppenish. The refuge's marshlands and thick riverside forests are excellent places to view the fall and spring migrations of Canada geese and ducks such as grebes, teals, scaups, and pintails. There are bald eagles, prairie falcons, and other wildlife that once populated the entire Yakima Valley area.

Orchards, Vineyards, & Railroads

A 10-mile, signed "Fruit Loop" route that circles the orchard-covered hills above the town of **Zillah** is an ideal way to discover the valley's agricultural opulence. To visit Zillah take I–82, exit 52 or 54, or follow the Yakima Valley Highway from Sunnyside through Granger and turn left onto Zillah's First Avenue. The loop starts from the downtown tourist information office at the corner of First Avenue and Fifth Street (509–829–5055), where you can pick up a route map during office hours, or just follow the colorful signs from downtown north on Roza Drive and left onto the Yakima Valley Highway. Along the way you'll enjoy grand views of the lower valley's patchwork quilt of farms, and you'll pass by at least seven wineries.

Of course, every winery claims to offer the best product, so it's up to you to determine your favorites. Each has a tasting room where visitors are offered a small sample of the many vintages available. Winery staff are glad to share their knowledge and offer suggestions for the best wine for various occasions. Most tasting rooms also sell nonalcoholic drinks, snacks, and gifts.

If wine tasting has given you an appetite and you forgot the picnic basket, you'll want to eat at *El Ranchito* (509–829–5880), the most authentic Mexican restaurant, bakery, and specialty store you are likely to find in this region. The much-loved restaurant is located at 1319 East First Avenue in Zillah, the last stop on the Fruit Loop tour. It has an informal atmosphere where farmworker families, local professionals, and tourists all enjoy fresh tamales, burritos, tostadas, and tempting specialty dishes. In warm weather the shaded patio offers a pleasant place to eat.

Worth a stop just a half mile from downtown is *Zillah Oakes Winery* (1001 Vintage Valley Parkway, Zillah 98953; 509–829–6990), which bears the name of the young girl the town was named for, the daughter of an early Yakima Valley resident. The tasting room is open from 10:00 A.M. to 5:00 P.M. daily.

For a nostalgic visit to an old-fashioned country store and orchard, stop by *Donald Fruit and Mercantile* (509–877–3115), just east of I–82 at exit 44 on Donald-Wapato Road. The building was constructed in 1911 and still has a wooden floor and most of the original store fixtures. Adjacent to the store is an orchard of antique variety apple trees, which visitors are welcome to explore. In the fall months you can taste the unique flavors of these old-style fruits. Donald Fruit and Mercantile is open 9:00 A.M. to 6:00 P.M. daily from May through December.

Near Wapato you'll find the *Staton Hills Winery,* where the vintner uses innovative techniques to grow premium grapes and produce excellent wines. Visitors can see up-to-date viticulture (grape growing) using three types of advanced trellising. The impressive French country–style winery, built of local stone and cedar, has a wine-tasting room, gift shop, and sophisticated wine-processing facilities, which use oak barrels imported from France and Germany. To reach the winery (509–877–2112), take I–84 exit 40, follow the road as it curves left toward the hill, then turn right onto Gangl Road.

This part of the valley is prime pepper-growing territory, and pepper afficionados shouldn't pass up a stop at Wapato's *Krueger Family Peppers & Produce* (362 Knights Lane). This roadside farm stand features a whopping seventy varieties of sweet and hot peppers, as well as fruit (delectable melons) and veggies. Bring your own container and venture out into the fields to pick your own, or buy from the stand. Hours are seasonal, so call (509) 877–3677 for current information.

Just south of Yakima is the town of Union Gap, the single gap in the line of hills that divides the upper and lower Yakima Valley. Next to the gap is the *Central Washington Agricultural Museum,* located at 4508 Main Street in Fulbright Park (509–457–8735). The large collection of farm equipment is arranged outdoors on spiral terraces in a mechanical parade around a windmill tower. You'll see horse-drawn plows and mowers, huge old steam tractors, antique threshers, and hop harvesters. In the fifteen-acre park you and the kids can also poke into some eighteen large display buildings to see such things as a blacksmith shop, furnished log cabin, fruit-packing line equipment, and the Museum Grange Library. You might even see working horse teams plowing the museum fields or an old steam harvester in use. To get to the museum from Union Gap, follow Main Street south 2 miles and across the Highway 97 overpass to the Fulbright Park turnoff. If you want to picnic, there are shaded tables on the grounds at Fulbright Park, or for a bite to eat in Union Gap, check out **Old Town Station Restaurant** at 2530 Main Street (509–453– 8485) and **Jean's Cottage Inn,** located at 3211 Main Street (509–575– 9709). For a jolt of java or espresso, try **Godfrey's Espresso** or **J. D.'s Coffee,** both drive-through locations in Union Gap's downtown area.

> ### Teapot Gas
>
> *Just east of Zillah is an unmistakable landmark, a true vintage roadside attraction just off I–82 exit 54. The big, white teapot with its red handle and spout is a gas station, circa the early 1920s. The joke here, which only old-timers or history buffs are likely to catch without explanation, is the name: the Teapot Dome Service Station. The reference is to the Wyoming oil-lease scandal of the same name, big news in the early '20s, as it sent Secretary of the Interior Albert Fall to prison.*

The city of Yakima offers many activities little-known to outsiders. For one, walking or bicycling along the 10-mile **Yakima Greenway Trail** is the perfect way to enjoy the Yakima and Naches Rivers. The path stretches from the quiet town of Selah at the north, past several riverfront parks, to the seventy-acre **Yakima Arboretum** at the southend. The arboretum includes hiking trails, a Japanese garden, and the new Jewett Interpretive Center. You can also access the Yakima Greenway Trail and a river landing for launching kayaks and canoes at **Sarg Hubbard Park** off I–82 or off South Eighteenth Street. Just next to the park find **Washington's Fruit Place Visitor Center** (509–576–3090), where you and the kids can taste samples of apple juice, apples, and other fruits and learn through hands-on exhibits all about the Yakima Valley's tree fruit industry. At Sarg Hubbard Park (509–453–8280) on Tuesday evenings in July and August, you can bring a picnic supper and take in free outdoor concerts at 7:00 P.M. that feature local performers including jazz, blues, country western, and blue grass musicians and singers. Folks find bleacher seating and lawn areas for blankets and folding chairs.

Railroad themes permeate Yakima. Along the old railroad line through downtown, find the renovated North Front Street and browse its eclectic shops, cafes, and pubs. Check out *The Barrel House* at 22 North First Street (509–453–3769), which offers fine food, wines, and microbrews. On North Second Street stop by *Yakima Cellars Winery* (509–577–0461), which offers an elegant tasting room. On Yakima Avenue between Fifth and Sixth Streets as well as on Second Street and A Avenue, you can browse a collection of delightful antiques shops. At 9 West Yakima Avenue, poke into *Crème De La Crème* (509–453–5335), a fun gift shop. For a quick snack stop by a local favorite, *Poochie's Gourmet Hot Dogs,* located at 301 South Third Avenue (509–452–3268), and choose from some thirty types of specialty hot dogs and sandwiches.

The circa 1885 Fire Station and Yakima City Hall building at 27 North Front Street now houses *Bob's Keg & Cork* (509–573–3691), serving a variety of microbrews and Yakima Valley wines Tuesday through Saturday from 11:30 A.M. The first railroad depot was constructed in 1886, then as the city grew, a larger depot was built in 1909. The main floor of this railroad station building, located at 32 North Front Street, houses *Bert Grant's Brewery Pub* (509–575–2922), one of the region's oldest brewpubs. Order up one of the pub's renowned stouts or ales along with gourmet pub-style vittles such as fish-and-chips, British bangers, Scotch eggs, and a variety of fresh salads and soups. The pub is smoke-free and open daily from 11:30 A.M.

In 1889 the Switzer Opera House was built at 5 North Front Street and housed Yakima's first performing arts and vaudeville theater. This structure also has been renovated and now houses a variety of shops, including *The Collector's Niche* (509–248–0940), which features unique jewelry, books, casual clothing and hats, and Victorian and old English-style linens and gifts. In 1902 came the Commercial Saloon building located at 7 North Front Street, which is now home to *Cafe Melange* (509–453–0571), serving outstanding Italian fare.

In 1898 the Lund building was constructed on the corner of North Front Street and Yakima Avenue. In those days it housed such colorful establishments as Sam's Cafe, The Alfalfa Saloon, The Chicago Clothing Company, and The Longbranch Saloon. All those early establishments are gone; nowadays, in place of Sam's Cafe, locals and travelers call ahead for reservations at the splendid *Greystone Restaurant* (5 North Front Street; 509–248–9801). The dining room is open Tuesday through Sunday evenings from 6:00 P.M.

The Capitol Theatre, located at 19 South Third Street (509–853–2787; www.capitoltheatre.org), is another historic structure restored to its 1920s splendor, including a resident ghost, Sparky, who apparently decided to stay on after the renovation. The theater is now home to the Yakima Symphony Orchestra and offers other concerts and road shows throughout the year. For lively local theater call **Warehouse Theatre Co.** in the Allied Arts Center in Gilbert Park at 5000 West Lincoln Avenue (509–966–0951 or 509–966–0930) for the current schedule produced by avid Yakima area thespians. Recent offerings included old favorites such as *Barefoot in the Park, Forever Plaid, On Golden Pond,* and the popular musical *Godspell.*

Be sure to plan a stop at the **Yakima Valley Museum** (2105 Tieton Drive; 509–248–0747; www.yakimavalleymuseum.org) for a soda and a hot dog ordered at the old-fashioned soda fountain. A bright neon sign greets visitors at the entry to the soda fountain, the floor sports black-and-white square tiled linoleum, and at the counter folks sit on round stools covered with bright red vinyl. In other sections of the museum you can browse a fine Native American collection, see a collection of wagons and carriages (from stagecoach to hearse), and turn the kids loose in the children's interactive center.

Located in a renovated fruit warehouse, **Glenwood Square** at 5001 Tieton Drive offers old, polished-wood floors and fun shops like **Twisted Sisters Gifts, Gotta Have It Resale Clothing, Inklings Books, Cedarberry Hollow Gifts & Treasures,** and **Asian Sensations Cafe.**

For those who get hungry not just for plain but for fine gourmet Mexican cooking, try the well-known **Santiago's Restaurant** at 111 East Yakima Avenue, 5 blocks west of the Convention Center. The eatery is open for lunch Monday through Friday from 11:00 A.M. until 2:00 P.M. and for dinner beginning at 5:00 P.M. daily; closed on Sunday. Call (509) 453–1644 for reservations. You could also call for dinner reservations at **The Apple Tree Restaurant,** located at **Apple Tree Golf Course,** 8804 Occidental Road (509–966–7140; www.appletreegolf.com), in the southwest section of Yakima. The chef cooks up apple wood–smoked prime rib to die for, and the best time to go is evening for sunset views of the golf course and surrounding hills. The course's signature hole is number 17, a large apple-shaped island green connected to the fairway by a footbridge "stem" and with an adjacent sand trap shaped like a large leaf.

Also plan to stay a day or two to further explore this interesting city of railroad memorabilia and this large region of fruit orchards, vineyards, wineries, and tasting rooms. To stay at a cozy bed-and-breakfast inn located in a scenic cherry orchard just west of downtown, check with innkeepers Ben and Shari Dover at **Orchard Inn Bed & Breakfast** (1207 Pecks Canyon Road, Yakima 98908; 509–966–1283 or

888–858–8284). You'll find three comfortable guest rooms with queen beds and whirlpool tubs along with a cozy common area and delicious breakfasts. At *A Touch of Europe Inn Bed and Breakfast* (220 North Sixteenth Avenue, Yakima 98908; 509–454–9775), innkeepers Erika and Jim offer elegant Victorian- and European-style decor in their three guest rooms on the second floor. Gourmet breakfasts are served in the morning room on the main floor.

Two miles east of Yakima, *Birchfield Manor Restaurant and Bed & Breakfast,* located at 2018 Birchfield Road (509–452–1960), offers elegant meals and overnight accommodations in a twenty-three-room Victorian-style mansion, complete with crystal chandeliers, a winding staircase, and flower garden. You'll find an abundance of genteel comforts (hot tub, pool, private baths) and a choice of eleven charming, antiques-filled guest rooms. If the notion of a sumptuous thirteen-course gourmet dinner including decadent desserts sounds appealing, call the Birchfield staff to inquire about reservations Thursday through Saturday. You'd like something simpler? It's easy; call *A Country Tea Garden* located a few miles north of Yakima in the community of Selah at 220 Johnson Road (509–697–7944), and make reservations for tea and crumpets outdoors in charming gazebos set in colorful gardens.

Highway 12 west of Yakima passes through the orchard-filled Naches Valley on its way to 14,000-foot snowy Mount Rainier and the central Cascade Mountain area. At the entrance to this valley, you can visit the ancient *Indian Painted Rocks* petroglyphs. A short hike up the hillside trail takes you to sheer rock walls where images painted by the valley's original inhabitants are still visible. You'll also enjoy wide views of the two fertile valleys stretching below. To reach the site, take Highway 12 west toward White Pass. At milepost 199, turn left on Ackley Road, then take an immediate right and park on the shoulder of the road near the large historical marker sign.

Just past the Naches Valley, 2 miles west of the Highway 410 turnoff, is the *Oak Creek Wildlife Area,* a feeding station for elk, deer, and mountain goats in winter and a popular spot for hunting and bird-watching. Continuing west, you'll ascend the Tieton River and climb through sagebrush-covered hills and the Gifford Pinchot National Forest up to White Pass at an elevation of 4,500 feet. Along the way you'll pass numerous lakes, fishing resorts, and campgrounds. This scenic route comes with more dramatic geology formations and mountain areas covered with Douglas fir, western red cedar, and alpine fir. White Pass has relatively light traffic and long stretches of undeveloped forest, making it a favorite route for bicyclists and a popular destination for all-season outdoor recreation.

To find a good place to eat and bed down for the night that's substantially farther off the beaten path, head northwest from Naches onto Highway 410 toward Mount Rainier National Park. You'll find *Whistlin' Jack Lodge* on the Naches River at 20800 State Route 410 (www. whistlinjacklodge.com). In the restaurant the chef features fresh mountain trout, prime rib, and select seafood served, if you wish, with Washington's best wines. During warm summer months, folks can eat a pleasant lunch outside on the deck. Accommodations include a convenience store and gasoline, a lodge, riverfront motel, and streamside cottages with private hot tubs. For further information, reservations, and road conditions and closures during snowy winter months, call the staff at (800) 827–2299 or (509) 658–2433.

If you're traveling RV-style, you could check for RV sites at *Squaw Rock Resort*, located on the Naches River at 15070 Highway 410; (509) 658–2926. Both the RV resort and Whistlin' Jack Lodge are about 40 miles northwest of Yakima and not far from 14,410-foot Mount Rainier. You can access scenic drives and campgrounds on Mount Rainier by crossing over 5,440-foot Chinook Pass. From Naches you could also travel southwest of the mountain on Highway 12, which winds over 4,500-foot White Pass and down toward Packwood and Randle, then connects with I–5 south of Chehalis and just north of 8,365-foot Mount St. Helens. At Randle you could inquire at the Cowlitz Valley Ranger Station (360–497–1100) for backroad directions to see sections of trees blown down when Mount St. Helens erupted in May 1980.

PLACES TO STAY IN SOUTH CENTRAL WASHINGTON

GLENWOOD
Ann's Place Bed & Breakfast
164 Mount Adam's Highway
Glenwood 98619
(509) 364–3580

GOLDENDALE
Timberframe Country Inn Bed & Breakfast
223 Golden Pine Drive
Goldendale 98620
(800) 861–8408

GRANDVIEW
Apple Valley Motel
903 West Wine Country Road
Grandview 98930
(509) 882–3003

STEVENSON
Dolce Skamania Lodge
P.O. Box 189
Stevenson 98648
(800) 221–7117

Econo Lodge
40 Northeast Second Street
Stevenson 98648
(800) 424–4777

Wind River Cabins
P.O. Box 777
Carson 98610
(509) 427–7777

SUNNYSIDE
Sunnyside Inn Bed
and Breakfast
804 East Edison Avenue
Sunnyside 98944
(800) 221–4195

TOPPENISH
Toppenish Inn
515 Elm Street
Toppenish 98948
(800) 222–3161

Yakama Nation RV Resort
280 Buster Road
Toppenish 98948
(800) 874–3087

TROUT LAKE
The Farm Bed & Breakfast
490 Sunnyside Road
Trout Lake 98650
(509) 395–2488

Serenity's Cottages
Highway 144
Trout Lake 98650
(800) 276–7993

VANCOUVER
Vintage Inn Bed &
Breakfast
310 West Eleventh Street
Vancouver 98660
(360) 693–6635

WHITE SALMON
Inn of the White Salmon
172 West Jewett Boulevard
White Salmon 98672
(800) 972–5226

Lakecliff Bed & Breakfast
3820 Westcliff Drive
Hood River, OR 97031
(541) 386–7000

Lothlorien Woods
Treehouse Hideway
222 Staats Road,
P.O. Box 1697
White Salmon 98672
(509) 493–8733

YAKIMA
Birchfield Manor Inn
2018 Birchfield Road
Yakima 98901
(509) 452–1960

Orchard Inn Bed &
Breakfast
1207 Pecks Canyon Road
Yakima 98908
(888) 858–8284

**PLACES TO EAT IN SOUTH
CENTRAL WASHINGTON**

BICKLETON
Bluebird Inn Tavern
121 Market Street
Bickleton 99322
(509) 896–2273

BINGEN
Loafer's Old World Bakery
& Coffee House
213 West Steuben
Bingen 98605
(509) 493–3100

Wild Berry Ice Cream
Shoppe
116 West Steuben
Bingen 98605
(509) 493–8655

GOLDENDALE
Cafe Maryhill
35 Maryhill Museum Drive
Goldendale 98620
(509) 773–3733

Dine & Dash Cafe
120 West Main Street
Goldendale 98620
(509) 773–4040

GRANDVIEW
Dykstra House Restaurant
114 Birch Avenue
Grandview 98930
(509) 882–2082

Helpful Web Sites in South Central Washington

Hood River–White Salmon Area
www.hoodriver.org

Klickitat County
www.klickitatcounty.org

Mount Adams Area
www.skamania.org

Visit Yakima
www.visityakima.com

Yakima Valley Wineries
www.yakimavalleywine.com

PROSSER
The Blue Goose Restaurant
306 Seventh Street
Prosser 99350
(509) 786-1774

Josephine's Restaurant &
Vault Room
602 Sixth Street
Prosser 99350
(509) 786-4556

STEVENSON
Big River Grill
192 Southwest
Second Street
Stevenson 98648
(509) 427-4888

SUNNYSIDE
Taqueria La Fogata
1204 Yakima Valley
Highway
Sunnyside 98944
(509) 839-9019

TOPPENISH
Cattlemen's Restaurant
2 Division Street
Toppenish 98948
(509) 865-5885

Los Murales Restaurant
202 First Avenue West
Toppenish 98948
(509) 865-7555

TROUT LAKE
KJ's Bear Creek Cafe
2376 Highway 141
Trout Lake 98650
(509) 395-2525

Selected Visitor Information Centers

Columbia River Gorge National Scenic Area
902 Wasco Avenue, Suite 200
Hood River, OR 97031
(541) 386-2333

Hood River Visitor Information Center
405 Portway Avenue
Hood River, OR 97031
(800) 366-3530

Prosser Visitor Information Center
1230 Bennett Avenue, Prosser 99350
(800) 408-1517; www.prosser.org

Toppenish Visitor Information Center
P.O. Box 28, Toppenish 98948
(509) 865-3262; www.toppenish.org

Yakima Valley Visitors and Convention Bureau
10 North Eighth Street, Yakima 98901
(800) 221-0751; www.visityakima.com

VANCOUVER
Dulin's Cafe & Espresso
1708 Main Street
Vancouver 98660
(360) 737-9907

Ice Cream Renaissance
2108 Main Street
Vancouver 98660
(360) 694-3892

WHITE SALMON
The Creamery
121 East Jewett
White Salmon 98672
(509) 493-4007

Holstein's Coffee Co.
12 Oak Street
Hood River, OR
(541) 386-4115

YAKIMA
Ballesteri's Coffee House
4001 Summitview
Yakima 98908
(509) 965-8592

Cafe Melange
7 North Front Street
Yakima 98901
(509) 453-0571

Some Bagels Cafe
1006 South Third Street
Yakima 98901
(509) 965-3218

The White House Cafe
3602 Kern Street
Yakima 98908
(509) 469-2644

ZILLAH
El Ranchito Restaurant
1319 East First Avenue
Zillah 98953
(509) 829–5880

Squeeze Inn Restaurant
611 First Street
Zillah 98953
(509) 829–6226

ALSO WORTH SEEING

Columbia Gorge Scenic
Highway 30 (Oregon)

Mount Hood Railroad
(Hood River, OR)

The Gorge Outdoor
Amphitheater,
Ellensburg
(206) 285–1970

Northeast Washington

ashington's northeast corner is a high desert and farming region of stark contrasts. In a few hours you can travel through steep basalt canyons thick with the spicy smell of sagebrush, over hills covered with wheat fields and dotted with farms, and through thick pine forests. The region's geological history is dynamic and readily visible in the layered walls of coulees and steep canyons cut deep by ancient glaciers and rivers.

You meet local residents at cafe lunch counters, at small restaurants, or at bistros and brewpubs. The people of this region are close to the earth and its seasonal changes, aware of their relationship to the farms, ranches, forests, and rivers upon which so much of the local economy depends. These hardy folks take pride in their Native American, farmer, rancher, and forestry heritages, which are very much alive in the current culture.

Northeast Washington also offers a variety of all-season outdoor activities, including hiking, bicycling, fishing, hunting, boating, snowmobiling, ice fishing, and skiing. On the shores of many rivers and lakes, secluded retreats and fishing resorts beckon local sportsmen and -women to rub shoulders with visitors from around the world.

Coulee Landscapes

good place to start your tour of the region is the town of Ephrata. From I–90 take Highway 283 northeast from George or Highway 17 northwest from Moses Lake. You'll pass enormous circular fields of corn, wheat, potatoes, and legumes kept green by massive central-pivot irrigation systems. This high plain is so wide you can glimpse hills to the north but only a hint of a southern ridge. Like many northeast Washington counties, Grant County preserves its past in a local historical museum. *Pioneer Village and Museum* (742 Basin Street North; 509–754–3334), located east of the highway at the far end of Ephrata, provides a three-dimensional view of pioneer life. Visitors walk through carefully re-created print, camera, and blacksmith shops;

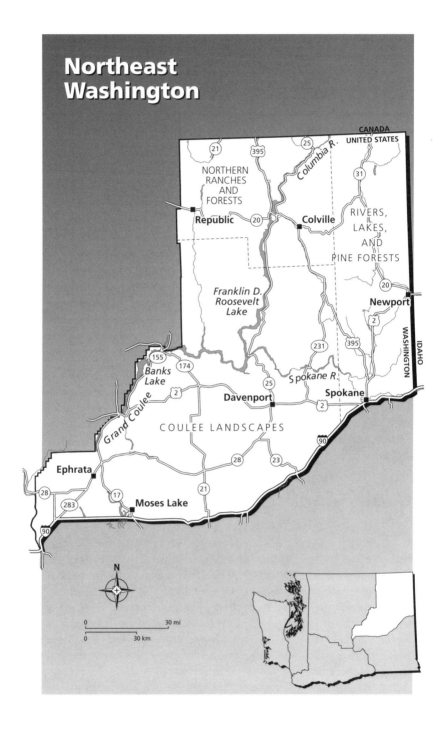

Northeast Washington

NORTHEAST WASHINGTON'S TOP HITS

Pioneer Village, Ephrata

Soap Lake

Lake Lenore Caves, Soap Lake

Dry Falls Interpretive
   Center, Coulee City

Wilbur

Gehrke Windmills, Grand Coulee

Keller Ferry

Colville Tribal Cultural Museum
   and Gift Shop, Coulee Dam

Steamboat Rock, Electric City

Fort Spokane, Creston

Lincoln County
   Historical Museum, Davenport

Silver Beach Resort, Valley

Spokane River
   Centennial Trail, Spokane

Northwest Museum of Arts and Culture
   and Historic Campbell House,
   Spokane

Bing Crosby Memorabilia Room,
   Ganzaga University, Spokane

Manito Park Gardens, Spokane

Pend Oreille County
   Historical Museum, Pend Oreille

Pioneer Park, Newport

Manresa Grotto, Usk

Sullivan Lake, Metaline Falls

Washington Hotel, Metaline Falls

North Pend Oreille Scenic Byway and
   Selkirk International Loop, Ione

Keller Heritage Center and Stevens
   County Historical Museum, Colville

Kettle Falls Historical Center

Lake Roosevelt Marina & Houseboats,
   Kettle Falls

Sherman Pass Scenic Byway,
   Sherman Pass

Stonerose Interpretive
   Center, Republic

saloons; a one-room schoolhouse; and homesteads. Outside is a collection of the big farm machines that made Grant County a major agricultural producer. The museum is open from early May to the end of September, 10:00 A.M. to 5:00 P.M. Monday through Saturday, 1:00 to 4:00 P.M. on Sunday, and closed on Wednesday. For another glimpse of local history, you can see the **Grant County Courthouse,** west of the highway at the corner of First NW and C Streets, built in 1917 and heated geothermally from a nearby hot spring.

Follow Highway 28 north to **Soap Lake.** Cherished by local tribes and early settlers for its healing properties, Soap Lake continues to draw people seeking rejuvenation from its buoyant waters. Seventeen minerals, with sodium bicarbonate the most common, give the water its soapy texture, although the frothy piles of suds that once accumulated on the lakeshore have disappeared due to dilution from irrigation. The popularity of this resort town is nothing like its heyday at the turn of the twentieth century, but the crowds still come. You can experience the water's effects with daily soaks at one of the town's two beaches or in baths piped from mineral waters deep in the lake to several of the town's motels. Both public beaches are crowded in summer when water temperatures can reach as high as 100° F. East Beach, located near the highway and motels, is the most popular with tourists. West Beach, separated by a small, rocky peninsula, is preferred by local residents and has a diving float. It also has public showers, helpful for removing the water's alkaline residue.

If you'd like to linger a day or two to soak in the soft mineral waters, you could ask about lodging facilities at *Notaras Lodge,* located in Soap Lake at 13 Canna Street (509–246–0462; www.notaraslodge.com). Folks choose from fifteen different rooms in four large log structures that offer outside entrances and small sitting decks. Your cozy room comes with handcrafted log walls, a comfortable sitting area with upholstered and oversized easy-chairs, and a small kitchenette. Several rooms offer handcrafted log beds and whirlpool tubs, and all rooms come with double plumbing that allows you to choose either the warm Soap Lake mineral water or freshwater for baths. One of the rooms, Eagles Nest, offers a balcony that frames morning sunrises. Another room, The Cabin, offers two queen beds, a lovely stained-glass window, and French doors that open to a balcony framing views of Soap Lake. All rooms are decorated with Western and antique memorabilia such as cattle brands, saddles, bridles, sombreros, old shotguns, railroad lanterns, and rodeo photographs. Several kinds of wood were used in the construction of the impressive log lodges including Tennessee red cedar, black walnut, and cherry. The handcrafted and scribed logs range in sizes from 12 to 24 inches or more in diameter.

Don's Restaurant, located just across the street from Notaras Lodge (509–246–1217), is a local favorite for steak, pasta, and seafood; open daily for lunch and dinner from 11:00 A.M. except for Saturday when it opens at 4:00 P.M. The large mural on the outside wall of cowboys around a campfire was painted by local artist Bill Robinson.

Soap Lake is the southernmost of the Grand Coulee's chain of mineral-rich lakes. The Grand Coulee was formed by glacial action that cut through layers of thick volcanic basalt. Highway 17, from Soap Lake to Coulee City, provides a scenic route through the lower end of the coulee. You'll follow secluded lake beds, cut deep into reddish brown cliffs, their shorelines often crusted white with minerals. Lake Lenore has public access, with several spots to launch a boat or to stop and watch the varied waterfowl in grassy lakeside wetlands.

Off the highway opposite Lake Lenore is the turnoff to *Lake Lenore*

FAVORITE ATTRACTIONS

Grand Coulee Dam

Lake Roosevelt

Steamboat Rock State Park and Banks Lake

Caves. A gravel road, open 10:00 A.M. to 6:00 P.M. daily, takes you to the trailhead for a short hike through fragrant sagebrush, up the cliff sides to the ancient caves. There, like ancient hunter-gatherers, you can find shelter from the heat in these cool, rocky overhangs. Watch graceful cliff swallows, listen to crickets, hear the dry scrub rustling in the breeze, and absorb the stark beauty of the wide coulee landscape.

Between Alkali and Blue Lakes, you can catch sight of the *Caribou Cattle Trail.* A roadside sign marks the point where the trail crosses the road. Originally a Native path, the 500-mile trail was used in the late nineteenth century as a supply route by miners and Blue Lake homesteaders. A few miles north on Blue Lake, *Coulee Lodge Resort,* located at 33017 Park Lake Road (509–632–5565), offers six cabins, nine well-equipped 40-foot mobile homes with tip-outs, and a number of campsites. Folks can rent 14-foot aluminum fishing boats for cruising the lake and fishing for rainbow and brown trout and for Donaldsons, a chubby trout-salmon mix with pinkish meat. "It's absolutely delicious," says Connie Bertsch, who co-owns and manages the resort with her husband, Larry. Visitors can rent Jet Skis and also find a nice swimming beach area for the kids. The resort is located 15 miles north of Ephrata. Nearby, *Sun Lakes State Park* (509–632–5583) offers lakeside camping with similar amenities, plus horseback riding, golf, and road access to the floor of Dry Falls.

The *Dry Falls Interpretive Center* (509–632–5214), open daily May to September and located near Coulee City at 34875 Park Lake Road, offers spectacular views of what was once a gigantic waterfall—possibly the largest that has ever existed on earth. Exhibits explain the geological forces that created this massive precipice and why it is now without water. You'll learn of the lush environment that covered this area twenty million years ago during the Miocene Epoch and how the largest basaltic lava flows on earth, up to a mile thick, eventually engulfed 200,000 square miles of the Pacific Northwest. Powerful forces buckled and warped the cooled lava plateau, followed by glaciation and massive flooding, creating the dramatic landscape before you.

Highway 2 and Highway 17 intersect near the *Dry Falls Cafe* (509–632–5634), then Highway 2 crosses the Dry Falls Dam at the south end of Banks Lake. Turn right off Highway 2 at *Coulee City* to explore this windblown western town, originally a watering hole along the Caribou Trail. Huge grain elevators now dominate downtown. For information on the town's history, pick up a walking-tour brochure at the *Country Mall Store* on Main Street. If you happen into town on Tuesday or Saturday between 10:00 A.M. and 3:00 P.M., you can learn about art and local history from members of the **Highlighters Art Club,** who meet at their gallery on Main between Fifth and Sixth (509–632–5373). The group encourages local artists and collects their work. The gallery, in a building constructed in 1905, features art produced by members, such as oil paintings, woodcarvings, dried-flower arrangements, and splendid carved ducks done by one member who uses old golf club woods as the base for her work. After all this browsing and perusing local artwork of Coulee City folks, you can pop into **Della's Espresso Alley** (509–632–5581) on Main Street at Robin's Cut & Curl for hot or cold beverages. Or just a mile north of Coulee City, you could hunker down for juicy hamburgers at **Big Wally's Gas Station** (509–632–5504) as well as find fishing tackle and information about local walleye fishing from owner and fishing enthusiast Gordon Speinmetz. You could also try one of the best eateries in town, **Steamboat Rock Restaurant** (509–632–5452), located on Main Street near the corner of Fifth Street; it's open daily, except Monday, from 11:00 A.M. to 8:00 P.M.

If you continue east, Highway 2 passes through a series of small farm towns at 10-mile intervals. The pleasant farm town of **Wilbur,** at the junction of Highway 2 and Highway 21, is worth a stop. The town's main park, located south of Main Street, is a shady oasis of mature trees and green lawns. If you're still hot, cross over Goose Creek on the rustic footbridge to swim with local families at the Wilbur outdoor pool. The facility is open throughout the summer and charges a small fee. The town displays its history at the **Big Bend Historical Society Museum** (509–647–5863), located in a 1915-era Lutheran church 1 block north of Main Street, on Wilbur's west side. The museum is open June through August on Saturday from 2:00 to 4:00 P.M., as well as during "Wild Goose Bill Days," named for the town's infamous founder and held the third weekend in May. The town of Wilbur has but one thoroughfare, Main Street, and there are a couple of good eateries here. Try **Billy Burger,** the **Pizza Barn,** or the **Alibi Tavern,** all located on Main Street.

The Gehrke Windmills

*E*rected in North Dam Park overlooking Banks Lake and near the city of Grand Coulee, more than 650 windmills have been built by local resident Emil Gehrke. He fashioned the folk-art treasures of old cast-off iron parts and painted them in bright colors. Take cameras and film for good shots of you and the kids and the fanciful windmills.

The Alibi opens daily from 6:30 A.M. to at least 9:00 P.M. "You really can't get lost in Wilbur," points out a longtime resident, who recently moved back to this, her hometown. You could also drive 8 miles east to Creston and try *Deb's Cafe* or *Corner Cafe,* both on Main Street in Creston. You can't get lost in Creston, either.

For another taste of Washington's varied topography, head north from Wilbur on Highway 21. You'll travel past trees and farms in distant clumps like islands in a sea of grain before the road winds abruptly down through layered coulee cliffs to the Columbia River and the *Lake Roosevelt National Recreation Area.* If you're traveling RV-style, plan to spend at least one night at Keller Ferry at the splendid *River Rue RV Campground* (509–647–2647). Folks will find full hookups, clean rest rooms, and a full-service deli here. You can also walk about, exercise Fido or Bowser, meet other travelers, and enjoy the bustling activity at the marina and at the ferry landing. At Keller Ferry Marina the Colville Confederated Tribes rent forty houseboats from 46 to 59 feet in length

The Colville Confederated Tribes

*N*amed for an Englishman who was in the rum and molasses business and who never set foot in America, the Colville Confederated Tribes is made up of eleven different bands: Chelan, Entiat, Lakes, Nez Perce (from North-east Oregon), Methow, Moses, Nespelem, Palus, San Poil, Sweelpoo, and Wenatchi.

Prior to 1826 these separate nomadic bands fished, hunted, and traded furs and goods with each other in the area of Kettle Falls. When Englishmen and white settlers learned of this, the Fort Colville trading post was established. From 1826 to 1887 the Indians traded the lush pelts and hides of beaver, brown and black bear, grizzly, muskrat, fisher, fox, lynx, martin, mink, otter, raccoon, wolverine, bad-ger, and wolf at the post. St. Paul's Mission near Kettle Falls includes the original site of Fort Colville and a rustic log missionary church. In 1872 the Colville Indian Reservation was formed, measuring today about 1.3 million acres. Travelers are invited to visit the tribal headquarters located near Nespelem about 20 miles north of Grand Coulee Dam. Here you can learn about the enterprises owned and operated by the tribes, including a timber and wood products opera-tion; a tree replanting program; a fish hatchery that provides fish for the lakes and streams in the region; and a fleet of thirty-six recreational house-boats on Lake Roosevelt launched from marinas at Keller Ferry and at Seven Bays Campground (800–648–5253 for rental information). To enjoy fishing certain lakes on the reserva-tion, contact the Tribal Fish and Wildlife Department in Nespelem (509–634–8845).

that sleep up to thirteen people. For information and current rates, check the Web site, www.colville-tribal.com/RRE, or call the Colville Tribe's Roosevelt Recreation Enterprise at (509) 633–0136. This is a popular Coulee Country vacation option; reservations are accepted in June for the following year. If you are hardy and adventurous, you could bring your own canoe or kayak to reach the isolated campsites along Lake Roosevelt's pristine shoreline. For houseboat rentals at the far north end of Lake Roosevelt, contact **Lake Roosevelt Vacations & Marina** in Kettle Falls (509–738–6121; www.lakeroosevelt.com). Lake Roosevelt and the Lake Roosevelt National Recreation Area extend 151 miles north from Grand Coulee Dam to the scenic Colville National Forest and to the U.S.–Canadian border into British Columbia. The lake offers 630 miles of shoreline, coves, and bays and offers year-round fishing for kokanee, walleye, large- and smallmouth bass, rainbow trout, perch, crappie, and sturgeon. Twenty-eight campgrounds on the west and east sides of Lake Roosevelt offer campsites, water, picnic tables, fire pits, and rest rooms. These campsites are available on a first-come basis, with no hookups for RVs. For some of the most scenic campgrounds, head north on Highway 25 into the northern section of the recreation area that borders the

Grand Coulee Dam

*O*ne of the most popular tourist attractions in Washington, and certainly one of the most impressive feats of engineering in the country, the Grand Coulee Dam just naturally attracts superlatives, comparisons, and illustrative examples to convey its sheer magnitude. Here are a few of its facts and figures:

- *The dam is one of the largest concrete structures in the world, containing nearly twelve million cubic yards of concrete. There is enough concrete in the dam to build a standard 6-foot-wide sidewalk around the world at the equator.*

- *The dam is 500 feet wide at its base, 4,173 feet across the crest, and stands 550 feet above bedrock—as high as* the Washington Monument and dwarfing the Great Pyramid of Egypt.

- *It is the country's largest hydroelectric producer and the world's third-largest, generating 6,494,000 kilowatts in a single instant—more power than a million locomotives.*

- *Each of the six conventional pumps in Grand Coulee's Pump-Generator Plant is powered by a 65,000-horsepower motor that can pump 1,600 cubic feet of water per second, or 781,128 gallons per minute. In addition, six pump-generators, each having a 67,500-horsepower rating, can pump 1,948 cubic feet of water per second. One of these twelve units can fill the water needs of a city the size of Chicago.*

Colville National Forest. Check out Hunters, Gifford, Bradbury Beach, Kettle Falls, Kettle River, and Evans campgrounds, which all have fresh drinking water and lakeside sites. For other specific campground information and maps, contact the National Park Service headquarters (509–633–9441), located in the town of Grand Coulee, or the district park service office in Kettle Falls (509–738–6266).

The *Keller Ferry* offers a free ten-minute crossing with runs every fifteen minutes between 6:00 A.M. and 11:00 P.M. We're talking very small ferry here; yours may be the only car on the ferry's small deck. Many of the large houseboats are launched nearby. The river is often so placid you can see the dry sage-covered cliffs and hills reflected in the water for a doubly scenic view. From the landing on the north side, you can turn left on Swawilla Basin Road to Grand Coulee Dam or continue north on scenic Highway 21 up the Sanpoil River to the old mining town of Republic. The 24-mile road west toward Grand Coulee Dam is a hilly one, surrounded by ponderosa pine, wild roses, purple lupine, and woolly mullein, with occasional old barns and glacial erratics along the way. You may even spot a bear cub or mule deer exploring the dry roadside. Grand Coulee Dam is located 4 miles south of the junction with Highway 155.

In the community of Coulee Dam, visit the *Colville Tribal Cultural Museum and Gift Shop,* at 512 Mead Way (509–633–0751); open 10:00 A.M. to 6:00 P.M. daily during summer. The museum recounts the story of tribal life when the salmon swam free, before the Columbia River was dammed. Exhibits feature ancient fishing scenes, tribal lodges, and tepees as well as cedar and beargrass basket displays. The gift shop highlights beadwork, paintings, prints, and ceramics by local Native artists and tribespeople as well as Pendleton, Perce, and Navajo blankets. Staff members are on hand to answer questions, and they can describe how to get to the grave site of the legendary Nez Perce leader Chief Joseph, buried in exile from northeastern Oregon on a hillside northeast of Nespelem, 13 miles north on Highway 155.

In contrast to the "before" picture glimpsed at the museum, you can stop by the *Grand Coulee Dam Interpretive Center* (509–633–9265) across the bridge to learn the story of one of the world's largest concrete structures, celebrated in Woody Guthrie's famous song, "Roll on Columbia," and the largest component of the Pacific Northwest's extensive hydroelectric system. Exhibits at the visitor center explain the dam's history and engineering. You can also inquire about the current status of tours of the dam facilities. The forty-minute laser light show of animated graphics projected on the dam's surface runs every night Memorial Day weekend through September.

Visitors to the Grand Coulee area can enjoy the extensive **Community Trail** system that connects all four towns (West and East Coulee Dam, Grand Coulee, and Electric City) and that offers exercise and spectacular views. The **Down River Trail**, a 6½-mile hiking, biking, wheelchair-accessible path, follows the Columbia River north from the dam. With gentle grades and landscaped rest stops, both trails offer relaxing strolls.

Within walking distance of the dam on a quiet residential hillside to the west, Fe and Dick Taylor welcome travelers to historic **Four Winds Guest House Bed & Breakfast** (301 Lincoln Street, Coulee Dam 99116; 800–786–3146). Guests find ten large rooms decorated in 1930s style when the structure housed engineers during the early construction days of Grand Coulee Dam. It is said that President Franklin D. Roosevelt met with engineers here in 1937 to review progress on the dam project. On this whirlwind trip through the northwest, FDR also visited Bonneville Dam in the Columbia River Gorge, and the Works Progress Administration (WPA)–constructed Timberline Lodge at the 6,000-foot elevation level on Mount Hood located 50 miles east of Portland, Oregon.

For another overnight option that offers expansive views of Grand Coulee Dam, including its grand evening Laser Light Show call innkeepers Bonnie and David Schmidt at romantic **Victoria's Cottage** (209 Columbia Street, Coulee Dam 99116; 509–633–2908). The elegant guest suite comes with a sitting area, spa tub, stereo and VCR, refrigerator stocked with sodas and juices, coffeemaker and fresh-ground coffee, microwave oven and toaster, pastries, and a fresh fruit basket. The oversized spa tub is located in a romantic enclosure in the bedroom that contains green plants and offers nighttime views of the moon and stars through large skylights. On the shaded lawn, step into the romantic gazebo for wide-angle views of the Columbia River and the dam, then inspect lovely plantings of roses and perennials. Guests also are invited to use the inn's mountain bikes and supply of fishing tackle. For information on other lodging including motor inns and RV resorts, contact the Grand Coulee Dam Area Chamber of Commerce at (509) 633–3074 or (800) 268–5332; www.grandcouleedam.org.

Highway 155 follows the eastern shore of Banks Lake back to Coulee City. It is preferable to drive south on this road so that you can easily pull over at viewpoints and appreciate the awesome geology and the varied wildlife. **Steamboat Rock,** a former island in an ancient river bed, rises like a solidified wave from the lake's north end. Picturesque **Northrup Canyon Trail** begins at the end of a half-mile road across the highway from the rest stop near Steamboat Rock's north end. This moderately difficult trail stretches from a sheltered canyon, through pine forests, and up a steep path to Northrup Lake atop the gorge. You'll see remnants of early days along the way and perhaps view eagles soaring overhead.

Steamboat Rock State Park offers 121 campsites with full hookups and day-use facilities on the shore of Banks Lake, located just south of Grand Coulee and Electric City. Reservations are recommended because this is one of the state's more popular campgrounds. A hiking trail to the rock's 640-acre summit offers excellent views of the surrounding terrain. Bring water for everyone in your group, and wear good walking shoes. Keep your distance from the edge of the cliff since basalt breaks easily, and though rattlesnakes in the area aren't considered particularly aggressive or lethal, a bite is still painful and dangerous. For more information on trails or campsites, contact Steamboat Rock State Park, (509) 633–1304, during business hours, May 1 through Labor Day. Also on scenic Banks Lake near Electric City, you can find beach and picnic areas, immaculate grounds, and RV spaces with hookups at *Sun Banks Resort* (509–633–3786). The resort hosts a popular jazz festival during the summer.

The town of *Creston,* east of Wilbur on Highway 2, begins and ends in wheat fields near the crest of the Columbia Plateau. Take the left fork 2 miles east of Creston to reach Seven Bays and Fort Spokane. Bachelor Drive (Miles Creston Road) zigzags through a narrow, wooded valley back to rolling wheat fields before it descends into pine forests near Lake Roosevelt and the Lake Roosevelt National Recreation Area.

Seven Bays Campground Resort (509–633–0136), owned by the Colville Confederated Tribes, offers a hilltop campground as well as a marina and store.

You can also visit and camp at nearby *Fort Spokane* and *Fort Spokane Campground* (509–725–2715). Built in 1880 after the overt wars against Native Americans ceased, Fort Spokane's main function was to maintain a truce between settlers and seminomadic tribes. Park volunteers and staff show what life was like back then through living-history programs each Sunday at 11:00 A.M. throughout the summer. The visitor center is located in the former guardhouse, one of the original fort buildings. An interpretive trail guides you through the grounds, and the camping and RV sites are rimmed by forest-covered hills.

You can continue north on scenic Highway 25 to Kettle Falls to access the scenic *Colville National Forest* area and the far north section of Lake Roosevelt (509–684–7000 for campground information). At this point travelers are some 100 miles north of Grand Coulee Dam and 40 miles south of the U.S.–Canadian border, where they can cross into the southeastern section of British Columbia. About 2 miles south of Kettle Falls, you can find another contact for houseboat vacations in this scenic lake area. Contact Ed and Carol Wimberly and their staff at *Lake Roosevelt Resort & Marina* in Kettle Falls, (509–738–6121; www.lakeroosevelt.com) to explore the costs and particulars on their fleet of fifteen luxurious houseboats. The staff provides complete orientation to the houseboat's facilities, safety instructions, and how to operate and handle the craft. There is a two-way marine radio on board in case of emergencies. For a small extra fee, folks can board their houseboat the night before sailing to save the cost of a motel room. The large crafts accommodate up to thirteen people and contain full kitchen facilities, baths, common areas, bedrooms and sleeping areas, and outside and topside decks. You bring your own bedding, bath linens, food, and beverages. What can you do on a floating houseboat with no TV and no telephone? Well, for starters, you relax into nature's time. Then you cruise the upper section of the lake and pull into a secluded cove or small bay and perhaps anchor for a day or two. Folks can fish for walleye or trout; dive and swim from the deck or paddle nearby on an inner tube or float tube; relax in the sun with a novel; enjoy a steak barbecue at sunset; and watch for wildlife such as eagles, osprey, deer, and even bear and wild turkeys. The summer season, late June through Labor Day, fills quickly. The value seasons are post–Labor Day through October 31 and May 1 through late June (excluding Memorial Day weekend). The houseboats are rented by the week, midweek, or weekends. For the most outrageous vacation option, ask about the Super Cruisers, which come with a six-person hot tub located on the topside deck right under the stars.

From Highway 25 you can also head south, away from the Lake Roosevelt National Recreation Area, and plunge back into rolling grain country proceeding to *Davenport.* This larger agricultural town west of Spokane is vibrant with daily farm life. The Davenport City Park, south of the highway, surrounds a natural spring where huge cottonwoods have grown for centuries. The sweet water made this an important campsite for Native tribes and, in the late nineteenth century, for settlers and miners traveling along the White Bluffs Road. The park is a pleasant spot for a picnic, with playground equipment, tables, shade, and a community pool. Nearby, at Seventh and Park, is the *Lincoln County Historical Museum* (509–725–6711), chock-full of items and images collected over the past century, including photos, farm machinery, a general store, and a blacksmith shop. The museum is open Monday through Saturday from 9:00 A.M. to 5:00 P.M. from May 1 to September 30.

The rolling landscape continues east along Highway 2. At the town of Reardan, you can continue to Spokane or turn north to Colville on Highway 231 for a scenic 70-mile drive up Spring Creek Canyon. Along this road you'll see a scattering of old farms, many of which still use windmills to pump water for irrigation. By the time you reach the Spokane River at Long Lake Dam, the wheat fields and farms have given way to ponderosa pine forests and meadows. At the tiny village of Ford, you can find a friendly pit stop at the *Ford Trading Post,* a post office, general store, rest stop, and gas station all jumbled together in a log building.

Continue on Highway 231 as the road curves west through Springdale. Nine miles north at the town of Valley, turn left on a 3-mile spur road to reach *Waitts Lake.* Waitts is a spring-fed lake surrounded by wetlands and pine forests. Scattered farms and fields dot its western shore, summer cabins and resorts hug the northeast, and public fishing spots offer recreation at the south end. The resorts are informal, catering to local families as well as visitors. *Silver Beach Resort* (3323 Waitts Lake Road, Valley 99181; 509–937–2811) offers travelers five cabins, a general store, boat rentals, swimming and picnic sites, and a pleasant restaurant with a patio overlooking the lake (open for dinner Thursday through Sunday, 5:00 to 9:00 P.M.). The family chef cooks up tasty entrees prepared with beef, chicken, salmon, and halibut.

Rivers, Lakes, and Pine Forests

Spokane, the largest city in the inland Northwest, is situated along the Spokane River near an ancient Indian campsite, where members of the Spo-kan-ee tribe gathered for centuries to fish at the river rapids. Although Spokane has grown into a major urban center, it retains much of its frontier identity. You'll see plenty of cowboy hats and pickup trucks even in downtown, and you don't have to go far past the city's suburban developments to find ranches and farms.

The Spokane River is still a dominant feature in the city. The *Spokane River Centennial Trail* (509–624–7188), which follows the Spokane River, offers an ideal path for walking, bicycling, running, or skating. The Washington portion of the Centennial Trail runs 37 miles—22 from the Idaho border to Spokane's *Riverfront Park* in the center of downtown, where you can see the churning rapids where the Spokane tribe fished for salmon. Nearby you'll find espresso and hot dog stands as well as many pleasant eateries.

Honor Thy Father

Father's Day was "invented" in Spokane in 1910 by a local housewife, Mrs. John Bruce Dodd. Mrs. Dodd wanted a special day to honor her father, William Smart, a Civil War veteran who had raised her and her five brothers after his wife's early death. She contacted the local YMCA and the Spokane Ministerial Association, who persuaded the city government to set aside the third Sunday in June to "honor thy father."

The recently renovated **Northwest Museum of Arts and Culture** and circa 1898 **Campbell House,** located in the city's historic Browne's addition at 2316 West First Avenue (509–456–3931), display the region's Native American and pioneer past and current culture. Early architect Kirtland Cutter designed the thirty-room English Tudor revival mansion, which showcased the opulent lifestyle of one of the region's mining barons. Both museum and house are open Tuesday through Sunday. See www.north westmuseum.org for current exhibits and current hours and admission fees.

Patsy Clark's Mansion and Restaurant (2208 West Second Avenue, Spokane 99204; 509–838–8300), another of architect Cutter's opulent designs, is located nearby and across from Coeur d'Alene Park. The restaurant offers elegant dinners and lunches as well as tours of the luxurious mansion. Lunch is served from 11:30 A.M. to 1:30 P.M. weekdays, Sunday brunch is from 10:00 A.M. to 1:30 P.M., and dinner is from 5:00 to 9:00 P.M. Monday through Thursday and until 10:00 P.M. on Friday and Saturday. The best time to tour the mansion is just after the doors open at 3:00 P.M. on Saturday, after Sunday brunch, or between lunch and dinner on weekdays.

Across the street from Patsy Clark's is the **Fotheringham House Bed and Breakfast** (2128 West Second Avenue, Spokane 99204; 509–838–1891; www.fotheringham.net). Spokane's first mayor, David B. Fotheringham, built the house in 1891 as his family home. Graham and Jackie Johnson, who purchased the house in 1993, restored both house and garden in classic Victorian style. Current owners Irene and Paul Jensen invite guests to relax in one of three rooms with shared or private bath, soak in an original claw-foot tub, enjoy evening tea and truffles, have a fireside chat in winter, or spend a quiet summer evening on the curved veranda overlooking the splendid perennial gardens. Travelers who love antique furniture and stained glass, combined with hand-carved woodwork, tin ceilings, and old world ambience, can make this a charming base from which to experience the Spokane area.

At **The Marianna Stoltz House Bed & Breakfast,** located in a shady residential neighborhood at 427 East Indiana Street (509–483–4316; www.mariannastoltzhouse.com), innkeepers Phyllis and Jim Maguire offer visitors four comfortable guest rooms on the second floor of their large, circa 1908 Craftsman-style home. The living room, dining room, and parlor all come with leaded-glass windows, high ceilings, and fine woodwork of polished fir. Roomy sofas and upholstered chairs are arranged in cozy groupings, with antique light fixtures and fringed lampshades mixing well with the other period furnishings. For breakfast you might enjoy such tasty fare as French toast with strawberry and mandarin orange sauce, Stoltz House Strada, or croissants with poached eggs topped with bacon and cheese sauce. The inn is located just 5 blocks from Gonzaga University (502 East Boone Avenue), where the **Bing Crosby Memorabilia Room** (509–328–4220), open to the public, is filled with photographs, letters, and musical memorabilia from the crooner's life. "He lived in the Spokane area as a boy," explains Phyllis.

Waverly Place Bed & Breakfast is located in the Corbin Park Historic District at 709 West Waverly Place; (509) 328–1856; www.waverlyplace. com. Guests find four guest rooms on the second floor with views of the park and grounds along with amenable comforts such as dormer window seats or turret sitting areas, stained-glass windows, gleaming fir floors, antique queen beds with down comforters and quilts, cozy common areas, and baths with claw-footed soaking tubs and tiled showers. A hearty and delicious breakfast, prepared by innkeeper Marge Arndt and daughter Tammy, amply prepares you for a fine day of exploring the Spokane area.

In the early 1900s **Corbin Park,** then the regional fairgrounds, housed a half-mile racing track, and the Gentlemen's Riding Club was soon established nearby. Sulky and harness racing were popular sports with many prominent gentlemen of Spokane and their ladies attending regularly. Locals as well as visitors especially enjoy the park and its shady walking paths that pass by many vintage homes built in the early 1900s.

Good eateries abound in the Spokane area; check out **The Onion Family Restaurant** at 302 West Riverside (509–747–3852) for pastas, fajitas, chicken, gourmet salads, and a variety of hamburgers; **Rock City Italian Grill** at 505 West Riverside (509–455–4400) for serious Italian food lovers; **Sawtooth Grill** at 801 West Main Street (509–363–1100) near River Park Square downtown for great burgers in a rustic mountain-cabin setting; and **Steam Plant Grill and Brew Pub,** located in historic Steam Plant Square (159 South Lincoln Street; 509–777–3900). Located near Manito Park, **Lindeman's Café** at 1235 South Grand Boulevard (509–838–3000) shouldn't be missed for freshly made entrees, great salads and sandwiches, and tempting desserts (if possible take a picnic along to the park); and **Paprika's** at 1228 South Grand Boulevard (509–455–7545) is frequented for its gourmet regional fare.

To get acquainted with the natural history of the area, go hiking at **Dishman Hills Natural Resource Conservation Area,** a 518-acre sanctuary with an easy $2^1/_2$-mile loop walk in the southeast hills. Spokane County Parks staff can provide more information (509–456–4730). Or walk in the splendid **John A. Finch Arboretum,** at 3404 West Woodland Boulevard (509–624–4832) with its stands of rhododendron, azaleas, and lilacs. The arboretum encompasses a mile-long natural area that stretches some sixty-five acres along the banks of Garden Springs Creek west of downtown Spokane off Sunset Boulevard. One of the best outdoor experiences awaits travelers at **Manito Park Gardens,** South Grand at Eighteenth Avenue (509–625–6622). Start your tour at Rose Hill, situated on a four-acre slope that overlooks the other garden sections. You'll see formal beds of some 1,500 roses representing over 150 varieties, as well as borders of old-fashioned scented roses. From here walk down to the **Joel E. Ferris Perennial Garden,** a three-acre oasis of lawns and large perennial beds where you'll see colorful hellebores, solidagos, and cosmos as well as salvias, poppies, spiky liatris, and phlox. Next visit the splendid Duncan Formal Gardens, just opposite Gaiser Conservatory. The conservatory houses collections of colorful begonias, fuchsias, and tropical plantings. Then access a meandering path just beyond the Lilac Garden and below Rose Hill to find the secluded **Nishinomiya Japanese Garden.** The graceful curved bridge over the reflecting pond, called a "ceremony bridge," is borrowed from the Oriental tradition. A small waterfall flows from the rising sun toward the setting sun; the three vertical stones in the central pond suggest cranes or ships at sea. Don't miss this splendid park and its wonderful gardens.

For more information about what to see and do in the Spokane area, contact the Visitor Information Center at 801 West Riverside, Suite 301, Spokane 99201; (509) 624–1341. You can also access the Web site, www.visitspokane.com.

From Spokane you can take Highway 2 north, but first detour onto High-way 395 and continue north to the community of Deer Park. Travelers would have difficulty missing *Love's Victorian Bed & Breakfast* (North 31317 Cedar Road, Deer Park 99006; 509–276–6939), an imposing Queen Anne Victorian–style structure complete with a handsome cupola, a miniature balcony, a large wraparound porch, and traditional gingerbread decorative trim. Innkeepers Bill and Leslie Love furnish afternoon tea in the sunroom. Three sumptuous guest rooms with private baths are located on the second floor; one guest room comes with a cozy gas fireplace. In the morning you sit at small round tables in the dining room, where the couple serves a romantic candlelit breakfast that may include heart-shaped French toast or waffles served with warm maple or berry syrups.

Backtrack a few miles to Highway 2 and head north on this route through lush farmlands to the gentle Pend Oreille (pond-er-RAY) River Valley. On the banks of the Pend Oreille River, you'll find the town of Newport and its Idaho neighbor, Oldtown. As you enter Newport from the southwest, you'll see *Centennial Plaza* to your right with its huge steam-engine wheel and the *Pend Oreille County Historical Museum* (509–447–5388) in the 1908 brick railroad passenger depot. The museum features antique quilts, kitchen items, books, photographs, tools, and news articles from local sources, as well as a settler's cabin, a one-room schoolhouse, and old farm machinery. It is open daily from 10:00 A.M. to 4:00 P.M. mid-May through September. Just 2 blocks from the museum, you can visit *The Lighthouse Gift Shop & Tea Room* located in a renovated circa 1905 Victorian house at South 519 Scott Avenue in Newport (509–447–3008). The dining room offers several small tables for tea lovers, and other rooms offer myriad gift items from Victorian and nautical to Western style and elegant contemporary. Call ahead for reservations for tea and freshly baked scones served with Devonshire cream.

Centennial Plaza also has a three-level drinking fountain "serving man, beast, and dog" since 1911. Across the street is Newport's oldest build-ing, *Kelly's Tavern* (324 West Fourth Street; 509–447–3526), a watering hole for miners, loggers, settlers, railway workers, and city folk since 1894. The tavern's impressive lead-glass bar was shipped around the Horn to San Francisco and then carried by wagon train to Newport.

For a scenic overnight option, consider *Inn at the Lake,* located at 581 South Shore Diamond Lake Road, Newport 99156 (509–447–5772). Travelers find four guest rooms in this Italian villa–style home constructed in 1993 and situated above the lake. The rooms offer superb lake views along with

Steam-Engine Wheel in Centennial Plaza

decks and gas-log fireplaces. The largest suite comes with an elegant four-poster bed and a couple-sized whirlpool tub. Newport is located 8 miles from the Idaho border and about 40 miles north of Spokane.

You can travel north on either side of the Pend Oreille River, but Le Clerc Road on the east bank is quieter and more scenic. A half mile north from the Newport/Oldtown Bridge, you can visit an ancient Indian campsite at *Pioneer Park.* Recent archaeological studies there have uncovered artifacts, earth ovens, and house pits that indicate use by the Kalispel tribe for at least 800 years and by prehistoric hunter-gatherers for possibly 2,000 to 4,000 years. The park offers quiet, forested camping and picnic spots and views of mergansers, herons, and other waterfowl in nearby wetlands and river islands.

As you continue north, watch for osprey, a small hawk that catches fish by speed-diving into water and builds large nests on river pilings and snags. A bridge crosses the river at Usk, a tiny mill town named for a Welsh river, where you can stay at *The Hotel Usk* (north on River Road just west of the bridge, 410 River Road, Usk 99180; 509–445–1526). Innkeepers Stan and Andrea Davey strive to re-create the ambience of Usk's early days, offering eight small guest rooms, seven with private baths.

A few miles north of the Usk bridge on Le Clerc Road, you may spot a herd of buffalo in pastures by the river. This is the *Kalispel Indian Reservation* (509–445–1147), the smallest reservation in Washington. The Kalispel people once numbered more than a thousand, spread out over the river valley. Now numbering in the hundreds, the tribe has worked to consolidate its small holdings and has developed community buildings, a bison herd raised for meat, and an aluminum plant in Cusick.

At the **Manresa Grotto,** located a few miles north, a short climb up a winding dirt pathway takes you to the dome-shaped grotto, formed by the waves of an ancient glacial lake. There you'll find rows of stone pews before an altar of mortared rock, site of religious ceremonies for more than a century. The view is enchanting—the peaceful river valley surrounded by forested hills, all framed by the gray stone arch of the grotto entrance.

Le Clerc Road ends across the bridge from the town of Ione, once the site of the most successful mill in northeast Washington. You can get a historic walking-tour brochure at the Ione Drug Store at Main and Fourth. Just west of the drugstore is the Old Railroad Depot, built in 1909. You can take in some breathtaking scenery on the historic **North Pend Oreille Valley Lion's Club Excursion Train** from Ione to Metaline Falls and back. Two-hour rides through forests, through two tunnels, and over Box Canyon trestle high above Pend Oreille River are scheduled during selected summer and fall weekends. Call (509) 442–5466 between noon and 6:00 P.M. for more information and reservations, which must be made at least two weeks before each ride. The current schedule and fees are also posted at www.povn.com/byway.

For more scenery, continue northeast on Sullivan Lake Road on the east side of the Pend Oreille River. **Sullivan Lake,** dammed in 1910 to run the cement plant at Metaline Falls, is situated at the foot of snow-capped peaks. There are forested campsites at Noisy Creek at the lake's south end and near the Sullivan Lake Ranger District Office at 12641 Sullivan Lake Road (509–446–7500) at the north end. In winter you can hike to the bighorn sheep observation area from the Noisy Creek Campsite. The 4.2-mile **Lakeshore Trail** connects the two campsites and offers great views, especially during autumn, as well as lakeshore access. The **Mill Pond Historic Site** includes a barrier-free interpretive trail from the western edge of Mill Pond, a small lake created in 1910 and located northwest on Sullivan Lake Road. The path follows a wooden flume that once ran between Sullivan Lake and Metaline Falls.

Continue west on Sullivan Lake Road to reach **Metaline Falls,** a small town nestled on the east bank of the Pend Oreille River that has attracted a lively artist community. The town's block-long main street (Fifth Street) ends at the city park and visitors center, a brightly painted railway car above terraced flower beds. To the left of the park is the vine-covered *Washington Hotel* (225 East Fifth Avenue, P.O. Box 2, Metaline Falls 99153; 509–446–4415). Built in 1910, the hotel has been restored to its earlier elegance as the centerpiece of a bustling turn-of-the-century mining town. Metaline Falls artist and former mayor Lee McGowan decorated the eighteen rooms, and she maintains a gallery, studio, and art study center on the hotel's first floor. Nearby, at 221 East Fifth Avenue, you can enjoy meeting the locals over breakfast, lunch, or dinner at *Cathy's Cafe* (509–446–2447), open daily from 5:30 A.M.

The building that houses *The Cutter Theater* at 302 Park Street in Metaline Falls (509–446–4108) was built early in the century and named for talented Spokane architect Kirtland Cutter. The historic school, built of locally kilned bricks, has been renovated as a performing arts center. Stop by to browse the permanent history exhibits and the traveling art exhibits in the Art Gallery. Visit the theater's Web site at www.povn.com/cutter for schedules of plays, performances, and upcoming events in the area.

For a spectacular view, follow Highway 31 north about 12 miles, then turn left on the ³/₄-mile access road to *Boundary Vista House.* There you'll have excellent views of Boundary Dam in its steep canyon as well as surrounding mountains. Cross back over the river west of Metaline Falls, and take the Boundary Road turnoff to Boundary Dam and Gardner Cave. Along the way you'll see beaver dams in the wetlands next to this scenic woodland road.

Boundary Road divides after 11¹/₂ miles. Take the left fork to reach the 1,055-foot *Gardner Cave* at *Crawford State Park.* The cave's limestone walls were formed from the bodies of ancient sea creatures that settled into ooze on the floor of an ancient ocean 500 million years ago. Groundwater seepage cut away the stone over the past seventy million years, creating the passage with its fantastic patterns. Visitors must be accompanied by a ranger to enter the cave. Tours are conducted Thursday through Monday from Memorial Day through Labor Day; they leave from the parking lot at 10:00 A.M., noon, and 2:00 and 4:00 P.M. and take about an hour. Bring along a light jacket or sweater, since the cave is always cool, and a flashlight. For current information contact Crawford State Park at North 26107 Mount Spokane Park Drive, Mead 99021; (509) 446–4065.

Northern Ranches and Forests

Three miles south of Ione at *Tiger,* Highway 20 turns west from the riverbank and heads over the Selkirk Mountains. As you drive through the small community of Tiger, stop at the *Tiger Historical*

Center Museum (509–446–2601). The building, the historic Tiger Store, was recently restored and converted to a historical center, museum, and visitor center gateway to the *North Pend Oreille Scenic Byway and Selkirk International Loop.* The original building, Tiger Store and Post Office, was constructed in 1912 and served the community until 1975, when the post office was moved to Cusick. The center is open June through September, Friday through Monday from 10:00 A.M. to 5:00 P.M. The road climbs and descends through evergreen forests and past a chain of glacial lakes cradled between the peaks. Among the biggest trees you'll see are Douglas fir, spruce, white pine, grand fir, and tamarack, all giant conifers. The aspen, birch, and mountain larch (tamarack) all turn vibrant colors of yellow, orange, and lime green in late September and October. The highway follows the Little Pend Oreille River through the Colville National Forest and past the *Little Pend Oreille Wildlife Area.* Leo, Thomas, Gillette, and Twin Lakes all have campsites with lakeshore access. The *Springboard Trail* from East Gillette Campground offers an easy 2.4-mile loop with interpretive highlights on the area's history and ecology as well as a platform with a view of the lakes.

Beaver Lodge Resort, situated on Lake Gillette at the 3,200-foot level on Tiger Pass, has miles of hiking, cross-country ski, and snowmobile trails nearby. The lodge features rustic wood cabins at the lake's edge, RV hookups, forested or lakeside campsites, laundry, swimming, boat rentals, a grocery store, and a deli overlooking the lake. for reservations For reservations contact proprietors Robert and Julie Beeck, Little Pend Oreille Lakes, 2430 Highway 20 East, Colville 99114 (509–684–5657).

The pine forest begins to thin as you continue winding west on Highway 20 and descend into the pastoral Colville River Valley. Colville is a large, bustling town at the junction of Highways 395 and 20. In town follow signs from the highway (Fifth Street) leading 2 blocks uphill on Wynne Street to reach the *Keller Heritage Center* and *Stevens County Historical Museum* (509–684–5968). A trail leads up from the museum to the Graves Mountain Fire Lookout at the top of a small hill, where you can enjoy a panoramic view of the valley, town, and mountains. Keller House Museum tells the area's story in chronological order from geological, Native American, and European perspectives. The museum is open June through September from 10:00 A.M. to 4:00 P.M. and on Sunday from 1:00 to 4:00 P.M. In May the facility is open from 1:00 to 4:00 P.M.

If you've worked up an appetite during your travels, consider a stop at nearby *Cafe Italiano* (153 West Second Avenue, Colville 99114; 509–684–5957). Serving tasty Italian dinners, the addition of outdoor seating on a patio with a fountain adds to the resaurant's Continental atmosphere. The cafe is open daily from 11:00 A.M. *Note:* Before leaving Colville and heading to Kettle Falls, gas up and load up on groceries, snacks, beverages, ice, and picnic items.

For a wonderfully fun adventure, you can drive 38 miles north of Colville into the Colville National Forest past the hamlets of Aladdin and Spirit, then continue past Deep Lake for another 8 miles. But first call and arrange to stay with Joann Bender, novelist, and Bud Budinger, geotechnical engineer, at **Lazy Bee Wilderness Retreat,** located at 3651 Deep Lake Boundary Road (509–732–8917). You're deep into the forests of pine, cedar, Douglas fir, larch, and birch and at a crisp elevation of 2,000 feet. And you're also not far from the U.S.–Canadian border crossing at the town of Boundary. The couple offers two comfy suites with shared bath, an incredible floor-to-ceiling library in the cozy common area, eight log-burning fireplaces, and delicious breakfasts along with quantities of solitude and relaxation. Inquire about meal options and costs.

The original site of **Kettle Falls** is believed to be one of the oldest continuously occupied spots in the Northwest. As long as 9,000 years ago, an ancient tribe known as the Shonitkwa fished the steep falls. Over the centuries Indians established permanent communities near the falls that existed until European settlement eroded traditional lifestyles. The actual falls and historic sites are now submerged under Lake Roosevelt. During the early spring drawdown in March or April, remnants of flooded islands and historic towns like **Old Marcus** (located about 5 miles north on Highway 25) are revealed.

You can learn more about the "People of the Falls" at the impressive

Sherman Alexie

*T*he Spokane Indian Reservation at Wellpinit is the home base of Sherman Alexie, one of the region's most celebrated young writers. Alexie is a Spokane/Coeur d'Alene Indian whose poems, short stories, and novels illuminate contemporary Native American reservation life, often bittersweetly.

Alexie, in his thirties, has earned numerous awards, including the PEN/Hemingway Award for the Best First Book of Fiction for The Lone Ranger and Tonto Fistfight in Heaven, *which served as the basis for* Smoke Signals, *a film that premiered at the 1998 Sundance Film Festival, and the Before Columbus Foundation's American Book Award for* Reservation Blues. *He was named as one of the best young novelists in America by* GRANTA *in 1995. Alexie currently lives in Seattle but says his roots will forever be in Wellpinit.*

Kettle Falls Historical Center, 1188 St. Paul's Mission Road (509–738–6964), on a spur road north of Highway 20 and 3 miles west of Kettle Falls, just before the bridge over Lake Roosevelt. The center features murals and models for each season of the year, telling the ancient story of tribal life near the falls. The exhibit and gift shop of local artwork are open from 11:00 A.M. to 5:00 P.M., Wednesday through Sunday, from May 15 through September 15.

Many family-owned farms and fruit orchards in the area offer berries, cherries, apricots, peaches, pears, apples, and grapes in season from June through September. Look for signs along nearby Peach Crest Road. Write to the Kettle Falls Chamber of Commerce, P.O. Box 119, Kettle Falls 99141, or call (509) 738–2300 for more information and an orchard directory and map of more than a dozen fruit-picking spots.

In late August you can take in the annual *Garlic Faire* at *China Bend Vineyards & Winery,* located about 23 miles north of Kettle Falls at 3596 Northport Flat Road (800–700–6123; www.chinabend.com). From roasted garlic and garlic corn to garlic soup and pizza, garlic lovers indulge in a festive day of tasting and buying garlic products. The winery produces delicious table and dessert wines that don't contain sulfites and also offers freshly made organic products such as salsa, pickled garlic, dilly beans, and a selection of tasty fruit preserves.

If you are traveling in winter when the lake is at its fullest, you'll find the best *bald eagle viewing area* around along Highway 25. Take the turnoff south before Kettle Falls Bridge and head toward the Gifford Ferry. The concentration of eagles reaches a peak in mid-February, when the striking white and black adults and mottled brown and white juveniles perch on top of gnarled snags and rocky outcroppings at the water's edge while on the lookout for fresh fish.

If the high desert, rolling hills, and pine forests beckon you to stay another night, you could call ahead to *River Bluff Log House* (509–722–3784; www.theriverbluff.com) located near Inchelium. Inquire about the self-contained log cabin with wraparound deck and non-stop views of Lake Roosevelt on this northern section of the Columbia River. These outrageous views are the kinds that fill the soul and urge stresses to melt away. Take the toll-free ferry at Gifford across the lake to Inchelium. For more stress-reducing scenery, the kind that even the locals don't tire of, from Inchelium take the county road heading west for about 35 miles past Twin Lakes to Highway 21. If you're tent camping, traveling by RV, or want a lakeside cabin, contact *Rainbow Beach Resort,* located on Twin Lakes (509–722–5901). Call well ahead for reservations—it's a popular spot during summer months. After crossing the Kettle River Range and intersecting with Highway 21, head north along the picturesque Sanpoil River for about 30 miles to the community of **Republic.** You can also reach Republic from Kettle Falls by continuing west on Highway 20, the **Sherman Pass Scenic Byway,** winding up and over 5,575-foot Sherman Pass.

Bicyclists, hikers, and hunters often make a beeline for the **Triangle J Ranch Hostel** (423 Old Kettle Falls Road, Republic 99166; 509–775–3933). In summer the fields next to the gardens and stables are often dotted with colorful tents and bicycles. The ranch has a four-bed dormitory with cooking facilities, a hot tub, and an outdoor swimming pool.

If you've ever hankered for wide open spaces, western hospitality, and delicious family-style meals at a guest ranch, contact the Konz family at **K-Diamond-K Guest Ranch,** located just south of Republic on the Sanpoil River at 15661 Highway 21 South (888–345–5355; www.kdiamondk.com). The family offers four spacious guest rooms in the large log-style home and offers a host of activities from horseback riding, mountain biking, and fishing to bird- and wildlife watching, stargazing, hunting, and winter snowmobiling and cross-country skiing. If you like, you could even go along on a seasonal cattle drive astride your steady steed. Autumn is one of the most memorable seasons on the ranch with vibrant fall colors, warm days, crisp evenings, and night skies jam-packed with glittering stars.

A loop around **Curlew Lake** to the north makes a pleasant bike ride or drive. The 7-mile-long lake is surrounded by mountains and rolling hills. Some early log cabins are still visible in the area. **Curlew Lake State Park** offers lakeside picnic sites, a swimming area, boat launches, and campsites. Several small lakeside resorts are scattered along the lake. **Fisherman's Cove Resort** (1157 Fisherman's Cove Road, Republic 99166; 509–775–3641) welcomes families and offers rustic cabins in a quiet, lakeside setting. **Tiffany's** (1026 Tiffany Road, Republic 99166; 509–775–3152), on the opposite shore, offers comparable amenities.

The Kettle River History Club's **Car and Truck Museum** is located at 1865 North Highway 21 (509–779–4204) between the towns of Malo and Curlew. This is an old-car aficionado's dream: dozens of carefully preserved and restored cars, including vintage Model T Fords, Buicks, actor Walter Brennan's 1928 Phaeton, the only 1917 Chevrolet Royal Mail Roadster still running, and one of the only three 1920 Howard Cooper Firetrucks ever made, all in operating condition. The museum is open from 10:00 A.M. to 5:00 P.M. daily in summer.

Kettle River History Club's Car and Truck Museum

The quiet town of *Curlew* is nestled between dry hills on the east bank of the Kettle River. Follow signs to the right off the highway, then left and right again into town. Curlew's main street, lined with dark-wood buildings with Western false fronts, overlooks the river through tall cottonwoods. The old ***Ansorge Hotel Museum*** on River Street (509–779–4808) no longer provides food or lodging, but you can tour the building, which is complete with period furnishings and clothing from its heyday in the early 1900s (weekends from mid-May to the end of September, 1:00 to 5:00 P.M.). The ***Curlew Riverside Restaurant*** (813 River Street; 509–779–4813) offers Mexican and American food prepared from fresh ingredients. The dining room, with its wood-burning stove, fans, and rustic wood furniture, overlooks the river. Dinner is served from 4:00 to 9:00 P.M. Wednesday through Sunday.

On your way back south on Highway 21 toward Republic, take the West Curlew Lake Road turnoff to your right (west) at Curlew Lake's north end for a less-traveled route along the lake's western shore. Klondike Road veers right about a mile south of the lake and then descends past pine trees and houses hugging the steep hillside into Republic.

Clark Avenue, the town's main street, was named for Republic Gold Mining and Milling Company president "Patsy" Clark. While most buildings' false fronts are recent additions to boost the town's already rustic feel, the **Republic Drug Store** (circa 1906), on the corner of Clark and Fourth Avenues, boasts an original storefront with hand-cranked awnings and pressed tin ceiling. At the north end of town, you'll pass a lovely stone Episcopal church, built in 1909, whose windows shimmer with stained-glass doves.

To participate in a paleontological treasure hunt, follow Sixth Avenue west a block onto Kean Street across from Patterson Park to the **Stonerose Interpretive Center** at 15 Kean Street (509–775–2295), open May through October, Tuesday through Saturday, from 10:00 A.M. to 5:00 P.M.; from June 14 through September 13, it's open Sunday 10:00 A.M. to 4:00 P.M. There, the curator and assistants can introduce you to the fascinating world of fifty million years ago, when an ancient lake covered the

Life on a Cattle Ranch, Northeastern Washington Style

*I*t's early morning and you squint at the bright yellow eastern horizon. The leather saddle creaks as you guide your horse along the stream toward the herd. You learn that the seasons come and go in a regular rhythm on a cattle ranch. The list of chores commands attention. Ranch life here is firmly anchored to the high desert, pine and fir forests, mountain ranges, and to the rivers and streams. Times for fun and frivolity come when the chores are done. Although we're not talking a rerun of City Slickers here, many ranch families now welcome travelers who seek a hearty dose of western hospitality and who hanker to sit astride a horse for a few days. Squinting at sunrises or gazing at sunsets and riding along a stream or meadow with friendly ranch hands is a good thing. Check out this host of seasonal chores and activities from

the K-Diamond-K Guest Ranch located near Republic:

January—*Winter feeding, snowmobile rides*

February—*New calves born*

March—*More calves, timber harvest*

April—*Branding calves, fishing*

May—*Spring roundups, barn dance*

June—*Rodeo & barn dance, Prospector Days*

July—*Rodeo & barn dance, draft horse show*

August—*Hay harvest, fiddle contest*

September—*County fair*

October—*Fall roundups, hunting*

November—*Calves weaned, timber harvest*

December—*Winter feeding*

town site of Republic. Fossil-hunting tours are permitted during the hours the center is open. Bring along a hammer and chisel, or rent some there, to use at the dig site north of town. The fossils you discover will be identified for you to take home, or, if you are lucky enough to find a new or rare species, you will be applauded as a paleontological hero, and your fossil will be kept for further study.

For good eats in the Republic area, try *Blondie's Cafe* at 644 South Clark Street (509–775–9992) for great breakfast omelets and excellent hamburgers; *Hometown Pizza* at 18 North Clark Street (509–775–2557) for good pizza and salad bar; *Esther's Mexican Restaurant* at 90 North Clark Street (509–775–2088) for super burritos, shredded beef taco salads, and homebaked pies; and *Small World Cafe* at Republic Trading Post located at 30277 Highway 20 (509–775–8005) for thick milkshakes and saucy barbecue chicken sandwiches. For great coffees, espresso, and homemade pastries, stop by *The Loose Blue Moose Coffee House* in Republic at 1015 South Clark Street (509–774–0441) and *River Street Espresso & Bakery* in Curlew at 9 River Street (509–779–4937).

PLACES TO STAY IN NORTHEAST WASHINGTON

COLVILLE
Beaver Lodge Resort
2430 Highway 20 East
Colville 99114
(509) 684–5657

Lazy Bee Wilderness Retreat
3651 Deep Lake Boundary Road
Colville 99114
(509) 732–8917

COULEE CITY
Coulee Lodge Resort
33017 Park Lake Road NE
Coulee City 99115
(509) 632–5565

COULEE DAM
Columbia River Inn
10 Lincoln Street
Coulee Dam 99116
(800) 633–6421
(509) 633–2100

Four Winds Guest House
301 Lincoln Street
Coulee Dam 99116
(509) 633–3146

CURLEW
Wolfgang's Riverview Inn
2320 Highway 21 North
Curlew 99118
(509) 779–4252

GRAND COULEE
The Gold House Bed and Breakfast
411 Partello Park
P.O. Box 76
Grand Coulee 99133
(509) 633–3276

ELECTRIC CITY
Sky Deck Motel
South Highway 155,
Cadillac Drive
Electric City 99123
(509) 633–0290

Sunbanks RV Resort & Marina
Banks Lake,
South Highway 155
Electric City 99123
(509) 633–3786

INCHELIUM
Rainbow Beach Resort at Twin Lakes
HC1 Box 146
Inchelium 99138
(509) 722–5901

METALINE FALLS
Washington Hotel
225 East Fifth Avenue
Metaline Falls 99153
(509) 446–4415

REPUBLIC
Fisherman's Cove Resort
1157 Fisherman's
Cove Road
Republic 99166
(509) 775–3641

K-Diamond-K Guest Ranch
404 Highway 21 South
Republic 99166
(509) 775–3536

Northern Motor Inn
852 South Clark Street
Republic 99166
(888) 801–1068

SOAP LAKE
Notaras Lodge
13 Canna Street
Soap Lake 98851
(509) 246–0462

SPOKANE
Cavanaugh's River Inn
700 North Division
Spokane 99204
(509) 326–5577

Marianna Stoltz House
Bed & Breakfast
427 East Indiana Avenue
Spokane 99204
(509) 483–4316

Waverly Place Bed &
Breakfast
709 West Waverly Place
Spokane 99204
(509) 328–1856

USK
The Hotel Usk
410 River Road
Usk 99180
(509) 445–1526

VALLEY
Silver Beach Resort
3323 Waitts Lake Road
Valley 99181
(509) 937–2811

**PLACES TO EAT IN
NORTHEAST WASHINGTON**

COLVILLE
Cafe al Mundo
100 South Main Street
Colville 99114
(509) 684–8092

Cookies Cafe
157 Oak Street
Colville 99114
(509) 684–8660

COULEE CITY
Fuller's Dry Falls Cafe
Junction of Highways 2
and 17
Coulee City 99115
(509) 632–5634

Steamboat Rock
Restaurant
420 West Main Street
Coulee City 99115
(509) 632–5452

CURLEW
Curlew Riverside
Restaurant
813 River Street
Curlew 99118
(509) 779–4813

DAVENPORT
Edna's Drive In
302 Morgan
Davenport 99122
(509) 725–1071

KETTLE FALLS
Sandy's Drive-Inn
1053 Highway 395 North
Kettle Falls 99141
(509) 738–6444

METALINE FALLS
Cathy's Cafe
221 East Fifth Avenue
Metaline Falls 99153
(509) 446–2447

Western Star Restaurant
202 North Highway 31
Metaline 99152
(509) 446–2105

Helpful Web Sites in Northeast Washington

Grand Coulee Dam Area
www.grandcouleedam.org

Experience Spokane
www.visitspokane.com

Republic-Curlew Area
www.ferrycountry.com

Kettle Range Conservation Group
www.kettlerange.org

NEWPORT
Grizzly Drive Inn
311 North Washington
Avenue
Newport 99156
(509) 447–3721

REPUBLIC
Blondie's Cafe
644 South Clark Street
Republic 99166
(509) 775–9992

Ike's Merchantile Cafe
15 North Clark Street
Republic 99166
(509) 775–2846

SOAP LAKE
Don's Restaurant
14 Canna Street
Soap Lake 98851
(509) 246–1217

SPOKANE
Lindeman's Restaurant
1235 South Grand
Boulevard
Spokane 99201
(509) 838–3000

The Onion Family
Restaurant
302 West Riverside
Spokane 99201
(509) 747–3852

Paprika Cafe
1228 South Grand
Boulevard
Spokane 99201
(509) 455–7545

Selected Visitor Information Centers

Grand Coulee Dam Area Visitor Information Center
306 Midway, Grand Coulee 99133
(800) 268–5332, (509) 633–3074

Spokane Area Convention & Visitors Bureau
801 West Riverside, Suite 301, Spokane 99201
(509) 747–3230

Republic Area Visitor Information Center
15 North Kean Street, P.O. Box 1024, Republic 99166
(509) 775–3387

Patsy Clark's Mansion
Restaurant
2208 West Second Avenue
Spokane 99204
(509) 838–8300

Steam Plant Grill
159 South Lincoln Street
Spokane 99204
(509) 777–3900

USK
X-Roads Cafe
Highways 20 and 211
Usk 99180
(509) 445–1515

VALLEY
Silver Beach Resort
Restaurant
3323 Waitts Lake Road
Valley 99181
(509) 937–2811

WILBUR
Alibi Tavern
4 Southwest Main Street
Wilbur 99185
(509) 647–2649

Billy Burger
804 Southeast Main Street
Wilbur 99185
(509) 647–5651

ALSO WORTH SEEING

Discovery Loop,
Curlew-Republic

Highland Heritage Loop,
Curlew

Selkirk International Loop,
North Pend Orielle County

Sherman Pass Scenic
Byway, Kettle Falls

Southeast Washington

Southeast Washington is a region of rolling hills and wide blue skies. Much of the terrain is covered with waving fields of dryland (unirrigated) wheat, offering endless variations of shapes, textures, and colors. The best way to explore this area is to get off the major highways and drive or bicycle along endless miles of farm roads that connect the area's small communities. Walking, bicycling, or sitting in a grassy park or meadow, you often will hear the melodious trill of a western meadowlark, catch sight of a soaring hawk, and smell the soil warmed in the sun.

Few corners of this fertile region have been left untouched by human enterprise, although the seasonal crops still depend on natural cycles of snow, rain, and sun. Hundreds of acres burst with new green shoots following spring rains or undulate tall and golden grains in the late summer sun. The lives of farm and ranch families are integrated with their land and the seasons. In early spring, huge eight-wheel-drive tractors comb the terrain for planting, pulling 20-foot-wide plows that raise spires of dust. In late summer, giant combines range in straight or curved rows to harvest wheat, lentils, and peas. Farmhouses and big old barns nestle in valleys surrounded by tall shade trees planted by previous generations.

The quiet towns of this region, devoted to serving the hardworking farm families, also welcome travelers. Walking down any main street, you'll see old brick buildings that once housed banks, stores, and fraternal organizations, many now empty and deserted. Tall grain elevators stand like sentinals next to rail depots. Many deserted rail depots throughout the region and the state have been, or are in the process of being, preserved and are coming to life again as local history museums and vibrant community art centers.

Stop at the local cafe (many towns have only one) where, for the price of a cup of coffee and a piece of homemade pie, you might hear stories of local history and gossip from fellow patrons eager to swap tales. The town cemetery, usually located on a nearby hilltop, is also a good place to learn about the community's past.

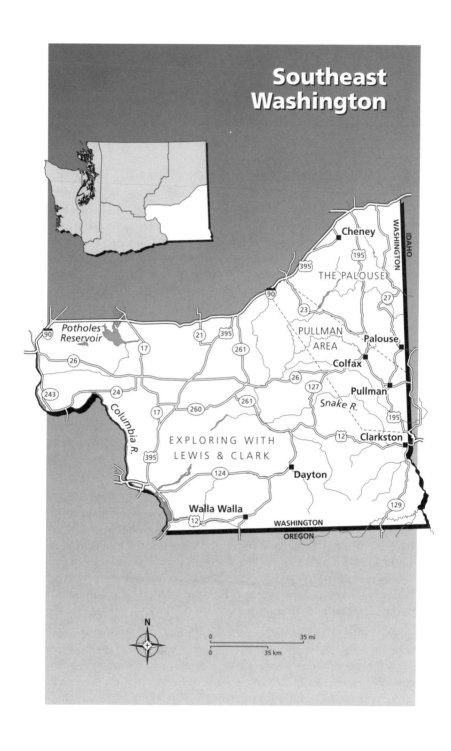

Southeast Washington

Cheney

THE PALOUSE

WASHINGTON

IDAHO

195

395

27

Potholes
Reservoir

90

21

495

PULLMAN
AREA

Palouse

90

23

17

261

Colfax

26

127

26

Pullman

195

Snake R.

243

24

17

260

261

Clarkston

12

Columbia R.

395

EXPLORING WITH
LEWIS & CLARK

124

Dayton

129

Walla Walla

12

WASHINGTON

OREGON

N

0   35 mi

0   35 km

The Palouse

Palouse is derived from the French word *pelouse,* meaning "green lawn," an appropriate name for one of the most fertile grain-growing regions in the world. The Appaloosa, a breed of horses distinguished by its spotted coat and gentle disposition, is a descendant of early horses used by the Native people of the Palouse.

Although most of this region is now farmed, there are still areas where the original Palouse environment is preserved. Chief of these is the **Turnbull National Wildlife Refuge** located at South 26010 Smith Road (509–235–4723) south of Spokane on the Cheney-Plaza Road. The refuge includes miles of lakes and marshes that attract a wide variety of wildlife. Generations before pioneers arrived, the Spokane tribe cherished this natural garden for its abundant roots and herbs, such as blue camas, wild onion, and kinnikinnick. Migrating and nesting water birds thrive in the rich wetlands.

Early farmers tried to drain these marsh areas but found the soil poor. Rescued from development in the 1920s, the area was set aside as a wildlife preserve in 1937. Now visitors to Turnbull can bicycle, walk, or drive on a 5-mile gravel loop road to experience the area's original beauty. Signs along the Pine Creek Trail help acquaint you with the area's background and natural history. A wooden boardwalk over shallow Black Horse Lake allows close-up viewing.

Heading south on Rock Lake Road, watch the landscape change from rocky pine-covered meadows to rolling wheat farms. The terrain changes again around **Rock Lake,** a quiet expanse of water surrounded by basalt outcroppings. This area was the home of Chief Kamiaken of the Yakama Indian Nation. Along the lake's southeast shore, you can see the **Milwaukee Road Corridor,** a railroad line until 1980, now converted to a public trail. This trail system, known as the Iron Horse Trail State Park west of the Columbia River, stretches from King County

SOUTHEAST WASHINGTON'S TOP HITS
Turnbull National Wildlife Refuge, Cheney
Rock Lake, Cheney
Kamiak Butte County Park, Palouse
Joseph's Flour, Oakesdale
Touch O'Country B&B, Tekoa
Bishop's U-Pick Orchard, Garfield
New Morning Glass Studio, Palouse
Boomerang Newspaper and Printing Museum, Palouse
Ferdinands Ice Cream Parlor, Pullman
Three Forks Pioneer Village Museum, Pullman
Perkins House, Pullman
Appaloosa Horse Club and Museum, Moscow
Premier Alpacas Ranch & Guest House, Uniontown
Dayton Depot, Dayton
Purple House Bed and Breakfast, Dayton
Weinhard Hotel, Dayton
Heritage Square, Walla Walla
Fort Walla Walla Museum Complex, Walla Walla
Whitman Mission National Historic Site, Walla Walla

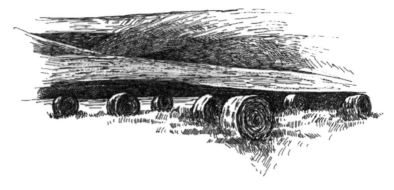

Palouse Fields

near Seattle across the Cascade Mountains and east to the Idaho border. The popular trail is used by hikers, bicyclists, equestrians, and even wagon trains. Such trails are a great way to experience the environment, removed from the impacts of motor traffic. Maps showing access points, and permits to use the trail (required east of the Columbia River), are available from the Washington Department of Natural Resources at 2211 Airport Road, Ellensburg 98926-9351 (800–527–3305). The corridor is open from June 15 to the end of September.

After traveling through the rolling hills of the Palouse, you can also enjoy seeing the region from two towering buttes that offer panoramic views of the quilted landscape. **Kamiak Butte County Park,** named for Chief Kamiaken, is a 3,650-foot-tall island of pine, fir, and larch surrounded by

Appaloosa Horse Museum

*F*or a closer look at the history surrounding the Palouse's namesake horse, head east from Pullman on Highway 8 to the Appaloosa Horse Club and Museum (2720 West Pullman Road; 208–882–5578; www. appaloosa.com). Straddling the state line, but technically in Moscow, Idaho, the museum explores the Nez Perce and Palouse tribes' connection with the breed with exhibits of Native

American artifacts. Other exhibits explore the Appaloosa's Asian and European roots, and there's a saddle collection, Western art, and Western tack and clothing on display. During the summer, you can see the horses in their fenced pasture. The museum is open Tuesday through Friday, from 10:00 A.M. to 5:00 P.M., year-round, and on summer Saturdays from 10:00 A.M. to 4:00 P.M.

FAVORITE ATTRACTIONS

Fort Walla Walla Museum Complex

Dayton Depot, Dayton

Appaloosa Horse Museum

Whitman Mission National Historic Site

Palouse Falls

wheat fields. The butte is 5 miles southeast of the town of Palouse near the Idaho border. The 3$^1/_2$-mile Pine Ridge Trail through the forest takes you on a self-guided nature walk to the top of the butte and back. The park has ten campsites, with campfire pits and cooking grills. Water is available May through October, but there is no electricity or showers. Picnic tables and three shelters with electricity, water, and barbeque make this a great spot for an impromptu outdoor feast. There is also an amphitheater for evening programs on local and natural history (beginning at 8:30 P.M., from late June through August). For current information contact Whitman County Parks, North 310 Main, Colfax 99111, or call (509) 397–6238.

Steptoe Butte, 15 miles north of Colfax, is, at 3,612 feet, the highest point in the region and a National Natural Landmark. Drive the road that spirals four times around the butte to the top to enjoy panoramic views of the Palouse's rolling fields and low hills as well as the distant Blue Mountains and Bitterroot Mountains. At the base you'll find a pleasant picnic area in an old apple orchard planted by one of the area's early homesteaders. In the 1880s another early entrepreneur operated a roadhouse at the bottom of the butte and a hotel at the top, which burned down in 1896.

Oakesdale, located a few miles north of Steptoe Butte, is home to *Joseph's Flour,* a processor of high-quality organic grain flour. Joseph Barron's father, J. C. Barron, owned and ran the Oakesdale flour mill starting in 1907, and Joseph spent most of his long life in various mill jobs. The huge timber-frame structure, which was moved piece by piece from Illinois in 1889, still contains the original milling and sifting equipment, which dates from the nineteenth century. Grain descended a labyrinth of perfectly fitted wooden chutes, through various processes on each of the building's four stories, to finish as flour on the ground floor. A central steam engine drove the complex network of belts and shafts powering conveyers, grinders, and sifters. The mill was used to produce flour until 1939 and continued as a grain cleaning and storage facility until the 1960s. Call the Oakesdale City Hall, (509) 285–4020, to inquire about tours that may be scheduled.

Travel northwest on Highway 27 from Oakesdale to reach the village of Tekoa, population 826. There you will find *Touch O'Country Bed and Breakfast* (509–284–5183), a Victorian farmhouse–style home built in 1900. Innkeeper Mary Heitt, who has lived in the house for more than thirty-five years, offers homey accommodations in the two upstairs

Joseph's Flour

rooms, with shared bath down the hall. An old-fashioned front porch welcomes travelers and offers a nostalgic yesteryears feeling.

Located south of Tekoa in Garfield (population 641), the **R.C. McCroskey House** at 803 North Fourth Street (509–635–1459) is a classical Revival-style Victorian mansion constructed in 1898. Owner Donna Gwinn has restored the century-old home to its original grandeur. Call ahead to inquire if tours of the historic house are currently offered.

Bishop's U-**Pick Orchard** (509–635–1276; www.bishop-orchard.com), in Garfield at Eighth and Adams Streets (follow Spokane Street west past Garfield's city park), offers a wealth of apples from mid-September through the end of October. People come from miles around to make their own fresh juice on Steven Bishop's four handmade oak cider presses, patterned after the ones his great-grandfather used when he homesteaded in Garfield.

South of Garfield is the town of **Palouse,** once a bustling commercial center supplying gold mining and logging camps in Idaho. The town's main street is lined with splendid old brick buildings, many now in the process of being renovated. Palouse's Main Street historic district is listed on the National Register of Historic Places. One old storefront now houses the **Boomerang Newspaper and Printing Museum,** a half block east of the town's only street light at 110 East Main Street.

The museum, named after the town's first (and current) newspaper, features old presses and other printing equipment dating from the late 1800s. Call Janet Barstow, editor of the *Boomerang Newspaper* at (509) 878–1742 for current hours.

Stop in at 110 South Bridge Street in the historic Bank Building in Palouse to visit **New Morning Glass Studio** (866–888–8425), a working glassblowers' shop where artists Jack Dobler and Mary Kernan use the old European tradition of mouth-blowing to craft goblets, vases, and other innovative objects. It's fascinating to watch the highly physical yet delicate process of the glass taking shape, and the finished works, signed by the artists, are available for purchase in the adjacent gallery. The studio is open Tuesday through Saturday from 10:00 A.M.

After visiting the glass studio, you can browse at **The Potpourri** located at 100 East Main Street (509–878–2171) for a splendid selection of Victorian gift items and then pop into **The Bunkhouse Antiques** at 108 North Bridge Street (509–878–1240) to meet owner Sue Akin and see her selection of antiques and collectibles. Cap off your tour of Palouse by stopping at **Sullivan's Restaurant** on Main Street (509–878–2171) for a tasty lunch or dinner (breakfast is served all day as well); open daily except Monday beginning at 11:00 A.M.

Bagels, English Muffins, Lentil or Split Pea Soup, Anyone?

In the morning I love a toasted bagel or English muffin with crunchy peanut butter topped with sprinkles of cinnamon and sugar. I also love steaming hot lentil or split pea soup for lunch. The ingredients for these tasty foods—wheat, lentils, and peas—are major crops grown in the Palouse region. After harvest they are barged about 200 miles down the Snake River from the Clarkston-Lewiston area to Pasco, passing through the scenic 2,000-foot-deep Snake River Canyon and negotiating through locks at Lower Granite Dam, Little Goose Dam, Lower Monumental Dam, and Ice Harbor Dam. At Pasco the large barges, pushed by fat tugboats, then enter the wide Columbia River and travel another 200 miles downriver passing The Dalles, Maryhill, Hood River, Cascade Locks, North Bonneville, Washougal, and Camas and detouring onto the Willamette River at the Portland-Vancouver area. Here the wheat, lentils, and peas are loaded onto huge transport ships at the Port of Portland. These vessels travel another 100 miles downriver on the Columbia River to Astoria and then out onto the Pacific Ocean for journeys to ports far and wide. Bagels, English muffins, lentil or split pea soup, anyone?

Pullman Area

Pullman is the Palouse region's largest city and a bustling mixture of agricultural businesses and student life. It is home to Washington State University (WSU, affectionately called *Wazzu*), which emphasizes agricultural sciences. Contact the Pullman Visitor Information Center (415 North Grand Avenue, Pullman 99163; 800–365–6948 or 509–334–3565) to receive the current Visitor Guide.

For a cozy bed-and-breakfast experience, contact Mary Lee and Bruce Tenwick at **Country Bed & Breakfast** located five miles south of town at 2701 Staley Road, Pullman 99163 (509–334–4453). The couple offers four comfortable guest rooms in their country house, one fifth-wheel suite just beyond the patio, and The Play Room, a separate cottage-suite that comes with a pool table, three antique beds, kitchenette, and private bath.

Also located close to Pullman, just across the nearby Idaho border, guests find two elegant suites at **Peacock Hill Bed & Breakfast** (1015 Joyce Road, Moscow, Idaho 83834; 208–882–1423). Moscow is located 8 miles east of Pullman, and the bed-and-breakfast is located 4 miles north of Moscow on a hill overlooking the rolling Palouse country. Here innkeeper Judi Elgar and resident Saint Bernard Jack Daniels welcome travelers to this scenic farm and ranch region. The innkeeper's large garden is filled with vegetables, herbs, and flowers. The views of the rolling countryside and distant hills are superb from the outside decks and grounds. For further information and photos check the Web site, www.users.moscow.com/peacock.

Love Those Lentils

Although the Palouse is widely known as wheat country, Pullman and the surrounding area also happen to be the U.S. leaders in lentil production. Up to 98 percent of the nation's lentils are harvested annually from farms hereabouts, totaling more than 135 million pounds of the culinarily versatile legumes. Just how versatile is displayed each year at the **National Lentil Festival,** held in Pullman's Reany Park in late August, where the main event is a cook-off featuring lentils as ingredients in everything from pizza and enchiladas to cake and cookies. The festivities kick off with the Tase T. Lentil 5Kfun Run. A microbrew tasting, live musical entertainment, and arts and crafts fair round out the day. For current information and a schedule of events, contact the Pullman Visitor Information Center at (800) 365–6948.

WSU has a splendid *Museum of Anthropology* featuring displays on human evolution and on the development of language and culture—and on the Northwest's mysterious Sasquatch. The museum is open weekdays during the school year (Monday to Thursday from 9:00 A.M. to 4:00 P.M., Friday from 9:00 A.M. to 3:00 P.M.). Tours can be scheduled two weeks in advance by calling (509) 335–3441. Art lovers can enjoy the University's *Museum of Art,* in the Fine Arts Center at the corner of Stadium Way and Farm Way. The gallery offers eleven changing exhibitions a year, featuring past and contemporary international, regional, and student artists working in painting, sculpture, photography, and architecture. There is something for every taste. The gallery is open daily from 10:00 A.M. to 4:00 P.M., and on Thursday until 9:00 P.M.

After you've worked up an appetite from museum touring, you'll want to stop at *Ferdinands* (509–335–2141), a campus ice-cream parlor named after the friendly, flower-sniffing bull. On the walls are quotations by author Munro Leaf and illustrations by Robert Lawson, from the classic book about Ferdinand beloved by generations of children. Ferdinands sells WSU's own Cougar brand of high-quality dairy products (such as the award-winning Cougar Gold cheese), produced by the Departments of Food Science and Human Nutrition of the College of Agriculture and Home Economics. Ferdinands is located behind the Human Nutrition building, next to the tennis courts on South Fairway Lane. Its hours are 9:30 A.M. to 4:30 P.M. weekdays and on special event weekends.

For a step back in time to the Old West, visit the *Three Forks Pioneer Village Museum,* located about 4 miles north of Pullman. This re-created

Rose Creek Preserve

A few miles northwest of Pullman and Albion is the Nature Conservancy's **Rose Creek Preserve.** Surrounded by rolling wheat fields, the preserve constitutes twenty-two acres of rare habitat, including black hawthorn, quaking aspen, and cow parsnip, as well as the rolling farmland of Smoot Hill. Donated by a local family in 1966, the land had been overgrazed but was allowed to recover to its natural state. It is now home to more than 250 plant species, more than 100 species of birds, and ample wildlife, including porcupine, coyote, and white-tailed deer. To get there from Pullman, head north on Route 27 and turn left on the Albion-Pullman Road. In Albion, turn right on Main Street, which becomes Old Albion Road (gravel), and proceed 2.8 miles. Turn left on Four Mile Road and continue bearing left for half a mile to the preserve, which is on the right.

TOP ANNUAL EVENTS IN SOUTHEAST WASHINGTON

Dogwood Festival,
Clarkston, throughout April;
(208) 799–2243

Balloon Stampede,
Walla Walla, early May;
(509) 525–0850

Muzzle Loader
Rendezvous, Asotin, early
May; (509) 758–4342

Dayton Days, Dayton, late
May; (800) 882–6299

Slippery Gulch Days &
Rodeo, Tekoa, late June;
(509) 284–3861

Sweet Onion Festival,
Walla Walla, mid-July;
(509) 525–0850

National Lentil Festival,
Pullman, mid-August;
(800) 365–6948

Lewis & Clark Days,
Clarkston, late August;
(800) 933–2128

Dayton Depot Festival,
Dayton, mid-September,
(800) 882–6299

Wings Over Walla Walla
Air Show, Walla Walla, early
October; (509) 527–3224

town, assembled during the past three decades by farmer Roger Rossebo, has a general store, barber shop, blacksmith's shop, jail, and hardware store, displaying thousands of antiques dating from the 1800s, including a piano shipped around Cape Horn, a pioneer kitchen, and a schoolhouse. The museum is open by appointment from May to September. There is a small fee. Call (509) 332–3889 for reservations and directions.

In *Colfax,* the Whitman County seat along the banks of the Palouse River, you could stop to see the splendid *Perkins House* at 623 North Perkins Street. The circa 1884 mansion listed on the National Register of Historic Places was built by city founder James Perkins, who established his fortune by constructing the region's first sawmill. It is open for tours from 1:00 to 5:00 P.M., Thursday and Sunday, from June to September. An old-fashioned ice-cream social is held at the mansion the last Sunday in June. For current information contact the Colfax Visitor Information Center, P.O. Box 166, Colfax 99111; (509) 397–3712.

The most unusual attraction in Colfax is indisputedly the *Codger Pole,* the world's largest chain-saw carving at 65 feet. The pole commemorates a grudge match played between the Colfax football team and its St. John rivals, wherein Colfax attained the victory that was snatched from it a quarter of a century earlier. The likenesses of the team members are carved on the pole, which occupies a prominent spot on John Crawford Boulevard, just off Main Street.

To bed down in the ponderosa pine and farm country, folks can call the Gilchrest family at *Union Creek Ranch,* located a few miles southwest via Highway 195 at 2501 Upper Union Flat Road, Colfax 99111 (509–397–3292). Penny and Jerry Gilchrest and son, Terry, welcome guests to their 2,200-acre ranch in the pines. Eight guest rooms in the main ranch house share three full baths, a one-acre fishing pond stocked with rainbow trout, a petting zoo of small farm animals, and stalls for your horses. "We have lots of trails for folks to ride with their own horses," says Penny. The family grows winter and spring wheat and barley, and they also grow the famous peas that come from this section of Washington State. "Folks often like to see the farm machinery, too," says Jerry. The kids love the petting zoo, which contains small horses, goats, sheep, and calves as well as a gaggle of geese, ducks, rabbits, and turkeys. Penny serves a hearty country breakfast of bacon, ham, eggs, and hash browns along with fresh fruit, juices, homemade cinnamon rolls, and her delicious apple crisp tortillas.

If you are traveling farther south via Highway 195 from Pullman, you can check with Leslee and Dale Miller at *Premier Alpacas Ranch & Guest House* (401 South Railroad Avenue, Uniontown 99179; 509–229–3655; www.premieralpacas.com). The remodeled guest bunkhouse contains sleeping quarters for four, with cozy quilts and comforters, and comes with a spiral staircase to the sleeping loft, a snack kitchen, a sofa bed on the main level, and a cheery woodstove. The couple raises alpacas, smaller cousins to the taller llama. "The alpacas stand about 36 inches in height and come in twenty-two different colors," says Leslee. This is a place to relax into farm and ranch time. An indoor lap pool, located in a sunroom at the main house, is available for guests to use to work out the kinks. Leslee serves a generous ranch breakfast of, perhaps, oven-baked French toast with Gran Marnier sauce or her special frittata made with fresh farm eggs, spinach, potatoes, roasted red peppers, and Parmesan cheese.

Another splendid option is to contact the innkeepers at *The Churchyard Inn Bed & Breakfast* (206 St. Boniface Street, Uniontown 99179; 509–229–3200). Guests find comfy bed-and-breakfast accommodations in the European Flemish–style convent (circa 1905) that once housed a group of Catholic nuns. The house and its interior were completely renovated including the fine hand-detailed woodwork, moldings, and doors of red fir; the impressive staircases and spacious hallways; and the seven bedrooms and several balconies. The inn is located next to historic Saint Boniface Catholic Church (circa 1904), one of the first such churches in the region.

The first Sunday in March brings the annual benefit *Sausage Feed* (since 1948 the men of Uniontown have made sausage from a renowned secret recipe). An old-fashioned *Threshing Bee* takes place in early September. Public golf links are located in nearby Lewiston and in Clarkston. For good eats ask about *Eleanor's Place,* a local saloon on Main Street (509–229–3389) in Uniontown that offers a good selection of microbrews and is reported to serve the best hamburgers on the Palouse. Located about 15 miles south of Uniontown in

Lewiston, Idaho, *Jonathan's Restaurant* at 1516 Main Street (208–746–3438) offers fine dining in a pleasant setting. Located about the same distance north, *Red Door Restaurant* at 215 South Main Street (208–882–7830) in Moscow, Idaho, also offers great dining. Also check out the newly opened *Sage Bakery & Deli* on Main Street in Uniontown, which offers crusty rustic breads as well as tasty pastries, coffee drinks, and deli fare (800–933–2128).

Exploring with Lewis & Clark

South of Pullman at the confluence of the Snake and Clearwater Rivers, you can visit *Clarkston* and, across the Snake River, *Lewiston,* Idaho. These twin cities are the embarking point for adventures at Hells Gate State Park, the Nez Perce Reservation, and boat or raft tours through Hells Canyon, the deepest river gorge in North America. Contact the Clarkston Chamber of Commerce at (800) 933–2128 or (509) 758–7712 for information on river trips, extensive bike paths, parks, and historical information on the levees that line both sides of the river. Innkeeper Doreen Bridgmount, who hails from England, fell in love with the area and now welcomes travelers to *Highland House Bed & Breakfast,* located at 707 Highland Street in Clarkston (509–758–3126). She can also direct you to the site of the community-developed *Lewis & Clark Expedition Timeline,* etched and painted in the pavement at Hells Canyon Marina, 1550 Port Drive. The nearly block long timeline illustrates key events from the Corps of Discovery's journey across the western half of the United States including canoeing down sections of the nearby Snake River and the Columbia River on their way to the Pacific Ocean. Highway 12 from Lewiston and Clarkston west toward Pomeroy and Dayton roughly parallels the party's return journey in 1806. For a state-by-state listing of Signature Events, happenings, and current activities celebrating the *Lewis & Clark Bicentennial,* browse www.lewisandclark200.org.

From Clarkston take Highway 12 west and stop in Pataha to see the historic *Pataha Flour Mill* (509–843–3799). Then, pull into the small community of Pomeroy where you're now roughly parallel to the historic Lewis & Clark Trail of 1806. Look for the circa 1916 Seeley building at 67 Seventh Street, which housed an early vaudeville theater. Across the street, you can inspect the progress being made on the renovation of the *Historic Hotel Revere* at the corner of Main and Seventh Streets.

At 99 Seventh Street peek into the windows at *Lost Highway Museum* to see a collection of vintage neon signs and nostalgic memorabilia from America's back roads. Park 1 block over on Columbia Street, where you'll see colorful flowerbeds planted down the center of the street where the train tracks once ran. Browse along Main Street and poke into inviting shops such as *Three Forks Art Gallery,* 804 Main Street; *Mangaboos Antiques,* 864 Main Street; *The Metro Antiques,* 847 Main Street; *Victorian Rose & Collectibles,* 741 Main Street; and *Pomeroy Pharmacy & Gifts,* 764 Main Street. Detour into eclectic *Meyer's Hardware,* 796 Main Street (509–843–3721), for coffee and espresso drinks.

Stop by *Pomeroy City Park* off Fifteenth Street to see a plaque that designates where the Lewis & Clark Corps of Discovery party camped in 1806 on their return trip to the east. You can also bed down in Pomeroy, but in a more comfy style, by checking on guest rooms at *The Picket Porch Bed & Breakfast* located at 266 Fourteenth Street (509–843–1150). If you're traveling RV-style and want hookups, call *The Last Resort RV Park,* located at 2005 Tucannon Road (509–843–1556) about 10 miles south of Pomeroy in the scenic Umatilla National Forest. The Forest Service ranger station at 71 West Main Street (509–843–1891) just west of Pomeroy can supply maps and information about forest camping, hiking, and fishing (including fly-fishing) along the Tucannon River.

The town of *Dayton* is another historic and charming community. When Lewis and Clark explored the region on their return trip in 1806, what is now Dayton's main street served as a racetrack for Native tribes who camped in the area. First homesteaded by cattle ranchers in 1859, grain farming took over within a few years. Dayton was also a stagecoach stop between Walla Walla and Lewiston. Logs from the Blue Mountains traveled down to the town mill by an 18-mile flume. By 1880 Dayton had become the Columbia County seat.

To see the *Dayton Depot,* the oldest existing railway station in the state, turn west from Main Street onto Commercial. The depot is open from 10:00 A.M. to 5:00 P.M., Tuesday through Saturday, year-round. For more information on self-guided historic walking tours and the lively *Dayton's Depot Days Festival* in mid-September, call the Dayton Visitor Information Center at (509) 382–4825 and browse the Web site at www.historicdayton.com.

The *Purple House Bed and Breakfast* (415 East Clay Street, Dayton 99328; 509–382–3159), built in 1882 by a pioneer physician and philanthropist, is one of Dayton's finest homes. Present owner Christine Williscroft has preserved the house's gracious past while adding her own European flair. Williscroft offers dinner by arrangement for her in-house guests, four charming rooms, a guest library, a lovely parlor, and a heated outdoor pool.

Just for fun stop by *Dingles of Dayton* located at 179 East Main Street (509–382–2581). In this old-fashioned general store, you'll find everything from nuts and bolts, nails and screws, and plumbing supplies, to teddy bears, coloring books, crystal glassware, and fishing rods. "If you can't find it at Dingles, you don't need it," proclaims the store motto.

If exploring makes you thirsty, stop at the *Elk Drug Store* at 270 Main Street to order milkshakes and sodas from an old-fashioned soda fountain. Step back in time in grand style at the circa 1889 *Weinhard Hotel* (235 East Main Street, Dayton 99328; 509–382–4032; www.weinhard.com), restored in a Victorian motif with 14-foot-high ceilings, elaborate antiques, and a rooftop garden. All fifteen rooms have private baths and antique furniture. Enjoy fine Italian specialties at Weinhard's Cafe located in the same building (509–382–1681). The cafe is open Wednesday through Sunday for lunch and dinner; breakfast is served on weekends only. For gourmet fare and great desserts in a comfortable setting, try the popular *Patit Creek Restaurant* at 725 East Dayton Avenue, on Highway 12 at the north end of town (509–382–2625). For casual eats try *Woodshed Bar & Grill,* 250 East Main Street (509–382–2004), for good pub fare with families welcomed and *Panhandlers Pizza & Pasta,* 400 West Main Street (509–382–4160), open daily from 7:00 A.M. to 8:00 P.M. and offering good breakfasts as well as steaks, burgers, salads, and tasty desserts. For espresso, cinnamon rolls, soups, and sandwiches, don't miss *Patit Valley Products Cafe* at 232 East Main Street (509–382–1998).

To rub shoulders with Dayton folks, check out what's playing at the restored circa 1920s *Liberty Theater* at 342 East Main Street (509–382–1380; www.libertytheater.org). Recent local theater productions included *Music Man, Steel Magnolias,* and *Oklahoma!*

Dayton is the access point for the Blue Mountains in the Umatilla National Forest, which includes the *Wenaha-Tucannon Wilderness,* an area of steep ridges, talus slopes, and tablelands accessible only by backcountry trails. Wildlife includes Rocky Mountain elk, white-tailed and mule deer, bighorn sheep, black bear, cougar, and bobcat. For information about backcountry camping and hiking, call the Pomeroy Ranger Station at (509) 843–1891. During the winter months, ski buffs enjoy *Ski Bluewood* (509–382–4725; www.bluewood.com) in the Blue Mountains, 22 miles southeast of Dayton. Its Skyline Express chair provides a vertical rise of 1,125 feet and more than twenty downhill runs. There are also runs for beginning and intermediate skiers.

Palouse Falls, 30 miles north of Dayton, is a spectacular waterfall offering a glimpse of what the many river canyons in the area looked like before most were dammed. The falls tumble 198 feet over basalt-column cliffs, surrounded by grass- and sage-covered hills. On your way north to the falls via Highway 261, those who love fly-fishing may want to pause in the small community of Starbuck to hunker down at **Darver Tackle Shop** on Main Street (509–399–2015). Fly-fishing gurus tie flies, tell stories, and offer gourmet flies for sale in this small shop that draws folks from all over the region. From here you cross the Snake River via a bridge rather than on the old Lyons Ferry that once carried vehicles across, then proceed about 7 miles to Palouse Falls State Park. Although this park offers only ten primitive campsites, nearby **Lyons Ferry State Park** on the Snake River offers fifty standard campsites with no hookups, a trailer dump station, and boat launch facilities (www.parks.wa.gov for current information and fees).

Palouse Falls

To the south, Walla Walla Valley is known primarily for fertile fields of grain, but since the late 1980s the valley also hosts some twenty wineries and large vineyards with such gourmet grapes as merlot, cabernet sauvignon, and syrah harvested each year. Tasting rooms abound in the valley. For lists and maps check with the Visitors Information Center in Walla Walla located at 29 East Sumach Street (509–525–0850 or 877–998–4748; www.wallawalla.com). You can also collect self-guided walking tour maps for the nostalgic downtown area and helpful information about the bustling arts scene in this farm and college town. The **Walla Walla Foundry** (509–522–2114) specializes in bronze but also produces works in gold, silver, and aluminum. You can visit more than twenty eclectic art galleries here and join the jazzy **ArtWalla** arts festival the last week of June. At **Whitman College** stroll the campus and its lovely grounds, and check with the **Harper Joy Theater** (509–527–5180; www.whitman.edu) for college plays and musical productions.

Downtown, after browsing a gaggle of art galleries, gift shops, historic buildings, and antiques shops that range along Main Street, join the locals and relax in **Heritage Square,** nestled in the heart of town. On one side of the square, you'll see a mural of nineteenth-century downtown Walla Walla. On the opposite wall is the 1902 Odd Fellows building facade. The park also has playground equipment, a picnic area, and rest rooms. Or, for a pleasant lunch on a sunny day, you can find an outdoor table under the striped awning at **Merchants Ltd.,** 21 East Main Street (509–525–0900), which also offers espresso, a take-out deli, freshly baked pastries, and regional wines. At **Grapefields,** 4 East Main Street (509–522–0345), you can order such tasty fare as quiche, homemade soup, a fresh salad, and bruschetta, and you can also sample local wines.

Walla Walla is home to several inviting bed-and-breakfast inns and guest ranches. The circa 1909 Craftsman-style **Green Gables Inn Bed and Breakfast** (922 Bonsella, Walla Walla 99362; 509–525–5501; www.greengablesinn.com) has served as a family home, a residence for nurses, and most recently renovated by Jim and Margaret Buchan with warm colors, handsome woodwork, splendid window treatments, and fine period antiques. Five guest rooms offer elegant and comfortable havens with private baths. Two of the rooms have private outside decks. A separate Carriage House Cottage sleeps four and comes equipped with a full kitchen.

For a back-to-nature experience just a short drive from town, call the innkeepers at **Mill Creek Inn Bed & Breakfast,** (509) 522–1234; www.millcreekbb.com. The hundred-year-old farmhouse is located at Route 4, Box 251 Mill Creek Road, Walla Walla 99362. On the extensive grounds filled with trees and flowers, travelers find a variety of pleasant country accommodations, including the Bunkhouse Cottage, Chicken House Cottage, Summer Kitchen Cottage, and Cottonwood Suite. The rooms are filled with light from wide expanses of windows and French doors and come with cozy sitting places and with comfortable beds equipped with down comforters and lovely linens.

For those who want to get even farther away from civilization, call the innkeepers at *Top of the Mountain Retreat* located at 9052 Mill Creek Road (509–529–4288; www.mountainretreats.com). You can even bring your horses. The retreat sits on 3,000 acres in the Strawberry Canyon area just a few miles from Walla Walla. In the Strawberry Canyon Lodge folks find a large master suite, two additional bedrooms, a fully equipped kitchen, and, on the adjoining patio, a soothing hot tub. If you need to get completely away from civilization, ask about the three secluded Mountain Top Cabins located at a crisp fresh-air elevation of 3,800 feet next to the Umatilla National Forest. The cabins come with bed and bath linens, cozy sitting areas, wood stoves, kitchenettes with eating and cooking utensils, and patio furniture. *Note:* Those who have four-wheel-drive vehicles can best reach the cabins. Facilities at the retreat include a corral for horses, horseback riding trails, walking and hiking trails, bird-watching, wildlife-watching, and fishing in nearby Mill Creek. For an extra cost, the staff can help guests who bring their horses with guided trail rides, evening steak-fry rides, and morning breakfast rides.

You don't have a horse and you don't relish eating at the top of a mountain? Not to worry—you can find great eateries in Walla Walla. Check out *Jacobi's Cafe* (416 North Second Street; 509–525–2677) in the historic train depot; *The Homestead* (1528 Isaacs Street; 509–522–0345)

Country-Western Music & Eastern Washington Go Together

While driving the highways and byways of the eastern section of the state, you'll most likely hear Country-Western singers and their tunes when you click on the radio and cruise the stations. It comes with the territory. Here are some favorite titles:

"Easy on the Eyes, Hard on the Heart"

"Let's Take It One Step at a Time"

"My Heart Has a History of Lettin' Go"

"I'm Old Enough to Know Better but Still Too Young to Care"

"All My Exes Live in Texas"

"Love Gets Me Every Time"

"Prop Me Up Beside the Juke Box When I Die"

for lunch, dinner, and Sunday breakfast; *Cookie Tree Bakery & Cafe* (23 South Spokane Street; 509–522–4826) for homemade sandwiches, espresso, cookies, and pastries; *Mill Creek Brew Pub & Restaurant* (11 South Palouse Street; 509–522–2440) for good pub food and regional ales; and *Pastime Cafe* (215 West Main Street; 509–525–0873) for Italian and American fare that folks in the Walla Walla area have enjoyed since 1927.

Southwest of town is the splendid *Fort Walla Walla Museum Complex* (509–525–7703; www.fortwallawallamuseum.org) located at 755 Myra Road on the grounds of Fort Walla Walla Park. The museum complex includes a re-created pioneer village with fourteen historic log buildings filled with antique household items and settlers' tools. There are also six large museum buildings with additional displays of pioneer life, equipment from horse-farming days, and railroad equipment. The historical complex is open daily from 10:00 A.M. to 5:00 P.M., from April to October. Nominal admission fees help maintain and support museum development.

Seven miles west of town is the *Whitman Mission National Historic Site* (509–522–6360; www.nps.gov/whmi), which commemorates the mission established there by Marcus and Narcissa Whitman in the early 1800s. Museum displays and an interpretive trail on the mission grounds describe the history of the region and bring to life activities in the Walla Walla Valley between 1836 and 1847, when waves of settlers stopped at the mission on their trek along the Oregon Trail. Crossing the Blue Mountains into what is now Washington State was one of the last major challenges of the journey west. The settlers found rest and care at Whitman Mansion. The large influx of settlers and the devastating epidemics spread to Native people created conflicts with the local Cayuse tribe, resulting in the missionaries' tragic deaths. For a panoramic view of the grounds, walk through the small grove of trees, past the tepee, and up the path to the nearby hilltop monument. Although the original buildings did not survive the years, their locations are outlined on the grounds. Regularly scheduled pioneer demonstrations and films supplement the artifacts and museum displays. The visitors center is open daily from 8:00 A.M. to 6:00 P.M. in summer and 8:00 A.M. to 4:30 P.M. in winter.

CLARKSTON
Best Western Rivertree Inn
1257 Bridge Street
Clarkston 99403
(509) 758–9551

Highland House Bed &
Breakfast
707 Highland Street
Clarkston 99403
(509) 758–3126

DAYTON
The Purple House Bed
& Breakfast
415 East Clay Street
Dayton 99328
(800) 486–2574
(590) 382–3159

The Weinhard Hotel
235 East Main Street
Dayton 99328
(509) 382–4032

POMEROY
The Picket Porch
Bed & Breakfast
266 Fourteenth Street
Pomeroy 99347

PULLMAN
Country Bed & Breakfast
Route 2 Box 666
Pullman 99163
(509) 334–4453

Hawthorne Inn & Suites
928 Northwest Olson
Pullman 99163
(509) 332–0928

Paradise Creek Quality Inn
Southeast 1050 Bishop
Boulevard
Pullman 99163
(509) 332–0500

TEKOA
Touch O'Country Bed
and Breakfast
218 South Broadway
Tekoa 99033
(509) 284–5183

UNIONTOWN
Premier Alpacas Ranch &
Guest House
401 South Railroad Avenue
Uniontown 99179
(509) 229–3655

WALLA WALLA
Green Gables Inn Bed &
Breakfast
922 Bonsella Street
Walla Walla 99362
(509) 525–5501

Inn at Blackberry Creek
Bed & Breakfast
1126 Pleasant Street
Walla Walla 99362
(509) 520–7372

Nendel's Whitman
Motor Inn
107 North Second Street
Walla Walla 99362
(509) 525–2200

CLARKSTON-LEWISTON
Bogey's Restaurant at
Quality Inn
700 Port Drive
Clarkston 99403
(509) 758–9500

Jonathan's Restaurant
1516 Main Street
Lewiston, ID 83501
(208) 746–3438

The Way Back Cafe
2138 Thirteenth Avenue
Lewiston, ID 83501
(208) 743–2396

Helpful Web Sites in Southeast Washington

Historic Dayton
www.historicdayton.com

Walla Walla Valley Visitor Information
www.wallawalla.com

Welcome to Pullman-Moscow
www.pullman-wa.com/
www.moscowchamber.com

Lewis & Clark Bicentennial
www.lewisandclark200.org

COLFAX
Colfax Coffee Shop
212 North Main Street
Colfax 99111
(509) 397-3572

DAYTON
Weinhard Cafe
235 East Main Street
Dayton 99328
(509) 382-1681

Patit Creek Restaurant
725 East Dayton Avenue
Dayton 99328
(509) 382-2625

Patit Valley Products Cafe
232 Main Street
Dayton 99328
(509) 382-1998

PULLMAN
The Hilltop Restaurant
920 Northwest Olson Street
Pullman 99163
(509) 332-0928

Swilly's
200 Northeast Kamiaken
Street
Pullman 99163
(509) 334-3395

UNIONTOWN
Eleanor's Place
Main Street (Highway 195)
Uniontown 99179
(509) 229-3389

TEKOA
The Feeding Station
205 North Crosby
Tekoa 99033
(509) 284-3141

WAITSBURG
Farmer's Cafe
216 Main Street
Waitsburg 99361
(509) 337-6845

WALLA WALLA
Jacobi's Cafe
416 North Second Street
Walla Walla 99362
(509) 525-2677

Merchant's Ltd. Cafe
21 East Main Street
Walla Walla 99362
(509) 525-0900

Mill Creek Brew Pub
11 South Palouse Street
Walla Walla 99362
(509) 522-2440

Whitehouse-Crawford
Restaurant
55 Cherry Street
Walla Walla 99362
(509) 525-2222

ALSO WORTH SEEING

Lawson Gardens, Pullman

Frazier Farmstead Museum
and Gardens,
Milton-Freewater, OR

Selected Visitor Information Centers

Colfax Chamber of Commerce
P.O. Box 166, Colfax 99111
(509) 397-3712

Dayton Visitor Information Center
P.O. Box 22, Dayton 99328
(509) 382-4825

Pullman Visitor Information Center
415 North Grand Avenue, Pullman 99163
(509) 334-3565, (800) 365-6948
www.pullman-wa.com

Clarkston Visitor Information Center
502 Bridge Street, Clarkston 99403
(509) 758-7712; (800) 933-2128

Walla Walla Area Visitor Information Center
P.O. Box 644, 29 East Sumach Street,
Walla Walla 99362
(509) 525-0850
www.wallawalla.com

Useful Resources

Government Agency Resources

Bicycle Program
Washington State Department of Transportation,
310 Maple Park Avenue, Olympia 98501; (360) 705–7277
Call this "bicycle hotline" for information on bicycling in Washington.

National Park Service, U.S. Forest Service Outdoor Recreation Information Center
222 Yale Avenue North, Seattle 98109; (206) 220–7450; www.nps.gov
and www.fs.fed.us/r6
Information on camping, hiking, and trail conditions for
western Washington's National Parks and Forests.

Washington State Department of Natural Resources
111 Washington Street SE, P.O. Box 47016, Olympia 98504;
(360) 902–1600; www.wadnr.gov
DNR manages more than 135 primitive recreation sites with hiking
trails, 4WD roads, and limited backcountry facilities.

Washington State Ferries
Colman Dock/Pier 52, 801 Alaskan Way, Seattle 98104-1487
For schedule information call (206) 464–6400 in Seattle or
in-state only (800) 808–7977; TDD, (800) 833–6385;
www.wsdot.wa.gov/ferries

Washington State Parks and Recreation Commission
7153 Cleanwater Lane, Olympia 98504; (360) 902–8844;
www.parks.wa.gov; Information on state parks and campgrounds
available for day and overnight stays.

Washington Tourist Information
off Capitol Way on the Capital grounds in Olympia; (360) 586–3460;
Call (800) 544–1800 to request a Washington Travel Kit that includes
the Washington State Traveler's Guide.

Other Resources

"Artguide Northwest"

Tipton Publishing Company, 13205 Ninth Avenue NW, Seattle 98177;
(206) 367–6831
This semiannual guide lists all galleries, museums, and antiques shops
west of the Cascades.

"Exploring Washington's Past: A Road Guide To History"

Ruth Kirk and Carmela Alexander
University of Washington Press, Seattle, 1989
This comprehensive handbook describes local history for much of
Washington, including fascinating stories and insights about many of
the places described in *Washington: Off the Beaten Path*.

North Cascades National Park Service Complex (U.S. Department of the Interior), Mount Baker Ranger District (U.S.D.A. Forest Service), and North Cascades Institute

810 Highway 20, Sedro-Woolley 98284; (360) 856–5700;
www.nps.gov/noca
Information about North Cascades National Park, Mt. Baker and Mt.
Baker Ranger District, Ross Lake, and Lake Chelan. Contact North
Cascades Institute for a current catalog of year-round seminars on Washington State's natural and cultural history. The complex, located about 5
miles east of I–5, is open daily 8:00 A.M. to 4:30 P.M. from Memorial Day
weekend through mid-October and Monday through Friday (same
hours) during the rest of the year. Farther east on Highway 20, and 14
miles east of Marblemount, the North Cascades Visitor Center in
Newhalem (206–386–4495) is open daily from 9:00 A.M. to 4:30 P.M.

Olympic Park Institute

111 Barnes Point Road, Port Angeles 98363; (800) 775–3720 or
(360) 928–3720; www.yni.org/opi
Call for a free catalog of backcountry courses in Olympic National Park
and courses at the institute located at the historic Rosemary Inn
complex on Lake Crescent.

"Plants and Animals of the Pacific Northwest"
Eugene Kozloff
University of Washington Press, Seattle, 1976
This interesting and informative guide is the ideal companion
for amateur naturalists.

Sierra Club, Cascade Chapter
Cascade Chapter, 1516 Melrose Avenue, Seattle 98122
Call (206) 523–2019 for the outings and events information hotline;
www.cascadeschapter.org.

Sound Experience
2310 Washington Street, Port Townsend 98368; (360) 379–0438;
www.soundexp.org
A nonprofit educational organization specializing in environmental,
marine science, and sailing programs for youths and adults aboard the
136-foot-long circa 1913 tall ship *Adventuress.*

Washington Atlas & Gazeteer
DeLorme Publishing
This atlas provides topographical maps covering all of Washington
State at approximately half an inch to the mile, making it ideal for
exploring back roads.

Washington Water Trails Association
4649 Sunnyside Avenue North, Room 305, Seattle 98103-6900;
(206) 545–9161; www.wwta.org
Promotes preservation of marine shorelines and the creation of
the Cascadia Marine Trail, a network of sites accessible to kayaks and
canoes throughout Puget Sound. At a cost of $25, membership
includes a trail guidebook and quarterly newsletter.

Index

Entries for Bed-and-Breakfasts, Inns, and Museums appear only in the special index on pages 219–21.

INDEX

INDEX

H

Heritage Square, 200
Historic Districts and Neighborhoods
  Downtown Ellensburg, 113
  Fairhaven District (Bellingham), 70
  North Front Street (Yakima), 147
  Old Town Tacoma, 45
Historic Sites
  American Camp (San Juan Island), 80
  Ansorge Hotel Museum, 179
  British Camp (San Juan Island), 80
  Cedar Creek Grist Mill, 125
  Dungeness Schoolhouse, 5
  Ebey's Landing National Historical
    Reserve, 65
  Fort Cascades Historic Site, 126
  Fort Simcoe State Park
    Heritage Site, 144
  Fort Spokane, 165
  Fort Vancouver National Historic
    Site, 123
  Grays Harbor Historical Seaport, 17
  Hovander Homestead Park, 73
  Indian Painted Rocks, 151
  Johnson Farm, 43
  Mill Pond Historic Site, 173
  New Dungeness Lighthouse, 6
  Officer's Row (Vancouver), 123
  Old Bell Tower, 58
  Perkins House, 194
  Rothschild House, 58
  She-Who-Watches, 134
  Stonehenge, 136
  Thorp Gristmill, 112
  Whitman Mission National
    Historic Site, 202
Horseback riding
  Bear Creek Homestead, 13
  Freestone Inn at Wilson Ranch, 95
  Northwestern Lake Riding
    Stables, 130

Sun Mountain Lodge, 95
Hostels
  Rain Forest Hostel, 15
  Triangle J Ranch Hostel, 178
Hotels, historic
  Fort Casey Inn, 64
  Hotel Usk, The, 172
  Tokeland Hotel & Restaurant, 19
  Washington Hotel, 174
  Weinhard Hotel, 198
Houseboats, Lake Roosevelt, 162
Hurricane Ridge, 8

I

Ilwaco, 20
Indian Reservations
  Hoh Tribal Center and Gallery, 15
  Kalispel, 172
  Makah, 12
  Yakama, 142
Institutes
  Chimpanzee and Human
    Communication Institute, 113
  North Cascades Institute, 87
  Olympic Park Institute, 10
Interpretive Centers
  Bald Eagle Interpretive Center, 89
  Breazeale–Padilla Bay Interpretive
    Center, 70
  Columbia Gorge, 127
  Colville Tribal Cultural
    Center, 163
  Dry Falls, 159
  Gingko Petrified Forest, 114
  Grand Coulee Dam, 163
  Hoh River Visitor Center and
    Nature Trail, 14
  Lewis and Clark, 21
  Seattle City Light Visitors Center, 91
  Steilacoom Tribal Cultural
    Center, 43

INDEX

Bed-and-Breakfasts, Inns

INDEX

Museums

Aberdeen Museum of History, 17
African American Museum, 45
American Hop Museum, 142
American Museum of Radio, the, 71
Anacortes History, 67
Anthropology and Art (Pullman), 193
Appaloosa Horse Museum, 188
Benton County Historical, 139
Big Bend Historical Society, 160
Bing Crosby Memorabilia Room,
    Gonzoga University, 169
Boomerang Newspaper and Printing
    Museum, 190
Car and Truck Museum, 178
Carpenter House Museum, 112
Central Washington Agricultural, 147
Colville Tribal Cultural Museum, 163
Dayton Depot museum, 197
Douglas County Historical, 106
Forks Timber Museum, 13
Fort Walla Walla Complex, 202
Hands-on Children's Museum, 38
Ilwaco Heritage Museum, 21
Island County Historical, 64
Jefferson County Historical, 58
Karpeles Manuscript Museum, 45
Keller Heritage Center, 175
Kettle Falls Historical Center, 177
Klickitat County Historical, 136
La Conner Quilt Museum, 69
Lincoln County Historical, 166
Log Cabin Museum, 53
Lopez Historical, 76
Lynden Pioneer Museum, 74
Makah, 12
Maryhill Museum, 136

Mason County Historical Society, 42
Molson School Museum, 100
Museum of Glass, 44
Northwest Museum of Arts and
    Culture, 168
Okanogan County Historical, 97
Old Molson Outdoor, 100
Oroville Depot Museum, 100
Pacific County Historical, 19
Pend Oreille County Historical
    Museum, 171
Pioneer Farm, 36
Pioneer Village, 155
Pioneer Village & Museum,
    Cashmere, 109
Schafer Museum, 96
Sidney Museum, 53
Skagit County Historical Museum, 69
Snoqualmie Valley Railroad &
    Northwest Railway Museum, 52
Steilacoom Historical, 43
Suquamish, 55
Tenino Depot, 41
Three Forks Pioneer Village, 193
Wahkiakum County Historical, 27
Washington State History Museum, 45
Westport Maritime Museum, 18
Whatcom Museum of History
    and Art, 71
Working Waterfront Museum, 45
World Kite Museum and Hall of
    Fame, 23
Yakama Nation Cultural Heritage
    Center, 143
Yakima Valley Rail and Steam
    Museum, 143

About the Author

Myrna Oakley has traveled the byways of the Northwest and western British Columbia since 1970, always with a camera in hand and an inquisitive eye for natural and scenic areas, as well as for wonderful inns, gardens, and places with historical character and significance. In this process she has developed an affinity for goosedown comforters, friendly conversations by the fire, and intriguing people who generally prefer to live somewhat off the beaten path.

In addition to *Washington: Off the Beaten Path,* she has written *Oregon: Off the Beaten Path, Recommended Bed & Breakfasts: Pacific Northwest, Public and Private Gardens of the Northwest,* and *Bed and Breakfast Northwest.* She teaches about the business of freelance writing, novel writing, and travel writing at local colleges and universities in the Portland environs. She also dreams about writing a mystery novel for young adults and plans to sneak away one of these days to one of the islands with her voluminous files and laptop computer.